REASON
LIBERTY
and
AUTHORITY

Riede *and* **Baker**

REASON, LIBERTY AND AUTHORITY

REASON
LIBERTY
and
AUTHORITY

David C. Riede
J. Wayne Baker

University of Akron

KENDALL/HUNT PUBLISHING COMPANY
DUBUQUE, IOWA

Contents

THE
EIGHTEENTH
CENTURY

René Descartes

René Descartes (1596-1650), the great French philosopher and mathematician, was a pioneer in the scientific revolution. Although he made significant contributions in mathematics, he is most famous for his methodology. His dream was to create a universal methodology which could be applied to all knowledge, including the sciences. He began with systematic doubt, rejecting everything except what could be proven beyond question. He felt that this method would sweep away past error, and provide a fresh beginning. In the following reading, we have the most important section of his *Discourse on Method,* in which he decided that the single thing he could not doubt was his own self-existence. From this self-certainty, he deduced the existence of God, using arguments not unlike those of Anselm. The proof of God's existence was an absolute necessity, for to Descartes God himself was the proof of a rational world and of the objective world of nature. How convincing do you find Descartes' argument?

A DISCOURSE ON METHOD

PART IV

I am in doubt as to the propriety of making my first meditations in the place above mentioned matter of discourse; for these are so metaphysical, and so uncommon, as not, perhaps, to be acceptable to every one. And yet, that it may be determined whether the foundations that I have laid are sufficiently secure, I find myself in a measure constrained to advert to them. I had long before remarked that, in relation to practice, it is sometimes necessary to adopt, as if above doubt, opinions which we discern to be highly uncertain, as has been already said; but as I then desired to give my attention solely to the search after truth, I thought that a procedure exactly the opposite was called for, and that I ought to reject as absolutely false all opinions in regard to which I could suppose the least ground for doubt, in order to ascertain whether after that there remained aught in my belief that was wholly indubitable. Accordingly, seeing that our senses sometimes deceive us, I was willing to suppose that there existed nothing really such as they presented to us; and because some men err in reasoning, and fall into paralogisms, even on the simplest matters of geometry, I, convinced that I was as open to error as any other, rejected as false all the reasonings I had hitherto taken for demonstrations; and finally, when I considered that the very same thoughts (presentations) which we experience when awake may also be experienced when we are asleep, while there is

at that time not one of them true, I supposed that all the objects (presentations) that had ever entered into my mind when awake, had in them no more truth than the illusions of my dreams. But immediately upon this I observed that, whilst I thus wished to think that all was false, it was absolutely necessary that I, who thus thought, should be somewhat; and as I observed that this truth, *I think, hence I am,* was so certain and of such evidence, that no ground of doubt, however extravagant, could be alleged by the sceptics capable of shaking it, I concluded that I might, without scruple, accept it as the first principle of the philosophy of which I was in search.

In the next place, I attentively examined that I was, and as I observed that I could suppose that I had no body, and that there was no world nor any place in which I might be; but that I could not therefore suppose that I was not; and that, on the contrary, from the very circumstance that I thought to doubt of the truth of other things, it most clearly and certainly followed that I was; while, on the other hand, if I had only ceased to think, although all the other objects which I had ever imagined had been in reality existent, I would have had no reason to believe that I existed; I

From the book *A Discourse on Method; Meditation on the First Philosophy; Principles of Philosophy* by Rene Descartes. Trans. by J. Veitch. Intro. by A. D. Lindsay. Everyman's Library Edition. Published by E. P. Dutton & Co., Inc. and used with their permission.

thence concluded that I was a substance whose whole essence or nature consists only in thinking, and which, that it may exist, has need of no place, nor is dependent on any material things; so that "I," that is to say, the mind by which I am what I am, is wholly distinct from the body, and is even more easily known than the latter, and is such, that although the latter were not, it would still continue to be all that it is.

After this I inquired in general into what is essential to the truth and certainty of a proposition; for since I had discovered one which I knew to be true, I thought that I must likewise be able to discover the ground of this certitude. And as I observed that in the words *I think, hence I am,* there is nothing at all which gives me assurance of their truth beyond this, that I see very clearly that in order to think it is necessary to exist, I concluded that I might take, as a general rule, the principle, that all the things which we very clearly and distinctly conceive are true, only observing, however, that there is some difficulty in rightly determining the objects which we distinctly conceive.

In the next place, from reflecting on the circumstance that I doubted, and that consequently my being was not wholly perfect (for I clearly saw that it was a greater perfection to know than to doubt), I was led to inquire whence I had learned to think of something more perfect than myself; and I clearly recognised that I must hold this notion from some nature which in reality was more perfect. As for the thoughts of many other objects external to me, as of the sky, the earth, light, heat, and a thousand more, I was less at a loss to know whence these came; for since I remarked in them nothing which seemed to render them superior to myself, I could believe that, if these were true, they were dependencies on my own nature, in so far as it possessed a certain perfection, and, if they were false, that I held them from nothing, that is to say, that they were in me because of a certain imperfection of my nature. But this could not be the case with the idea of a nature more perfect than myself; for to receive it from nothing was a thing manifestly impossible; and, because it is not less repugnant that the more perfect should be an effect of, and dependence on the less perfect, than that something should proceed from nothing, it was equally impossible that I could hold it from myself: accordingly, it but remained that it had been placed in me by a nature which was in reality more perfect than mine, and which even possessed within itself all the perfec-

tions of which I could form any idea; that is to say, in a single word, which was God. And to this I added that, since I knew some perfections which I did not possess, I was not the only being in existence (I will here, with your permission, freely use the terms of the schools); but, on the contrary, that there was of necessity some other more perfect Being upon whom I was dependent, and from whom I had received all that I possessed; for if I had existed alone, and independently of every other being, so as to have had from myself all the perfection, however little, which I actually possessed, I should have been able, for the same reason, to have had from myself the whole remainder of perfection, of the want of which I was conscious, and thus could of myself have become infinite, eternal, immutable, omniscient, all-powerful, and, in fine, have possessed all the perfections which I could recognise in God. For in order to know the nature of God (whose existence has been established by the preceding reasonings), as far as my own nature permitted, I had only to consider in reference to all the properties of which I found in my mind some idea, whether their possession was a mark of perfection; and I was assured that no one which indicated any imperfection was in him, and that none of the rest was awanting. Thus I perceived that doubt, inconstancy, sadness, and such like, could not be found in God, since I myself would have been happy to be free from them. Besides, I had ideas of many sensible and corporeal things; for although I might suppose that I was dreaming, and that all which I saw or imagined was false, I could not, nevertheless, deny that the ideas were in reality in my thoughts. But, because I had already very clearly recognised in myself that the intelligent nature is distinct from the corporeal, and as I observed that all composition is an evidence of dependency, and that a state of dependency is manifestly a state of imperfection, I therefore determined that it could not be a perfection in God to be compounded of these two natures, and that consequently he was not so compounded; but that if there were any bodies in the world, or even any intelligences, or other natures that were not wholly perfect, their existence depended on his power in such a way that they could not subsist without him for a single moment.

I was disposed straightway to search for other truths; and when I had represented to myself the object of the geometers, which I conceived to be a continuous body, or a space indefinitely extended in length, breadth, and height or depth, divisible into divers parts which admit of different figures and sizes, and of being moved or transposed in all manner of ways (for all this the geometers suppose to be in the object they contemplate), I went over some of their simplest demonstrations. And, in the first place, I observed, that the great certitude which by common consent is accorded to these demonstrations, is founded solely upon this, that they are clearly conceived in accordance with the rules I have already laid down. In the next place, I perceived that there was nothing at all in these demonstrations which could assure me of the existence of their object: thus, for example, supposing a triangle to be given, I distinctly perceived that its three angles were necessarily equal to two right angles, but I did not on that account perceive anything which could assure me that any triangle existed: while, on the contrary, recurring to the examination of the idea of a Perfect Being, I found that the existence of the Being was comprised in the idea in the same way that the equality of its three angles to two right angles is comprised in the idea of a triangle, or as in the idea of a sphere, the equidistance of all points on its surface from the centre, or even still more clearly; and that consequently it is at least as certain that God, who is this Perfect Being, is, or exists, as any demonstration of geometry can be.

But the reason which leads many to persuade themselves that there is a difficulty in knowing this truth, and even also in knowing what their mind really is, is that they never raise their thoughts above sensible objects, and are so accustomed to consider nothing except by way of imagination, which is a mode of thinking limited to material objects, that all that is not imaginable seems to them not intelligible. The truth of this is sufficiently manifest from the single circumstance, that the philosophers of the schools accept as a maxim that there is nothing in the understanding which was not previously in the senses, in which however it is certain that the ideas of God and of the soul have never been; and it appears to me that they who make use of their imagination to comprehend these ideas do exactly the same thing as if, in order to hear sounds or smell odours, they strove to avail themselves of their eyes; unless indeed that there is this difference, that the sense of sight does not afford us an inferior assurance to those of smell or hearing; in place of which neither our imagination nor our senses can give us assurance of anything unless our understanding intervene.

Finally, if there be still persons who are not sufficiently persuaded of the existence of God and of the soul, by the reasons I have adduced, I am desirous that they should know that all the other propositions, of the truth of which they deem themselves perhaps more assured, as that we have a body, and that there exist stars and an earth, and such like, are less certain; for, although we have a moral assurance of these things, which is so strong that there is an appearance of extravagance in doubting of their existence, yet at the same time no one, unless his intellect is impaired, can deny, when the question relates to a metaphysical certitude, that there is sufficient reason to exclude entire assurance, in the observation that when asleep we can in the same way imagine ourselves possessed of another body and that we see other stars and another earth, when there is nothing of the kind. For how do we know that the thoughts which occur in dreaming are false rather than those other which we experience when awake, since the former are often not less vivid and distinct than the latter? And though men of the highest genius study this question as long as they please, I do not believe that they will be able to give any reason which can be sufficient to remove this doubt, unless they presuppose the existence of God. For, in the first place, even the principle which I have already taken as a rule, viz., that all the things which we clearly and distinctly conceive are true, is certain only because God is or exists and because he is a Perfect Being, and because all that we possess is derived from him: whence it follows that our ideas or notions, which to the extent of their clearness and distinctness are real, and proceed from God, must to that extent be true. Accordingly, whereas we not unfrequently have ideas or notions in which some falsity is contained, this can only be the case with such as are to some extent confused and obscure, and in this proceed from nothing (participate of negation), that is, exist in us thus confused because we are not wholly perfect. And it is evident that it is not less repugnant that falsity or imperfection, in so far as it is imperfection, should proceed from God, than that truth or perfection should proceed from nothing. But if we did not know that all which we possess of real and true proceeds from a Perfect and Infinite Being, however clear and distinct our ideas might be, we should have no ground on that account for the assurance that they possessed the perfection of being true.

But after the knowledge of God and of the soul has rendered us certain of this rule, we can easily understand that the truth of the thoughts we experience when awake, ought not in the slightest degree to be called in question on account of the illusions of our dreams. For if it happened that an individual, even when asleep, had some very distinct idea, as, for example, if a geometer should discover some new demonstration, the circumstance of his being asleep would not militate against its truth; and as for the most ordinary error of our dreams, which consists in their representing to us various objects in the same way as our external senses, this is not prejudicial, since it leads us very properly to suspect the truth of the ideas of sense; for we are not unfrequently deceived in the same manner when awake; as when persons in the jaundice see all objects yellow, or when the stars or bodies at a great distance appear to us much smaller than they are. For, in fine, whether awake or asleep, we ought never to allow ourselves to be persuaded of the truth of anything unless on the evidence of our reason. And it must be noted that I say of our *reason,* and not of our imagination or of our senses: thus, for example, although

we very clearly see the sun, we ought not therefore to determine that it is only of the size which our sense of sight presents; and we may very distinctly imagine the head of a lion joined to the body of a goat, without being therefore shut up to the conclusion that a chimaera exists; for it is not a dictate of reason that what we thus see or imagine is in reality existent; but it plainly tells us that all our ideas or notions contain in them some truth; for otherwise it could not be that God, who is wholly perfect and veracious, should have placed them in us. And because our reasonings are never so clear or so complete during sleep as when we awake, although sometimes the acts of our imagination are then as lively and distinct, if not more than in our waking moments, reason further dictates that, since all our thoughts cannot be true because of our partial imperfection, those possessing truth must infallibly be found in the experience of our waking moments rather than in that of our dreams.

John Locke

John Locke (1632-1704), essayist, philosopher and political theorist, was the father of the English enlightenment. His *Essay Concerning Human Understanding,* a portion of which constitutes the following reading, was particularly important for both the English and French enlightenment. In the *Essay,* Locke argued that all human knowledge resulted from experience, from sense perception. At birth the mind was like a blank sheet of paper; there was no innate knowledge. Thus Locke provided for the enlightenment a theory of knowledge, an epistemology, which was sympathetic to the new mechanistic world view then emerging from the Newtonian synthesis. The Lockean theory of knowledge became an enlightened article of faith, on which the philosophers based their attacks on Christian "superstition." It also reinforced the emerging idea of progress because it placed the emphasis on man's environment.

AN ESSAY CONCERNING HUMAN UNDERSTANDING

BOOK I

CHAPTER I

No Innate Speculative Principles

It is an established opinion amongst some men, that there are in the understanding certain *innate principles*; some primary notions, characters, as it were stamped upon the mind of man; which the soul receives in its very first being, and brings into

the world with it. It would be sufficient to convince unprejudiced readers of the falseness of this supposition, if I should only show (as I hope I shall in the following parts of this Discourse) how

From *An Essay Concerning Human Understanding* by John Locke. Collated and annotated, with prolegomena, biographical, critical, and historical by Alexander Campbell Fraser, Volume 1. Copyright 1894 by the Clarendon Press, Oxford.

men, barely by the use of their natural faculties, may attain to all the knowledge they have, without the help of any innate impressions; and may arrive at certainty, without any such original notions or principles. For I imagine any one will easily grant that it would be impertinent to suppose the ideas of colours innate in a creature to whom God hath given sight, and a power to receive them by the eyes from external objects: and no less unreasonable would it be to attribute several truths to the impressions of nature, and innate characters, when we may observe in ourselves faculties fit to attain as easy and certain knowledge of them as if they were originally imprinted on the mind.

But because a man is not permitted without censure to follow his own thoughts in the search of truth, when they lead him ever so little out of the common road, I shall set down the reasons that made me doubt of the truth of that opinion, as an excuse for my mistake, if I be in one; which I leave to be considered by those who, with me, dispose themselves to embrace truth wherever they find it.

There is nothing more commonly taken for granted than that there are certain *principles,* both *speculative* and *practical,* (for they speak of both), universally agreed upon by all mankind: which therefore, they argue, must needs be the constant impressions which the souls of men receive in their first beings, and which they bring into the world with them, as necessarily and really as they do any of their inherent faculties.

This argument, drawn from universal consent, has this misfortune in it, that if it were true in matter of fact, that there were certain truths wherein all mankind agreed, it would not prove them innate, if there can be any other way shown how men may come to that universal agreement, in the things they do consent in, which I presume may be done.

But, which is worse, this argument of universal consent, which is made use of to prove innate principles, seems to me a demonstration that there are none such: because there are none to which all mankind give an universal assent. I shall begin with the speculative, and instance in those magnified principles of demonstration, 'Whatsoever is, is,' and 'It is impossible for the same thing to be and not to be'; which, of all others, I think have the most allowed title to innate. These have so settled a reputation of maxims universally received, that it will no doubt be thought strange if any one should seem to question it. But yet I take liberty to say, that these propositions are so far from having an universal assent, that there are a great part of mankind to whom they are not so much as known.

For, first, it is evident, that all children and idiots have not the least apprehension or thought of them. And the want of that is enough to destroy that universal assent which must needs be the necessary concomitant of all innate truths: it seeming to me near a contradiction to say, that there are truths imprinted on the soul, which it perceives or understands not: imprinting, if it signify anything, being nothing else but the making certain truths to be perceived. For to imprint anything on the mind without the mind's perceiving it, seems to me hardly intelligible. If therefore children and idiots have souls, have minds, with those impressions upon them, *they* must unavoidably perceive them, and necessarily know and assent to these truths; which since they do not, it is evident that there are no such impressions. For if they are not notions naturally imprinted, how can they be innate? and if they are notions imprinted, how can they be unknown? To say a notion is imprinted on the mind, and yet at the same time to say, that the mind is ignorant of it, and never yet took notice of it, is to make this impression nothing. No proposition can be said to be in the mind which it was never yet conscious of. For if any one may, then, by the same reason, all propositions that are true, and the mind is capable ever of assenting to, may be said to be in the mind, and to be imprinted: since, if any one can be said to be in the mind, which it never yet knew, it must be only because it is capable of knowing it; and so the mind is of all truths it ever shall know. Nay, thus truths may be imprinted on the mind which it never did, nor ever shall know; for a man may live long, and die at last in ignorance of many truths which his mind was capable of knowing, and that with certainty. So that if the capacity of knowing be the natural impression contended for, all the truths a man ever comes to know will, by this account, be every one of them innate; and this great point will amount to no more, but only to a very improper way of speaking; which, whilst it pretends to assert the contrary, says nothing different from those who deny innate principles. For nobody, I think, ever denied that the mind was capable of knowing several truths. The capacity, they say, is innate; the knowledge acquired. But then to what end such contest for certain innate maxims? If truths can be imprinted on the understanding without being perceived, I can see no difference there can be between any truths the mind is *capable* of knowing in respect of their original: they must all be innate or all adventitious: in vain shall a man go about to distinguish them. He therefore that talks of innate notions in the understanding, cannot (if he intend thereby any distinct sort of truths) mean such truths to be in the understanding as it never perceived, and is yet wholly ignorant of. For if these words 'to be in the understanding' have any propriety, they signify to be understood. So that to be in the understanding, and not to be understood; to be in the mind and never to be perceived, is all one as to say anything is and is not in the mind or understanding. If therefore these two propositions, 'Whatsoever is, is,' and 'It is impossible for the same thing to be and not to be,' are by nature imprinted, children cannot be ignorant of them: infants, and all that have souls, must necessarily have them in their understandings, know the truth of them, and assent to it.

To avoid this, it is usually answered, that all men know and assent to them, *when they come to the use of reason;* and this is enough to prove them innate. I answer:

Doubtful expressions, that have scarce any signification, go for clear reasons to those who, being prepossessed, take not the pains to examine even what they themselves say. For, to apply this answer with any tolerable sense to our present purpose, it must signify one of these two things: either that as soon as men come to the use of reason these supposed native inscriptions come to be known and observed by them; or else, that the use and exercise of men's reason, assists them in the discovery of these principles, and certainly makes them known to them.

If they mean, that by the use of reason men may discover these principles, and that this is sufficient to prove them innate; their way of arguing will stand thus, viz. that whatever truths reason can certainly discover to us, and make us firmly assent to, those are all naturally imprinted on the mind; since that universal assent, which is made the mark of them, amounts to no more but this,—that by the use of reason we are capable to come to a certain knowledge of and assent to them; and, by this means, there will be no difference between the maxims of the mathematicians, and theorems they deduce from them: all must be equally allowed innate; they being all discoveries made by the use of reason, and truths that a rational creature may certainly come to know, if he apply his thoughts rightly that way.

But how can these men think the use of reason necessary to discover principles that are supposed innate, when reason (if we may believe them) is nothing else but the faculty of deducing unknown truths from principles or propositions that are already known? That certainty can never be thought innate which we have need of reason to discover; unless, as I have said, we will have all the certain truths that reason ever teaches us, to be innate. We may as well think the use of reason necessary to make our eyes discover visible objects, as that there should be need of reason, or the exercise thereof, to make the understanding see what is originally engraven on it, and cannot be in the understanding before it be perceived by it. So that to make reason discover those truths thus imprinted, is to say, that the use of reason discovers to a man what he knew before: and if men have those innate impressed truths originally, and before the use of reason, and yet are always ignorant of them till they come to the use of reason, it is in effect to say, that men know and know them not at the same time.

BOOK II

CHAPTER I

Of Ideas in General, and Their Original

Every man being conscious to himself that he thinks; and that which his mind is applied about whilst thinking being the *ideas* that are there, it is past doubt that men have in thier minds several ideas,—such as are those expressed by the words *whiteness, hardness, sweetness, thinking, motion, man, elephant, army, drunkenness,* and others: it is the first place then to be inquired, *How he comes by them?*

I know it is a received doctrine, that men have native ideas, and original characters, stamped upon their minds in their very first being. This opinion I have at large examined already; and, I suppose what I have said in the foregoing Book will be much more easily admitted, when I have shown whence the understanding may get all the ideas it has; and by what ways and degrees they may come into the mind;—for which I shall appeal to every one's own observation and experience.

Let us then suppose the mind to be, as we say, white paper, void of all characters, without any ideas:—How comes it to be furnished? Whence comes it by that vast store which the busy and boundless fancy of man has painted on it with an almost endless variety? Whence has it all the *materials* of reason and knowledge? To this I answer, in one word, from EXPERIENCE. In that all our knowledge is founded; and from that it ultimately derives itself. Our observation employed either, about external sensible objects, or about the internal operations of our minds perceived and reflected on by ourselves, is that which supplies our understandings with all the *materials* of thinking. These two are the fountains of knowledge, from whence all the ideas we have, or can naturally have, do spring.

First, our Senses, conversant about particular sensible objects, do convey into the mind several distinct perceptions of things, according to those various ways wherein those objects do affect them. And thus we come by those *ideas* we have of *yellow, white, heat, cold, soft, hard, bitter, sweet,* and all those which we call sensible qualities; which when I say the senses convey into the mind, I mean, they from external objects convey into the mind what produces there those perceptions. This great source of most of the ideas we have, depending wholly upon our senses, and derived by them to the understanding, I call SENSATION.

Secondly, the other fountain from which experience furnisheth the understanding with ideas is,— the perception of the operations of our own mind within us, as it is employed about the ideas it has got;—which operations, when the soul comes to reflect on and consider, do furnish the understanding with another set of ideas, which could not be had from things without. And such are *perception, thinking, doubting, believing, reasoning, knowing, willing,* and all the different actings of our own minds;— which we being conscious of, and observing in ourselves, do from these receive into our understandings as distinct ideas as we do from bodies affecting our senses. This source of ideas every man has wholly in himself; and though it be not sense, as having nothing to do with external objects, yet it is very like it, and might properly enough be called *internal sense.* But as I call the other Sensation, so I call this REFLECTION, the ideas it affords being such only as the mind gets by reflecting on its own operations within itself. By reflection then, in the following part of this discourse, I would be understood to mean, that notice which the mind takes of its own operations, and the manner of them, by reason whereof there come to be ideas of these operations in the understanding. These two, I say, viz. external material things, as the objects of SENSATION, and the operations of our own minds within, as the objects of REFLECTION, are to me the only originals from whence all our ideas take their beginnings. The term *operations* here I use in a

large sense, as comprehending not barely the actions of the mind about its ideas, but some sort of passions arising sometimes from them, such as is the satisfaction or uneasiness arising from any thought.

The understanding seems to me not to have the least glimmering of any ideas which it doth not receive from one of these two. *External objects* furnish the mind with the ideas of sensible qualities, which are all those different perceptions they produce in us; and *the mind* furnishes the understanding with ideas of its own operations.

These, when we have taken a full survey of them, and their several modes, [combinations, and relations,] we shall find to contain all our whole stock of ideas; and that we have nothing in our minds which did not come in one of these two ways. Let any one examine his own thoughts, and thoroughly search into his understanding; and then let him tell me, whether all the original ideas he has there, are any other than of the objects of his senses, or of the operations of his mind, considered as objects of his reflection. And how great a mass of knowledge soever he imagines to be lodged there, he will, upon taking a strict view, see that he has not any idea in his mind but what one of these two have imprinted;—though perhaps, with infinite variety compounded and enlarged by the understanding, as we shall see hereafter.

He that attentively considers the state of a child, at his first coming into the world, will have little reason to think him stored with plenty of ideas, that are to be the matter of his future knowledge. It is *by degrees* he comes to be furnished with them. And though the ideas of obvious and familiar qualities imprint themselves before the memory begins to keep a register of time or order, yet it is often so late before some unusual qualities come in the way, that there are few men that cannot recollect the beginning of their acquaintance with them. And if it were worth while, no doubt a child might be so ordered as to have but a very few, even of the ordinary ideas, till he were grown up to a man. But all that are born into the world, being surrounded with bodies that perpetually and diversely affect them, variety of ideas, whether care be taken of it or not, are imprinted on the minds of children. Light and colours are busy at hand everywhere, when the eye is but open; sounds and some tangible qualities fail not to solicit their proper senses, and force an entrance to the mind;—but yet, I think, it will be granted easily, that if a child were kept in a place where he never saw any other but black and white till he were a man, he would have no more ideas of scarlet or green, than he that from his childhood never tasted an oyster, or a pine-apple, has of those particular relishes.

Men then come to be furnished with fewer or more simple ideas from without, according as the objects they converse with afford greater or less variety; and from the operations of their minds within, according as they more or less reflect on them. For, though he that contemplates the operations of his mind, cannot but have plain and clear ideas of them; yet, unless he turns his thoughts that way, and considers them *attentively,* he will no more have clear and distinct ideas of all the operations of his mind, and all that may be observed therein, than he will have all the particular ideas of any landscape, or of the parts and motions of a clock, who will not turn his eyes to it, and with attention heed all the parts of it. The picture, or clock may be so placed, that they may come in his way every day; but yet he will have but a confused idea of all the parts they are made up of, till he applies himself with attention, to consider them each in particular.

And hence we see the reason why it is pretty late before most children get ideas of the operations of their own minds; and some have not any very clear or perfect ideas of the greatest part of them all their lives. Because, though they pass there continually, yet, like floating visions, they make not deep impressions enough to leave in their mind clear, distinct, lasting ideas, till the understanding turns inward upon itself, reflects on its own operations, and makes them the objects of its own contemplation. Children [when they come first into it, are surrounded with a world of new things, which, by a constant solicitation of their senses, draw the mind constantly to them; forward to take notice of new, and apt to be delighted with the variety of changing objects. Thus the first years are usually employed and diverted in looking abroad. Men's business in them is to acquaint themselves with what is to be found without;] and so growing up in a constant attention to outward sensations seldom make any considerable reflection on what passes within them, till they come to be of riper years; and some scarce ever at all.

Voltaire

Francois Marie Arouet, better known as Voltaire (1694-1778), was the supreme figure of the Enlightenment. A life long champion of individual liberty, he hated the smug optimism of his day which viewed the world as the best of all possible worlds. He wrote scathing articles against the church, governments, rulers and all those who disagreed with his enlightened ideas. *Candide,* his most famous satire in which he ridiculed religion, government and society, appeared in 1759. The hero of the story is an incurable optimist who has been taught by a muddle-headed philosopher-teacher. Candide moves from one incredible adventure to the next, but never seems to lose his optimism. Check the conclusion of the story and decide if you think Voltaire gives any deep answer to the problems which he satirizes throughout the tale. Is this what you would expect from such a prominent man of letters in the Age of Enlightenment?

CANDIDE

In a castle of Westphalia, belonging to the Baron of Thunder-ten-Tronckh, lived a youth whom nature had endowed with the most gentle manners. His countenance was a true picture of his soul. He combined a true judgment with simplicity of spirit, which was the reason, I apprehend, of his being called Candide. The old servants of the family suspected him to have been the son of the Baron's sister, by a good, honest gentleman of the neighborhood, whom that young lady would never marry because he had been able to prove only seventy-one quarterings, the rest of his genealogical tree having been lost through the injuries of time.

The Baron was one of the most powerful lords

in Westphalia, for his castle had not only a gate, but windows. His great hall, even, was hung with tapestry. All the dogs of his farmyards formed a pack of hounds at need; his grooms were his huntsmen; and the curate of the village was his grand almoner. They called him "My Lord," and laughed at all his stories.

The Baron's lady weighed about three hundred and fifty pounds, and was therefore a person of great consideration, and she did the honors of the house with a dignity that commanded still greater respect. Her daughter Cunegonde was seventeen years of age, fresh-colored, comely, plump, and desirable. The Baron's son seemed to be in every respect worthy of his father. The Preceptor Pangloss was the oracle of the family, and little Candide heard his lessons with all the good faith of his age and character.

Pangloss was professor of metaphysicotheologico-cosmolo-nigology. He proved admirably that there is no effect without a cause, and that in this best of all possible worlds, the Baron's castle was the most magnificent of castles, and his lady the best of all possible Baronesses.

"It is demonstrable," said he, "that things cannot be otherwise than as they are; for all being created for an end, all is necessarily for the best end. Observe, that the nose has been formed to bear spectacles—thus we have spectacles. Legs are visibly designed for stockings—and we have stockings. Stones were made to be hewn, and to construct castles—therefore my lord has a magnificent castle; for the greatest baron in the province ought to be the best lodged. Pigs were made to be eaten—therefore we eat pork all the year round. Consequently they who assert that all is well have said a foolish thing; they should have said all is for the best."

Candide listened attentively and believed innocently; for he thought Miss Cunegonde extremely beautiful, though he never had the courage to tell her so. He concluded that after the happiness of being born of the Baron of Thunder-ten-Tronckh, the second degree of happiness was to be Miss Cunegonde, the third that of seeing her every day, and the fourth that of hearing Master Pangloss, the greatest philosopher of the whole province, and consequently of the whole world.

One day Cunegonde, while walking near the castle, in a little wood which they called a park, . . . became quite pensive, and filled with the desire to be loved, dreamed that she might well be a *sufficient reason* for young Candide, her cousin, and he for her.

She met Candide on reaching the castle and blushed; Candide blushed also, she wished him good morrow in a faltering tone, and Candide spoke to her without knowing what he said. The next day after dinner, as they went from table, Conegonde and Candide found themselves behind a screen; Cunegonde let fall her handkerchief, Candide picked it up, she took him innocently by the hand, the youth as innocently kissed the young lady's hand with particular vivacity, sensibility, and grace; their lips met, their eyes sparkled, their knees trembled. Baron Thunder-ten-Tronckh passed near the screen and beholding this cause and effect chased Candide from the castle with great kicks; Cunegonde fainted away; she was boxed on the ears by the Baroness, as soon as she came to herself; and all was consternation in this most magnificent and most agreeable of all possible castles.

Candide, driven from this terrestrial paradise, walked a long while without knowing where, weeping, raising his eyes to heaven, turning them often towards the most magnificent of castles which imprisoned the purest of noble young ladies. He lay down to sleep without supper, in the middle of a field between two furrows. The snow fell in large flakes. Next day Candide, all benumbed, dragged himself towards the neighboring town which was called Waldberghofftrarbkdikdorff. Having no money, dying of hunger and fatigue, he stopped sorrowfully at the door of an inn. Two men dressed in blue observed him.

"Comrade," said one, "here is a well-built young fellow, and of proper height."

They went up to Candide and very civilly invited him to dinner.

"Gentlemen," replied Candide, with a most engaging modesty, "you do me great honor, but I have not wherewithal to pay my share."

"Oh, sir," said one of the blues to him, "people of your appearance and of your merit never pay anything: are you not five feet five inches high?"

"Yes, sir, that is my height," answered he, making a low bow.

"Come, sir, seat yourself; not only will we pay your reckoning, but we will never suffer such a man as you to want money; men are only born to assist one another."

"You are right," said Candide; "this is what I was always taught by Mr. Pangloss, and I see plainly that all is for the best."

They begged of him to accept a few crowns. He took them, and wished to give them his note; they refused; they seated themselves at table.

"Love you not deeply?"

"Oh, yes," answered he; "I deeply love Miss Cunegonde."

"No," said one of the gentle, "we ask you if you do not deeply love the King of the Bulgarians?"

"Not at all," said he; "for I have never seen him."

"What! he is the best of kings, and we must drink his health.

"Oh! very willingly, gentlemen," and he drank.

"That is enough," they told him. "Now you are the help, the support, the defender, the hero of the Bulgarians. Your fortune is made, and your glory is assured."

Instantly they fettered him, and carried him away to the regiment. There he was made to wheel about to the right, and to the left, to draw his rammer, to return his rammer, to present, to fire, to march, and they gave him thirty blows with a cudgel. The next day he did his exercise a little less badly, and he received but twenty blows. The following they gave him only ten, and he was regarded by his comrades as a prodigy.

Candide, all stupefied, could not yet very well realize how he was a hero. He resolved one fine day in spring to go for a walk, marching straight before him, believing that it was a privilege of the human as well as of the animal species to make use of their legs as they pleased. He had advanced two leagues when he was overtaken by four others, heroes of six feet, who bound him and carried him to a dungeon. He was asked which he would like the best, to be whipped six-and-thirty times through all the regiment, or to receive at once twelve balls of lead in his brain. He vainly said that human will is free, and that he chose neither the one nor the other. He was forced to make a choice; he determined, in virtue of that gift of God called liberty, to run the gauntlet six-and-thirty times. He bore this twice. The regiment was composed of two thousand men; that composed for him four thousand strokes, which laid bare all his muscles and nerves, from the nape of his neck quite down to his rump. As they were going to proceed to a third whipping Candide, able to bear no more, begged as a favor that they would be so good as to shoot him. He obtained this favor; they bandaged his eyes and bade him kneel down. The King of the Bulgarians passed at this moment and ascertained the nature of the crime. As he had great talent, he understood from all that he learned of Candide that he was a young metaphysician, extremely ignorant of the things of this world, and he accorded him his pardon with a clemency which

will bring him praise in all the journals, and throughout all ages.

An able surgeon cured Candide in three weeks by means of emollients taught by Dioscordies. He had already a little skin, and was able to march when the King of the Bulgarians gave battle to the King of the Abares.

There was never anything so gallant, so spruce, so brilliant, and so well disposed as the two armies. Trumpets, fifes, hautboys, drums, and cannon made music such as Hell itself had never heard. The cannons first of all laid flat about six thousand men on each side; the muskets swept away from this best of worlds nine or ten thousand ruffians who infested its surface. The bayonet was also a *sufficient reason* for the death of several thousands. The whole might amount to thirty thousand souls. Candide, who trembled like a philosopher, hid himself as well as he could during this heroic butchery.

At length, while the two kings were causing *Te Deum* to be sung each in his own camp, Candide resolved to go and reason elsewhere on effects and causes. He passed over heaps of dead and dying, and first reached a neighboring village; it was in cinders; it was an Abare village which the Bulgarians had burnt according to the laws of war. Here, old men covered with wounds beheld their wives, hugging their children to their bloody breasts, massacred before their faces; there, their daughters, disemboweled and breathing their last after having satisfied the natural wants of Bulgarian heroes, while others, half burnt in the flames, begged to be dispatched. The earth was strewn with brains, arms, and legs.

Candide fled quickly to another village; it belonged to the Bulgarians; and the Abarian heroes had treated it in the same way. Candide, walking always over palpitating limbs or across ruins, arrived at last beyond the seat of war, with a few provisions in his knapsack, and Miss Cunegonde always in his heart. His provisions failed him when he arrived in Holland; but having heard that everybody was rich in that country, and that they were Christians, he did not doubt but he should meet with the same treatment from them as he had met with in the Baron's castle, before Miss Cunegonde's bright eyes were the cause of his expulsion thence.

He asked alms of several grave-looking people, who all answered him that if he continued to follow this trade they would confine him to the house of correction, where he should be taught to get a living.

The next he addressed was a man who had been haranguing a large assembly for a whole hour on the subject of charity. But the orator, looking askew, said:

"What are you doing here? Are you for the good cause?"

"There can be no effect without a cause," modestly answered Candide; "the whole is necessarily concatenated and arranged for the best. It was necessary for me to have been banished from the presence of Miss Cunegonde, to have afterwards run the gauntlet, and now it is necessary I should beg my bread until I learn to earn it; all this cannot be otherwise."

"My friend," said the orator to him, "do you believe the Pope to be Anti-Christ?"

"I have not heard it," answered Candide; "but whether he be, or whether he be not, I want bread."

"Thou dost not deserve to eat," said the other. "Begone, rogue; begone, wretch; do not come near me again."

The orator's wife, putting her head out of the window, and spying a man that doubted whether the Pope was Anti-Christ, poured over him a full bucket of slops. Oh, heavens! to what excess does religious zeal carry the ladies.

A man who had never been christened, a good Anabaptist, named James, beholding the cruel and ignominious treatment shown to one of his brethren, an unfeathered biped with a rational soul, he took him home, cleaned him, gave him bread and beer, presented him with two florins, and even wished to teach him the manufacture of Persian stuffs, which they make in Holland. Candide, almost prostrating himself before him, cried:

"Master Pangloss has well said that all is for the best in this world, for I am infinitely more touched by your extreme generosity than with the inhumanity of that gentleman in the black coat and his lady."

The next day, as he took a walk, he met a beggar all covered with scabs, his eyes diseased, the end of his nose eaten away, his mouth distorted, his teeth black, choking in his throat, tormented with a violent cough, and spitting out a tooth at each effort.

Candide, yet more moved with compassion than with horror, gave to this shocking beggar the two florins which he had received from the honest Anabaptist James. The specter looked at him very earnestly, dropped a few tears, and fell upon his neck. Candide recoiled in disgust.

"Alas!" said one wretch to the other, "do you no longer know your dear Pangloss?"

"What do I hear? You, my dear master! You in this terrible plight! What misfortune has happened to you? Why are you no longer in the most magnificent of castles? What has become of Miss Cunegonde, the pearl of girls, and nature's masterpiece?"

"I am so weak that I cannot stand," said Pangloss.

Upon which Candide carried him to the Anabaptist's stable, and gave him a crust of bread. As soon as Pangloss had refreshed himself a little:

"Well," said Candide, "Cunegonde?"

"She is dead," replied the other.

Candide fainted at this word; his friend recalled his senses with a little bad vinegar which he found by chance in the stable. Candide reopened his eyes.

"Cunegonde is dead! Ah, best of worlds, where art thou? But what illness did she die? Was it not for grief, upon seeing her father kick me out of his magnificent castle?"

"No," said Pangloss, "she was stabbed by the Bulgarian soldiers; they broke the Baron's head for attempting to defend her; my lady, her mother, was cut in pieces; my poor pupil was served just in the same manner as his sister; and as for the castle, they have not left one stone upon another, not a bar, nor a sheep, nor a duck, nor a tree; but we have had our revenge, for the Abares have done the very same thing to a neighboring barony, which belonged to a Bulgarian lord. . . . "

"Well, this is wonderful!" said Candide, "but you must be cured."

"Alas! how can I?" said Panglos. "I have not a farthing, my friend, and all over the globe there is no letting of blood or taking a gloster without paying, or somebody paying for you."

These last words determined Candide; he went and flung himself at the feet of the charitable Anabaptist James, and gave him so touching a picture of the state to which his friend was reduced that the good man did not scruple to take Dr. Pangloss into his house, and had him cured at his expense. In the cure Pangloss lost only an eye and an ear. He wrote well, and knew arithmetic perfectly. The Anabaptist James made him his bookkeeper. At the end of two months, being obliged to go by sea to Lisbon about some mercantile affairs, he took the two philosophers with him in his ship. Pangloss explained to him how everything was so constituted that it could not be better. James was not of this opinion.

"It is more likely," said he, "mankind have a little corrupted nature, for men were not born wolves, and they have become wolves; God has given them neither cannon or four-and-twenty pounders nor bayonets; and yet they have made cannon and bayonets to destroy one another. Into this account I might throw not only bankrupts, but Justice which seizes on the effects of bankrupts to cheat the creditors."

"All this was indispensable," replied the one-eyed doctor, "for private misfortunes make the general good, so that the more private misfortunes there are the greater is the general good."

While he reasoned, the sky darkened, the winds blew from the four quarters, and the ship was assailed by a most terrible tempest within sight of the port of Lisbon.

Half dead of that inconceivable anguish which the rolling of a ship produces, one half of the passengers were not even sensible of the danger. The other half shrieked and prayed. The sheets were rent, the masts broken, the vessel gaped. Work who would, no one heard, no one commanded. The Anabaptist, being upon deck, bore a hand; then a brutish sailor struck him roughly and laid him sprawling; but with the violence of the blow he himself tumbled head foremost overboard, and struck upon a piece of the broken mast. Honest James ran to his assistance, hauled him up, and from the effort he made was precipitated into the sea in sight of the sailor, who left him to perish, without deigning to look at him. Candide drew near and saw his benefactor, who rose above the water one moment and was then swallowed up forever. He was just going to jump after him, but was prevented by the philosopher Pangloss, who demonstrated to him that the Bay of Lisbon had been made on purpose for the Anabaptist to be drowned. While he was proving this *a priori*, the ship foundered; all perished except Pangloss, Candide, and the brutal sailor who had drowned the good Anabaptist. The villain swam safely to shore, while Pangloss and Candide were borne thither upon a plank.

As soon as they recovered themselves a little, they walked toward Lisbon. They had some money left, with which they hoped to save themselves from starving, after they had escaped drowning. Scarcely had they reached the city, lamenting the death of their benefactor, when they felt the earth tremble under their feet. The sea swelled and foamed in the harbor and beat to pieces the vessels riding at anchor. Whirlwinds of fire and ashes covered the streets and public places; houses fell,

roofs were flung upon the pavements, and the pavements were scattered. Thirty thousand inhabitants of all ages and sexes were crushed under the ruins. The sailor, whistling and swearing, said booty was to be gained here.

"What can be the *sufficient reason* of this phenomenon?" said Pangloss.

"This is the Last Day!" cried Candide.

The sailor ran among the ruins, facing death to find money; finding it, he took it, and got drunk . . .

Some falling stones had wounded Candide. He lay stretched in the street covered with rubbish.

"Alas!" said he to Pangloss, "get me a little wine and oil; I am dying."

"This concussion of the earth is no new thing," answered Pangloss. "The city of Lima, in America, experienced the same convulsions last year; the same cause, the same effects; there is certainly a train of sulphur underground from Lima to Lisbon."

"Nothing more probable," said Candide; "but for the love of God get me a little oil and wine."

"How, probable?" replied the philosopher. "I maintain that the point is capable of being demonstrated."

Candide fainted away, and Pangloss fetched him some water from a neighboring fountain. The following day they rummaged among the ruins and found provisions, with which they repaired their exhausted strength. After this they joined with others in relieving those inhabitants who had escaped death. Some, whom they had succored, gave them as good a dinner as they could in such disastrous circumstances; true, the repast was mournful, and the company moistened their bread with tears; but Pangloss consoled them, assuring them that things could not be otherwise.

"For," said he, "all that is is for the best. If there is a volcano at Lisbon it cannot be elsewhere. It is impossible that things should be other than they are; for everything is right." . . .

Candide and Pangloss are then seized, Candide is publicly whipped and Pangloss is hanged. Candide, half dead, is nursed by an old woman who finally takes him to Cunegonde, who miraculously was not killed in Westphalia. Candide then kills two men who break into Cunegonde's room and the three, Cunegonde, the old woman and Candide, are forced to flee to Spain.

Candide, Cunegonde, and the old woman, having passed through Lucena, Chillas, and Lebrixa, arrived at length at Cadiz. A fleet was there getting ready, and troops assembling to bring to reason the reverend Jesuit Fathers of Paraguay, accused of having made one of the native tribes in the neighborhood of San Sacrament revolt against the kings of Spain and Portugal. Candide, having been in the Bulgarian service, performed the military exercise before the general of this little army with so graceful an address, with so intrepid an air, and with such agility and expedition, that he was given the command of a company of foot. Now, he was a captain! He set sail with Miss Cunegonde, the old woman, two valets, and two Andalusian horses, which had belonged to the Grand Inquisitor of Portugal.

During their voyage they reasoned a good deal on the philosophy of poor Pangloss.

"We are going into another world," said Candide; "and surely it must be there that all is for the best. For I must confess there is reason to complain a little of what passeth in our world in regard to both natural and moral philosophy."

"I love you with all my heart," said Cunegonde; "but my soul is still full of fright at that which I have seen and experienced."

"All will be well," replied Candide; "the sea of this new world is already better than our European sea; it is calmer, the winds more regular. It is certainly the New World which is the best of all possible worlds." . . .

The party lands in Buenos Aires, but Candide is pursued by those seeking the murderer of the two men. He flees again with his valet, Cacambo, leaving Cunegonde behind with the Governor. As the two enter Paraguay they meet a Jesuit priest, Cunegonde's brother, but during an argument Candide kills him. The pair escapes but soon they encounter the savage Oreillons, who make ready to roast them on a spit. However Cacambo pleads successfully for their freedom and they are allowed to leave.

"You see," said Cacambo to Candide, as soon as they had reached the frontiers of the Oreillons, "that this hemisphere is not better than the other, take my word for it; let us go back to Europe by the shortest way."

"How go back?" said Candide, "and where shall we go? to my own country? The Bulgarians and the Abares are slaying all; to Portugal? there I shall be burnt; and if we abide here, we are every moment in danger of being pitted. But how can I resolve to quit a part of the world where my dear Cunegonde resides?"

"Let us turn towards Cayenne," said Cacambo; "there we shall find Frenchmen, who wander all over the world; they may assist us; God will perhaps have pity on us."

It was not easy to get to Cayenne; they knew vaguely in which direction to go, but rivers, precipices, robbers, savages obstructed them all the way. Their horses died of fatigue. Their provisions were consumed; they fed a whole month upon wild fruits, and found themselves at last near a little river bordered with cocoa trees, which sustained their lives and their hopes.

Cacambo, who was a good counselor, said to Candide:

"We are able to hold out no longer; we have walked enough. I see an empty canoe near the riverside; let us fill it with cocoanuts, throw ourselves into it, and go with the current; a river always leads to some inhabited spot. If we do not find pleasant things, we shall at least find new things."

"With all my heart," said Candide; "Let us recommend ourselves to Providence."

They rowed a few leagues, between banks, in some places flowery, in others barren; in some parts smooth, in others rugged. The stream widened, and at length lost itself under an arch of frightful rocks which reached to the sky. The two travelers had the courage to commit themselves to the current. The river, suddenly contracting at this place, whirled them along with a dreadful noise and rapidity. At the end of four-and-twenty hours they saw daylight again, but their canoe was dashed to pieces against the rocks. For a league they had to creep from rock to rock, until at length they discovered an extensive plain, bounded by inaccessible mountains. The country was cultivated as much for pleasure as for necessity. On all sides the useful was also the beautiful. The roads were covered, or rather adorned, with carriages of a glittering form and substance, in which were men and women of surprising beauty, drawn by large red sheep which surpassed in fleetness the finest coursers of Andalusia, Tetuan, and Mequinez.

"Here, however, is a country," said Candide, "which is better than Westphalia."

He stepped out with Cacambo toward the first village which he saw. Some children dressed in tattered brocades played at quoits on the outskirts. Our travelers from the other world amused themselves by looking on. The quoits were large round pieces, yellow, red, and green, which cast a singular luster! The travelers picked a few of them off the ground; this was of gold, that of emeralds, the other of rubies—the least of them would have been the greatest ornament on the Mogul's throne.

"Without doubt," said Cacambo, "these children must be the kings's sons that are playing at quoits!"

The village schoolmaster appeared at this moment and called them to school.

"There," said Candide, "is the preceptor of the royal family."

The little truants immediately quitted their game, leaving the quoits on the ground with all their other playthings. Candide gathered them up, ran to the master, and presented them to him in a most humble manner, giving him to understand by signs that their royal highnesses had forgotten their gold and jewels. The schoolmaster, smiling, flung them upon the ground; then, looking at Candide with a good deal of surprise, went about his business.

The travelers, however, took care to gather up the gold, the rubies, and the emeralds.

"Where are we?" cried Candide. "The king's children in this country must be well brought up, since they are taught to despise gold and precious stones."

Cacambo was as much surprised as Candide. At length they drew near the first house in the village. It was built like an European palace. A crowd of people pressed about the door, and there were still more in the house. They heard most agreeable music, and were aware of a delicious odor of cooking. Cacambo went up to the door and heard they were talking Peruvian; it was his mother tongue, for it is well known that Cacambo was born in Tucuman, in a village where no other language was spoken.

"I will be your interpreter here," said he to Candide; "Let us go in; it is a public house."

Immediately two waiters and two girls, dressed in cloth of gold, and their hair tied up with ribbons, invited them to sit down to table with the landlord. They served four dishes of soup, each garnished with two young parrots; a boiled condor which weighed two hundred pounds; two roasted monkeys, of excellent flavor; three hundred hummingbirds in one dish, and six hundred fly-birds in another; exquisite ragouts; delicious pastries; the whole served up in dishes of a kind of rock crystal. The waiters and girls poured out several liqueurs drawn from the sugar cane.

Most of the company were chapmen and wagoners, all extremely polite; they asked Cacambo a few questions with the greatest circumspection, and answered his in the most obliging manner.

As soon as dinner was over, Cacambo believed as well as Candide that they might well pay their reckoning by laying down two of those large gold pieces which they had picked up. The landlord and landlady shouted with laughter and held their sides. When the fit was over:

"Gentlemen," said the landlord, "it is plain you are strangers, and such guests we are not accustomed to see; pardon us therefore for laughing when you offered us the pebbles from our highroads in payment of your reckoning. You doubtless have not the money of the country; but it is not necessary to have any money at all to dine in this house. All hostelries established for the convenience of commerce are paid by the government. You have fared but very indifferently because this is a poor village; but everywhere else, you will be received as you deserve."

Cacambo explained this whole discourse with great astonishment to Candide, who was as greatly astonished to hear it.

"What sort of a country then is this," said they to one another; "a country unknown to all the rest of the world, and where nature is of a kind so different from ours? It is probably the country where all is well; for there absolutely must be one such place. And, whatever Master Pangloss might say, I often found that things went very ill in Westphalia."

Cacambo expressed his curiosity to the landlord, who made answer:

"I am very ignorant, but not the worse on that account. However, we have in this neighborhood an old man retired from Court who is the most learned and most communicative person in the kingdom."

At once he took Cacambo to the old man. Candide acted now only a second character, and accompanied his valet. They entered a very plain house, for the door was only of silver, and the ceilings were only of gold, but wrought in so elegant a taste as to vie with the richest. The antechamber, indeed, was only encrusted with rubies and emeralds, but the order in which everything was arranged made amends for this great simplicity.

The old man received the strangers on his sofa, which was stuffed with hummingbirds' feathers, and ordered his servants to present them with liqueurs in diamond goblets; after which he satisfied their curiosity in the following terms:

"I am now one hundred and seventy-two years old, and I learned of my late father, Master of the Horse to the King, the amazing revolutions of Peru, of which he had been an eyewitness. The kingdom we now inhabit is the ancient country of the Incas, who quitted it very imprudently to conquer another part of the world, and were at length destroyed by the Spaniards.

"More wise by far were the princes of their family, who remained in their native country; and they ordained, with the consent of the whole nation, that none of the inhabitants should ever be permitted to quit this little kingdom; and this has preserved our innocence and happiness. The Spaniards have had a confused notion of this country, and have called it *El Dorado;* and an Englishman, whose name was Sir Walter Raleigh, came very near it about a hundred years ago; but being surrounded by inaccessible rocks and precipices, we have hitherto been sheltered from the rapaciousness of European nations, who have an inconceivable passion for the pebbles and dirt of our land, for the sake of which they would murder us to the last man.

The conversation was long: it turned chiefly on their form of government, their manners, their women, their public entertainments, and the arts. At length Candide, having always had a taste for metaphysics, made Cacambo ask whether there was any religion in that country.

The old man reddened a little.

"How then," said he, "can you doubt it? Do you take us for ungrateful wretches?"

Cacambo humbly asked, "What is the religion in El Dorado?"

The old man reddened again, but continued.

"Can there be two religions?" said he. "We have, I believe, the religion of all the world: we worship God night and morning."

"Do you worship but one God?" said Cacambo, who still acted as interpreter in representing Candide's doubts.

"Surely," said the old man, "there are not two, nor three, nor four. I must confess the people from your side of the world ask very extraordinary questions."

Candide was not yet tired of interrogating the good old man; he wanted to know in what manner they prayed to God in El Dorado.

"We do not pray to Him," said the worthy sage; "we have nothing to ask of Him; He has given us all we need, and we return Him with thanks without ceasing."

Candide, having a curiosity to see the priests, asked where they were. The good old man smiled.

"My friend," said he, "we are all priests. The King and all the heads of families sing solemn canticles of thanksgiving every morning, accompanied by five or six thousand musicians . . ."

During this whole discourse Candide was in raptures, and he said to himself:

"This is vastly different from Westphalia and the Baron's castle. Had our friend Pangloss seen El Dorado he would no longer have said that the castle of Thunder-ten-Tronckh was the finest upon earth. It is evident that one must travel."

After this long conversation the old man ordered a coach and six sheep to be got ready, and twelve of his domestics to conduct the travelers to Court . . .

They spent a month in this hospitable place. Candide frequently said to Cacambo:

"I own, my friend, once more that the castle where I was born is nothing in comparison with this; but, after all, Miss Cunegonde is not here, and you have, without doubt, some mistress in Europe. If we abide here we shall only be upon a footing with the rest, whereas, if we return to our old world, only with twelve sheep laden with the pebbles of El Dorado, we shall be richer than all the kings in Europe. We shall have no more Inquisitors to fear, and we may easily recover Miss Cunegonde."

This speech was agreeable to Cacambo; mankind are so fond of roving, of making a figure in their own country, and of boasting of what they have seen in their travels that the two happy ones resolved to be no longer so, but to ask His Majesty's leave to quit the country.

"You are foolish," said the King. "I am sensible that my kingdom is but a small place, but when a person is comfortably settled in any part he should abide there. I have not the right to detain strangers. It is a tyranny which neither our manners nor our laws permit. All men are free. Go when you wish, but the going will be very difficult. It is impossible to ascend that rapid river on which you came as by a miracle, and which runs under vaulted rocks. The mountains which surround my kingdom are ten thousand feet high, and as steep as walls; they are each over ten leagues in breadth, and there is no other way to descend them than by precipices. However, since you absolutely wish to depart, I shall give orders to my engineers to construct a machine that will convey you very safely. When we have conducted you over the mountains no one can accompany you further, for my subjects have made a vow never to quit the kingdom, and they are too wise to break it. Ask me besides anything that you please."

"We desire nothing of Your Majesty," said

Candide, "but a few sheep laden with provisions, pebbles, and the earth of this country."

The King laughed.

"I cannot conceive," said he, "what pleasure you Europeans find in our yellow clay, but take as much as you like, and great good may it do you!"

At once he gave directions that his engineers should construct a machine to hoist up these two extraordinary men out of the kingdom. Three thousand good mathematicians went to work; it was ready in fifteen days, and did not cost more than twenty million sterling in the specie of that country. They placed Candide and Cacambo on the machine. There were two great red sheep saddled and bridled to ride upon as soon as they were beyond the mountains, twenty pack-sheep laden with provisions, thirty with presents of the curiosities of the country, and fifty with gold, diamonds, and precious stones. The King embraced the two wanderers very tenderly.

Their departure, with the ingenious manner in which they and their sheep were hoisted over the mountains, was a splendid spectacle. The mathematicians took their leave after conveying them to a place of safety, and Candide had no other desire, no other aim, than to present his sheep to Miss Cunegonde.

"Now," said he, "we are able to pay the Governor of Buenos Aires if Miss Cunegonde can be ransomed. Let us journey towards Cayenne. Let us embark, and we will afterwards see what kingdom we shall be able to purchase."

Our travelers spent the first day very agreeably. They were delighted with possessing more treasure than all Asia, Europe, and Africa could scrape together. Candide, in his raptures, cut Cunegonde's name on the trees. The second day two of their sheep plunged into a morass, where they and their burdens were lost; two more died of fatigue a few days after; seven or eight perished with hunger in a desert; and others subsequently fell down precipices. At length, after traveling a hundred days, only two sheep remained. Said Candide to Cacambo:

"My friend, you see how perishable are the riches of the world; there is nothing solid but virtue, and the happiness of seeing Cunegonde once more."

"I grant all you say," said Cacambo, "but we have still two sheep remaining, with more treasure than the King of Spain will ever have; and I see a town which I take to be Surinam, belonging to the Dutch. We are at the end of all our troubles, and at the beginning of happiness."

As they drew near the town, they saw a Negro stretched upon the ground, with only one moiety of his clothes, that is, of his blue linen drawers; the poor man had lost his left leg and his right hand.

"Good God!" said Candide in Dutch, "what are thou doing there, friend, in that shocking condition?"

"I am waiting for my master, Mynheer Vanderdendur, the famous merchant," answered the Negro.

"Was it Mynheer Vanderdendur," said Candide, "that treated thee thus?"

"Yes, sir," said the Negro, "it is the custom. They give us a pair of linen drawers for our whole garment twice a year. When we work at the sugar canes, and the mill snatches hold of a finger, they cut off the hand; and when we attempt to run away, they cut off the leg; both cases have happened to me. This is the price at which you eat sugar in Europe. Yet when my mother sold me for ten patagons on the coast of Guinea, she said to me: 'My child, bless your fetishes, adore them forever; they will make thee live happily; thou hast the honor of being the slave of our lords, the whites, which is making the fortune of thy father and mother.' Alas! I know not whether I have made their fortunes; this I know, that they have not made mine. Dogs, monkeys, and parrots are a thousand times less wretched than I. The Dutch fetishes, who have converted me, declare every Sunday that we are all of us children of Adam—blacks as well as whites. I am not a genealogist, but if these preachers tell truth, we are all second cousins. Now, you must agree with me it is impossible to treat one's relations in a more barbarous manner."

"Oh, Pangloss!" cried Candide, "thou hadst not guessed at this abomination; it is the end. I must at last renounce thy optimism."

"What is this optimism?" said Cacambo.

"Alas!" said Candide, "it is the madness of maintaining that everything is right when it is wrong."

Looking at the Negro, he shed tears, and weeping, he entered Surinam.

The first thing they inquired after was whether there was a vessel in the harbor which could be sent to Buenos Aires. The person to whom they applied was a Spanish sea-captain, who offered to take them there upon reasonable terms. He appointed to meet them at a public house, whither Candide and the faithful Cacambo went with their two sheep, and awaited his coming.

Candide, who had his heart upon his lips, told

the Spaniard all his adventures, and avowed that he intended to elope with Miss Cunegonde.

"Then I will take good care not to carry you to Buenos Aires," said the seaman. "I should be hanged, and so would you. The fair Cunegonde is my lord's favorite mistress!"

This was a thunderclap for Candide: he wept for a long while. At last he drew Cacambo aside.

"Here, my dear friend," said he to him, "this thou must do. We have, each of us in his pocket, five or six millions in diamonds; you are more clever than I; you must go and bring Miss Cunegonde from Buenos Aires. If the Governor makes any difficulty, give him a million; if he will not relinquish her, give him two; as you have not killed an Inquisitor, they will have no suspicion of you; I'll get another ship, and go and wait for you at Venice; that's a free country, where there is no danger either from Bulgarians, Abares, Jews, or Inquisitors."

Cacambo applauded this wise resolution. He despaired at parting from so good a master, who had become his intimate friend; but the pleasure of serving him prevailed over the pain of leaving him. They embraced with tears; Candide charged him not to forget the good old woman who had aided them to escape to South America. Cacambo set out that very same day. This Cacambo was a very honest fellow.

Candide stayed some time longer in Surinam, waiting for another captain to carry him and the two remaining sheep to Italy. After he had hired domestics, and purchased everything necessary for a long voyage, Mynheer Vanderdendur, captain of a large vessel, came and offered his services.

"How much will you charge," said he to this man, "to carry me straight to Venice—me, my servants, my baggage, and these two sheep?"

The skipper asked ten thousand piastres. Candide did not hesitate.

"Oh! oh!" said the prudent Vanderdendur to himself, "this stranger gives ten thousand piastres unhesitatingly! He must be very rich."

Returning a little while after, he let him know that, upon second consideration, he could not undertake the voyage for less than twenty thousand piastres.

"Well, you shall have them," said Candide.

"Ay!" said the skipper to himself, "this man agrees to pay twenty thousand piastres with as much ease as ten."

He went back to him again, and declared that he could not carry him to Venice for less than thirty thousand piastres.

"Then you shall have thirty thousand," replied Candide.

"Oh! oh!" said the Dutch skipper once more to himself, "thirty thousand piastres are a trifle to this man; surely these sheep must be laden with an immense treasure; let us say no more about it. First of all, let him pay down the thirty thousand piastres; then we shall see."

Candide sold two small diamonds, the least of which was worth more than what the skipper asked for his freight. He paid him the money in advance.

The two sheep were put on board. Candide followed in a little boat to join the vessel in the roads. The skipper seized his opportunity, set sail, and put out to sea, the wind favoring him. Candide, dismayed and stupefied, soon lost sight of the vessel.

"Alas!" said he, "this is a trick worthy of the old world!"

Candide, after losing his fortune, has more adventures while visiting England, France, and other parts of Europe. Eventually he buys a small farm in Turkey and there is reunited with all his friends. Pangloss who really was not hanged because the wet rope did not slip properly, the Jesuit priest and brother of Cunegonde whom Candide had not really killed, Cunegonde whom Candide marries, the old woman, the valet Cacambo and several others live and work on the farm.

In the neighborhood there lived a very famous Dervish who was esteemed the best philosopher in all Turkey, and so they went to consult him. Pangloss was the speaker.

"Master," said he, "we come to beg you to tell why so strange an animal as man was made."

"With what meddlest thou?" said the Dervish. "Is it thy business?"

"But, reverend father," said Candide, "there is horrible evil in this world."

"What signifies it," said the Dervish, "whether there be evil or good? When His Highness sends a ship to Egypt, does he trouble his head whether the mice on board are at their ease or not?"

"What, then, must we do?" said Pangloss.

"Hold your tongue," answered the Dervish.

"I was in hopes," said Pangloss, "that I should reason with you a little about causes and effects, about the best of possible worlds, the origin or evil, the nature of the soul, and the pre-established harmony."

At these words, the Dervish shut the door in their faces.

During this conversation, the news was spread that two Viziers and the Mufti had been strangled at Constantinople, and that several of their friends had been impaled. This catastrophe made a great noise for some hours. Pangloss, Candide, and Martin, returning to the little farm, saw a good old man taking the fresh air at his door under an orange bower. Pangloss, who was as inquisitive as he was argumentative, asked the old man what was the name of the strangled Mufti.

"I do not know," answered the worthy man, "and I have not known the name of any Mufti, nor of any Vizier. I am entirely ignorant of the event you mention; I presume in general that they who meddle with the administration of public affairs die sometimes miserably, and that they deserve it; but I never trouble my head about what is transacting at Constantinople; I content myself with sending there for sale the fruits of the garden which I cultivate."

Having said these words, he invited the strangers into his house; his two sons and two daughters presented them with several sorts of sherbet, which they made themselves, with Kaimak enriched with the candied peel of citrons, with oranges, lemons, pineapples, pistachio nuts, and Mocha coffee unadulterated with the bad coffee of Batavia or the American islands; after which the two daughters of the honest Mussulman perfumed the strangers' beards.

"You must have a vast and magnificent estate," said Candide to the Turk.

"I have only twenty acres," replied the old man, "I and my children cultivate them; our labor preserves us from three great evils—weariness, vice, and want."

Candide, on his way home, made profound reflections on the old man's conversation.

"This honest Turk," said he to Pangloss and Martin, "seems to be in a situation far preferable to that of the six kings with whom we had the honor of supping."

"Grandeur," said Pangloss, "is extremely dangerous, according to the testimony of philosophers . . ."

"I know also," said Candide, "that we must cultivate our garden."

"You are right," said Pangloss, "for when man was first placed in the Garden of Eden, he was put there *ut operaretur enum,* that he might cultivate it; which shows that man was not born to be idle."

"Let us work," said Martin, "without disputing; it is the only way to render life tolerable."

The whole little society entered into this laudable design, according to their different abilities. Their little plot of land produced plentiful crops . . . They were all of some service or other. . . .

Pangloss sometimes said to Candide:

"There is a concatenation of events in this best of all possible worlds: for if you had not been kicked out of a magnificent castle for love of Miss Cunegonde; if you had not suffered misfortune in Portugal; if you had not walked over America; if you had not stabbed the Baron; if you had not lost all your sheep from the fine country of El Dorado, you would not be here eating preserved citrons and pistachio nuts."

"All that is very well," answered Candide, "but let us cultivate our garden."

Jean-Jacques Rousseau

Jean-Jacques Rousseau (1712-1778) was a man of the Enlightenment and generally in sympathy with the beliefs of the *Philosophes*. He was, however, exceedingly sensitive and impulsive as well as highly emotional, and is often looked upon as a transitional figure between rationalism and romanticism. His most famous work, *The Social Contract,* appeared in 1762. Although Rousseau, like Hobbes and Locke, believed in the state of nature, he thought of it as a Paradise which was ruined when a few men staked off some land and claimed ownership of this property. Because Rousseau was an eloquent writer, but often a confused thinker, he has been considered by many as a dangerous man. His influence, however, has been widespread. He has been called the Father of Romanticism as well as the founder of democracy; he not only influenced the German Romantic Idealists, but also provided the dictators of the 20th century with many political concepts. In these selections from *The Social Contract* note in particular the type of political community envisioned by Rousseau and the concept which he calls the General Will. Find the connection between Rousseau's General Will and the theories of Adolph Hitler and Benito Mussolini who claimed to embody the feelings and desires of the people of their country.

THE SOCIAL CONTRACT

BOOK I

I mean to inquire if, in the civil order, there can be any sure and legitimate rule of administration, men being taken as they are and laws as they might be. In this inquiry I shall endeavour always to unite what right sanctions with what is prescribed by interest, in order that justice and utility may in no case be divided.

I enter upon my task without proving the importance of the subject. I shall be asked if I am a prince of a legislator, to write on politics. I answer that I am neither, and that is why I do so. If I were a prince or a legislator, I should not waste time in saying what wants doing; I should do it, or hold my peace.

As I was born a citizen of a free State, and a member of the Sovereign, I feel that, however feeble the influence my voice can have on public affairs, the right of voting on them makes it my duty to study them: and I am happy, when I reflect upon governments, to find my inquiries always furnish me with new reasons for loving that of my own country.

Subject of the First Book

Man is born free; and everywhere he is in chains. One thinks himself the master of others, and still remains a greater slave than they. How did this change come about? I do not know. What can make it legitimate? That question I think I can answer.

If I took into account only force, and the effects derived from it, I should say: "As long as a people is compelled to obey, and obeys, it does well; as soon as it can shake off the yoke, and shakes it off, it does still better; for, regaining its liberty by the same right as took it away, either it is justified in resuming it, or there was no justification for those who took it away." But the social order is a sacred right which is the basis of all other rights. Nevertheless, this right does not come from nature, and must therefore be founded on conventions. Before coming to that, I have to prove what I have just asserted. . . .

The Right of the Strongest

The strongest is never strong enough to be always the master, unless he transforms strength into right, and obedience into duty. Hence the right of the strongest, which, though to all seeming

From *The Social Contract & Discourses* by Jean Jacques Rousseau. Published by J. M. Dent & Sons Ltd in London & Tronto and in New York by E. P. Dutton & Co. Copyright 1913.

meant ironically, is really laid down as a fundamental principle. But are we never to have an explanation of this phrase? Force is a physical power, and I fail to see what moral effect it can have. To yield to force is an act of necessity, not of will—at the most, an act of prudence. In what sense can it be a duty?

Suppose for a moment that this so-called "right" exists. I maintain that the sole result is a mass of inexplicable nonsense. For, if force creates right, the effect changes with the cause: every force that is greater than the first succeeds to its right. As soon as it is possible to disobey with impunity, disobedience is legitimate; and, the strongest being always in the right, the only thing that matters is to act so as to become the strongest. But what kind of right is that which perishes when force fails? If we must obey perforce, there is no need to obey because we ought; and if we are not forced to obey, we are under no obligation to do so. Clearly, the word "right" adds nothing to force: in this connection, it means absolutely nothing.

Obey the powers that be. If this means yield to force, it is a good precept, but superfluous: I can answer for its never being violated. All power comes from God, I admit; but so does all sickness: does that mean that we are forbidden to call in the doctor? A brigand surprises me at the edge of a wood: must I not merely surrender my purse on compulsion; but, even if I could withhold it, am I in conscience bound to give it up? For certainly the pistol he holds is also a power.

Let us then admit that force does not create right, and that we are obliged to obey only legitimate powers. In that case, my original question recurs.

Slavery

Since no man has a natural authority over his fellow, and force creates no right, we must conclude that conventions form the basis of all legitimate authority among men.

If an individual, says Grotius, can alienate his liberty and make himself the slave of a master, why could not a whole people do the same and make itself subject to a king? There are in this passage plenty of ambiguous words which would need explaining; but let us confine ourselves to the word *alienate.* To alienate is to give or to sell. Now, a man who becomes the slave of another does not give himself; he sells himself, at the least for his subsistence: but for what does a people sell itself? A king is so far from furnishing his subjects with their subsistence that he gets his own only from them; and, according to Rabelais, kings do not live on nothing. Do subjects then give their persons on condition that the king takes their goods also? I fail to see what they have left to preserve.

It will be said that the despot assures his subjects civil tranquility. Granted; but what do they gain, if the wars his ambition brings down upon them, his insatiable avidity, and the vexatious conduct of his ministers press harder on them than their own dissensions would have done? What do they gain, if the very tranquility they enjoy is one of their miseries? Tranquility is found also in dungeons; but is that enough to make them desirable places to live in? The Greeks imprisoned in the cave of the Cyclops the minority to submit to the choice of the majority? How have a hundred men who wish for a master the right to vote on behalf of ten who do not? The law of majority voting is itself something established by convention, and presupposes unanimity, on one occasion at least.

The Social Compact

I suppose men to have reached the point at which the obstacles in the way of their preservation in the state of nature show their power of resistance to be greater than the resources at the disposal of each individual for his maintenance in that state. That primitive condition can then subsist no longer; and the human race would perish unless it changed its manner of existence.

But, as men cannot engender new forces, but only unite and direct existing ones, they have no other means of preserving themselves than the formation, by aggregation, of a sum of forces great enough to overcome the resistance. These they have to bring into play by means of a single motive power, and cause to act in concert.

This sum of forces can arise only where several persons come together: but, as the force and liberty of each man are the chief instruments of his self-preservation, how can he pledge them without harming his own interests, and neglecting the care he owes to himself? This difficulty, in its bearing on my present subject, may be stated in the following terms—

"The problem is to find a form of association which will defend and protect with the whole common force the person and goods of each associate, and in which each, while uniting himself with all, may still obey himself alone, and remain as free as before." This is the fundamental problem of which the *Social Contract* provides the solution.

The clauses of this contract are so determined by the nature of the act that the slightest modification would make them vain and ineffective; so that, although they have perhaps never been formally set forth, they are everywhere the same and everywhere tacitly admitted and recognised, until, on the violation of the social compact, each regains his original rights and resumes his natural liberty, while losing the conventional liberty in favour of which he renounced it.

These clauses, properly understood, may be reduced to one—the total alienation of each associate, together with all his rights, to the whole community; for, in the first place, as each gives himself absolutely, the conditions are the same for all; and, this being so, no one has any interest in making them burdensome to others.

Moreover, the alienation being without reserve, the union is as perfect as it can be, and no associate has anything more to demand: for, if the individuals retained certain rights, as there would be no common superior to decide between them and the public, each, being on one point his own judge, would ask to be so on all; the state of nature would thus continue, and the association would necessarily become inoperative or tyrannical.

Finally, each man, in giving himself to all, gives himself to nobody; and as there is no associate over whom he does not acquire the same right as he yields others over himself, he gains an equivalent for everything he loses, and an increase of force for the preservation of what he has.

If then we discard from the social compact what is not of its essence, we shall find that it reduces itself to the following terms—

"Each of us puts his person and all his power in common under the supreme direction of the general will, and, in our corporate capacity, we receive each member as an indivisible part of the whole."

At once, in place of the individual personality of each contracting party, this act of association creates a moral and collective body, composed of as many members as the assembly contains votes, and receiving from this act its unity, its common identity, its life and its will. This public person, so formed by the union of all other persons, formerly took the name of *city,* and now takes that of *Republic* or *body politic;* it is called by its members *State* when passive, *Sovereign* when active, and *Power* when compared with others like itself. Those who are associated in it take collectively the name of *people,* and severally are called *citizens,* as sharing in the sovereign power, and

subjects, as being under the laws of the State. But these terms are often confused and taken one for another: it is enough to know how to distinguish them when they are being used with precision.

The Sovereign

This formula shows us that the act of association comprises a mutual undertaking between the public and the individuals, and that each individual, in making a contract, as we may say, with himself, is bound in a double capacity; as a member of the Sovereign he is bound to the individuals, and as a member of the State to the Sovereign. But the maxim of civil right, that no one is bound by undertakings made to himself, does not apply in this case; for there is a great difference between incurring an obligation to yourself and incurring one to a whole of which you form a part.

Attention must further be called to the fact that public deliberation, while competent to bind all the subjects to the Sovereign, because of the two different capacities in which each of them may be regarded, cannot, for the opposite reason, bind the Sovereign to itself; and that it is consequently against the nature of the body politic for the Sovereign to impose on itself a law which it cannot infringe. Being able to regard itself in only one capacity, it is in the position of an individual who makes a contract with himself; and this makes it clear that there neither is nor can be any kind of fundamental law binding on the body of the people—not even the social contract itself. This does not mean that the body politic cannot enter into undertakings with others, provided the contract is not infringed by them; for in relation to what is external to it, it becomes a simple being, an individual.

But the body politic or the Sovereign, drawing its being wholly from the sanctity of the contract, can never bind itself, even to an outsider, to do anything derogatory to the original act, for instance, to alienate any part of itself, or to submit to another Sovereign. Violation of the act by which it exists would be self-annihilation; and that which is itself nothing can create nothing.

As soon as this multitude is so united in one body, it is impossible to offend against one of the members without attacking the body, and still more to offend against the body without the members resenting it. Duty and interest therefore equally oblige the two contracting parties to give each other help; and the same men should seek to combine, in their double capacity, all the advantages dependent upon that capacity.

Again, the Sovereign, being formed wholly of the individuals who compose it, neither has nor can have any interest contrary to theirs; and consequently the sovereign power need give no guarantee to its subjects, because it is impossible for the body to wish to hurt all its members. We shall also see later on that it cannot hurt any in particular. The Sovereign, merely by virtue of what it is, is always what it should be.

This, however, is not the case with the relation of the subjects to the Sovereign, which, despite the common interest, would have no security that they would fulfil their undertakings, unless it found means to assure itself of their fidelity.

In fact, each individual, as a man, may have a particular will contrary or dissimilar to the general will which he has as a citizen. His particular interest may speak to him quite differently from the common interest: his absolute and naturally independent existence may make him look upon what he owes to the common cause as a gratuitous contribution, the loss of which will do less harm to others than the payment of it is burdensome to himself; and, regarding the moral person which constitutes the State as a *persona ficta,* because not a man, he may wish to enjoy the rights of citizenship without being ready to fulfil the duties of a subject. The continuance of such an injustice could not but prove the undoing of the body politic.

In order then that the social compact may not be an empty formula, it tacitly includes the undertaking, which alone can give force to the rest, that whoever refuses to obey the general will shall be compelled to do so by the whole body. This means nothing less than that he will be forced to be free: for this is the condition which, by giving each citizen to his country, secures him against all personal dependence. In this lies the key to the working of the political machine; this alone legitimises civil undertakings, which, without it, would be absurd, tyrannical, and liable to the most frightful abuses.

The Civil State

The passage from the state of nature to the civil state produces a very remarkable change in man, by substituting justice for instinct in his conduct, and giving his actions the morality they had formerly lacked. Then only, when the voice of duty takes the place of physical impulses and right of appetite, does man, who so far had considered only himself, find that he is forced to act on different principles, and to consult his reason before listening to his inclinations. Although, in this state, he deprives himself of some advantages which he got from nature, he gains in return others so great, his faculties are so stimulated and developed, his ideas so extended, his feelings so ennobled, and his whole soul so uplifted, that, did not the abuses of this new condition often degrade him below that which he left, he would be bound to bless continually the happy moment which took him from it for ever, and, instead of a stupid and unimaginative animal, made him an intelligent being and a man.

Let us draw up the whole account in terms easily commensurable. What man loses by the social contract is his natural liberty and an unlimited right to everything he tries to get and succeeds in getting; what he gains is civil liberty and the proprietorship of all he possesses. If we are to avoid mistake in weighing one against the other, we must clearly distinguish natural liberty, which is bounded only by the strength of the individual, from civil liberty, which is limited by the general will; and possession, which is merely the effect of force or the right of the first occupier, from property, which can be founded only a positive title.

We might, over and above all this, add, to what man acquires in the civil state, moral liberty, which alone makes him truly master of himself; for the mere impulse of appetite is slavery, while obedience to a law which we prescribe to ourselves is liberty. But I have already said too much on this head, and the philosophical meaning of the word liberty does not now concern us.

Real Property

Each member of the community gives himself to it, at the moment of its foundation, just as he is, with all the resources at his command, including the goods he possesses. This act does not make possession, in changing hands, change its nature, and become property in the hands of the Sovereign; but, as the forces of the city are incomparably greater than those of an individual, public possession is also, in fact, stronger and more irrevocable, without being any more legitimate, at any rate from the point of view of foreigners. For the State, in relation to its members, is master of all their goods by the social contract, which, within the State, is the basis of all rights but, in relation to other powers, it is so only by the right of the first occupier, which it holds from its members.

The right of the first occupier, though more real than the right of the strongest, becomes a real right only when the right of property has already been established. Every man has naturally a right to everything he needs; but the positive act which makes him proprietor of one thing excludes him from everything else. Having his share, he ought to keep to it, and can have no further right against the community. This is why the right of the first occupier, which in the state of nature is so weak, claims the respect of every man in civil society. In this right we are respecting not so much what belongs to another as what does not belong to ourselves.

In general, to establish the right of the first occupier over a plot of ground, the following conditions are necessary: first, the land must not yet be inhabited; secondly, a man must occupy only the amount he needs for his subsistence; and, in the third place, possession must be taken, not by an empty ceremony, but by labour and cultivation, the only sign of proprietorship that should be respected by others, in default of a legal title.

In granting the right of first occupancy to necessity and labour, are we not really stretching it as far as it can go? Is it possible to leave such a right unlimited? Is it to be enough to set foot on a plot of common ground, in order to be able to call yourself at once the master of it? Is it to be enough that a man has the strength to expel others for a moment, in order to establish his right to prevent them from ever returning? How can a man or a people seize an immense territory and keep it from the rest of the world except by a punishable usurpation, since all others are being robbed, by such an act, of the place of habitation and the means of subsistence which nature gave them in common? When Nũnez Balbao, standing on the sea-shore, took possession of the South Seas and the whole of South America in the name of the crown of Castile, was that enough to dispossess all their actual inhabitants, and to shut out from them all the princes of the world? On such a showing, these ceremonies are idly multiplied, and the Catholic King need only take possession all at once, from his apartment, of the whole universe, merely making a subsequent reservation about what was already in the possession of other princes.

We can imagine how the lands of individuals, where they were contiguous and came to be united, became the public territory, and how the right of Sovereignty, extending from the subjects over the lands they held, became at once real and personal. The possessors were thus made more dependent, and the forces at their command used to guarantee their fidelity. The advantage of this does not seem to have been felt by ancient monarchs, who called themselves King of the Persians, Scythians, or Macedonians, and seemed to regard themselves more as rulers of men than as masters of a country. Those of the present day more cleverly call themselves Kings of France, Spain, England, etc.: thus holding the land, they are quite confident of holding the inhabitants.

The peculiar fact about this alienation is that, in taking over the goods of individuals, the community, so far from despoiling them, only assures them legitimate possession, and changes usurpation into a true right and enjoyment into proprietorship. Thus the possessors, being regarded as depositaries of the public good, and having their rights respected by all the members of the State and maintained against foreign aggression by all its forces, have, by a cession which benefits both the public and still more themselves, acquired, so to speak, all that they gave up. This paradox may easily be explained by the distinction between the rights which the Sovereign and the proprietor have over the same estate, as we shall see later on.

It may also happen that men begin to unite one with another before they possess anything, and that, subsequently occupying a tract of country which is enough for all, they enjoy it in common, or share it out among themselves, either equally or according to a scale fixed by the Sovereign. However the acquisition be made, the right which each individual has to his own estate is always subordinate to the right which the community has over all: without this, there would be neither stability in the social tie, nor real force in the exercise of Sovereignty.

I shall end this chapter and this book by remarking on a fact on which the whole social system should rest: *i.e.* that, instead of destroying natural inequality, the fundamental compact substitutes, for such physical inequality as nature may have set up between men, an equality that is moral and legitimate, and that men, who may be unequal in strength or intelligence, become every one equal by convention and legal right.

BOOK II

That Sovereignty is Inalienable

The first and most important deduction from the principles we have so far laid down is that the general will alone can direct the State according to the object for which it was instituted, *i.e.* the common good: for if the clashing of particular interests made the establishment of societies necessary, the agreement of these very interests made it possible. The common element in these different interests is what forms the social tie; and, were there no point of agreement between them all, no society could exist. It is solely on the basis of this common interest that every society should be governed.

I hold then that Sovereignty, being nothing less than the exercise of the general will, can never be alienated, and that the Sovereign, who is no less than a collective being, cannot be represented except by himself: the power indeed may be transmitted, but not the will.

In reality, if it is not impossible for a particular will to agree on some point with the general will, it is at least impossible for the agreement to be lasting and constant; for the particular will tends, by its very nature, to partiality, while the general will tends to equality. It is even more impossible to have any guarantee of this agreement; for even if it should always exist, it would be the effect not of art, but of chance. The Sovereign may indeed say: "I now will actually what this man wills, or at least what he says he wills"; but it cannot say: "What he wills tomorrow, I too shall will" because it is absurd for the will to bind itself for the future, nor is it incumbent on any will to consent to anything that is not for the good of the being who wills. If then the people promises simply to obey, by that very act it dissolves itself and loses what makes it a people; the moment a master exists, there is no longer a Sovereign, and from that moment the body politic has ceased to exist.

This does not mean that the commands of the rulers cannot pass for general wills, so long as the Sovereign, being free to oppose them, offers no opposition. In such a case, universal silence is taken to imply the consent of the people. . . .

Whether the General Will is Fallible

It follows from what has gone before that the general will is always right and tends to the public advantage; but it does not follow that the deliberations of the people are always equally correct. Our will is always for our own good, but we do not always see what that is; the people is never corrupted, but it is often deceived, and on such occasions only does it seem to will what is bad.

There is often a great deal of difference between the will of all and the general will; the latter considers only the common interest, while the former takes private interest into account, and is no more than a sum of particular wills: but take away from these same wills the pluses and minuses that cancel one another, and the general will remains as the sum of the differences.

If, when the people, being furnished with adequate information, held its deliberations, the citizens had no communication one with another, the grand total of the small differences would always give the general will, and the decision would always be good. But when factions arise, and partial associations are formed at the expense of the great association, the will of each of these associations becomes general in relation to its members, while it remains particular in relation to the State: it may then be said that there are no longer as many votes as there are men, but only as many as there are associations. The differences become less numerous and give a less general result. Lastly, when one of these associations is so great as to prevail over all the rest, the result is no longer a sum of small differences, but a single difference; in this case there is no longer a general will, and the opinion which prevails is purely particular.

It is therefore essential, if the general will is to be able to express itself, that there should be no partial society within the State, and that each citizen should think only his own thoughts: which was indeed the sublime and unique system established by the great Lycurgus. But if there are partial societies, it is best to have as many as possible and to prevent them from being unequal, as was done by Solon, Numa and Servius. These precautions are the only ones that can guarantee that the general will shall be always enlightened, and that the people shall in no way deceive itself.

The Limits of the Sovereign Power

If the State is a moral person whose life is in the union of its members, and if the most important of its cares is the care for its own preservation, it must have a universal and compelling force, in order to move and dispose each part as may be most advantageous to the whole. As nature gives each man absolute power over all his members, the social compact gives the body politic absolute power over all its members also; and it is this power which, under the direction of the general will, bears, as I have said, the name of Sovereignty.

But, besides the public person, we have to consider the private persons composing it, whose life and liberty are naturally independent of it. We are bound then to distinguish clearly between the respective rights of the citizens and the Sovereign, and between the duties the former have to fulfil as subjects, and the natural rights they should enjoy as men.

Each man alienates, I admit, by the social compact, only such part of his powers, goods and liberty as it is important for the community to control; but it must also be granted that the Sovereign is sole judge of what is important.

Every service a citizen can render the State he ought to render as soon as the Sovereign demands it; but the Sovereign, for its part, cannot impose upon its subjects any fetters that are useless to the community, nor can it even wish to do so; for no more by the law of reason than by the law of nature can anything occur without a cause.

The undertakings which bind us to the social body are obligatory only because they are mutual; and their nature is such that in fulfilling them we cannot work for others without working for ourselves. Why is it that the general will is always in the right, and that all continually will the happiness of each one, unless it is because there is not a man who does not think of "each" as meaning him, and consider himself in voting for all? This proves that equality of rights and the idea of justice which such equality creates originate in the preference each man gives to himself, and accordingly in the very nature of man. It proves that the general will, to be really such, must be general in its object as well as its essence; that it must both come from all and apply to all; and that it loses its natural rectitude when it is directed to some particular and determinate object, because in such a case we are judging of something foreign to us, and have no true principle of equity to guide us.

Indeed, as soon as a question of particular fact or right arises on a point not previously regulated by a general convention, the matter becomes contentious. It is a case in which the individuals concerned are one party, and the public the other, but in which I can see neither the law that ought to be followed nor the judge who ought to give the decision. In such a case, it would be absurd to propose to refer the question to an express decision of the general will, which can be only the conclusion reached by one of the parties and in consequence will be, for the other party, merely an external and particular will, inclined on this occasion to injustice and subject to error. Thus, just as a particular will cannot stand for the general will, the general will, in turn, changes its nature, when

its object is particular, and, as general, cannot pronounce on a man or a fact. When, for instance, the people of Athens nominated or displaced its rulers, decreed honours to one, and imposed penalties on another, and, by a multitude of particular decrees, exercised all the functions of government indiscriminately, it had in such cases no longer a general will in the strict sense; it was acting no longer as Sovereign, but as magistrate. This will seem contrary to current views; but I must be given time to expound my own.

It should be seen from the foregoing that what makes the will general is less the number of voters than the common interest uniting them; for, under this system, each necessarily submits to the conditions he imposes on others: and this admirable agreement between interest and justice gives to the common deliberations an equitable character which at once vanishes when any particular question is discussed, in the absence of a common interest to unite and identify the ruling of the judge with that of the party.

From whatever side we approach our principle, we reach the same conclusion, that the social compact sets up among the citizens an equality of such a kind, that they all bind themselves to observe the same conditions and should therefore all enjoy the same rights. Thus, from the very nature of the compact, every act of Sovereignty, *i.e.* every authentic act of the general will, binds or favours all the citizens equally; so that the Sovereign recognises only the body of the nation, and draws no distinctions between those of whom it is made up. What, then, strictly speaking, is an act of Sovereignty? It is not a convention between a superior and an inferior, but a convention between the body and each of its members. It is legitimate, because based on the social contract, and equitable, because common to all; useful, because it can have no other object than the general good, and stable, because guaranteed by the public force and the supreme power. So long as the subjects have to submit only to conventions of this sort, they obey no-one but their own will; and to ask how far the respective rights of the Sovereign and the citizens extend, is to ask up to what point the latter can enter into undertakings with themselves, each with all, and all with each.

We can see from this that the sovereign power, absolute, sacred and inviolable as it is, does not and cannot exceed the limits of general conventions, and that every man may dispose at will of such goods and liberty as these conventions leave him; so that the Sovereign never has a right to lay more charges on one subject than on another, because, in that case, the question becomes particular, and ceases to be within its competency.

When these distinctions have once been admitted, it is seen to be so untrue that there is, in the social contract, any real renunciation on the part of the individuals, that the position in which they find themselves as a result of the contract is really preferable to that in which they were before. Instead of a renunciation, they have made an advantageous exchange: instead of an uncertain and precarious way of living they have got one that is better and more secure; instead of natural independence they have got liberty, instead of the power to harm others security for themselves, and instead of their strength, which others might overcome, a right which social union makes invincible. Their very life, which they have devoted to the State, is by it constantly protected; and when they risk it in the State's defence, what more are they doing than giving back what they have received from it? What are they doing that they would not do more often and with greater danger in the state of nature, in which they would inevitably have to fight battles at the peril of their lives in defence of that which is the means of their preservation? All have indeed to fight when their country needs them; but then no one has ever to fight for himself. Do we not gain something by running, on behalf of what gives us our security, only some of the risks we should have to run for ourselves, as soon as we lost it? . . .

The Marks of a Good Government

The question "What absolutely is the best government?" is unanswerable as well as indeterminate; or rather, there are as many good answers as there are possible combinations in the absolute and relative situation of all nations.

But if it is asked by what sign we may know that a given people is well or ill governed, that is another matter, and the question, being one of fact, admits of an answer.

It is not, however, answered, because every-one wants to answer it in his own way. Subjects extol public tranquillity, citizens individual liberty; the one class prefers security of possessions, the other that of person; the one regards as the best government that which is most severe, the other maintains that the mildest is the best; the one wants crimes punished, the other wants them prevented; the one wants the State to be feared by its neighbours, the other prefers that it should be ignored; the one is content if money circulates, the other demands that the people shall have bread. Even if an agreement were come to on these and similar points, should we have got any further? As moral qualities do not admit of exact measurement, agreement about the mark does not mean agreement about the valuation.

For my part, I am continually astonished that a mark so simple is not recognised, or that men are of so bad faith as not to admit it. What is the end of political association? The preservation and prosperity of its members. And what is the surest mark of their preservation and prosperity? Their numbers and population. Seek then nowhere else this mark that is in dispute. The rest being equal, the government under which, without external aids, without naturalisation or colonies, the citizens increase and multiply most, is beyond question the best. The government under which a people wanes and diminishes is the worst. Calculators, it is left for you to count, to measure, to compare. . . .

How to Check the Usurpations of Government

What we have just said confirms Chapter XVI, and makes it clear the the institution of government is not a contract, but a law; that the depositaries of the executive power are not the people's masters, but its officers; that it can set them up and pull them down when it likes; that for them there is no question of contract, but of obedience; and that in taking charge of the functions the State imposes on them they are doing no more than fulfilling their duty as citizens, without having the remotest right to argue about the conditions.

When therefore the people sets up an hereditary government, whether it be monarchical and confined to one family, or aristocratic and confined to a class, what it enters into is not an undertaking; the administration is given a provisional form, until the people chooses to order it otherwise.

It is true that such changes are always dangerous, and that the established government should never be touched except when it comes to be incompatible with the public good; but the circumspection this involves is a maxim of policy and not a rule of right, and the State is no more bound to leave civil authority in the hands of its rulers than military authority in the hands of its generals.

It is also true that it is impossible to be too careful to observe, in such cases, all the formalities necessary to distinguish a regular and legitimate act from a seditious tumult, and the will of a whole people from the clamour of a faction. Here above all no further concession should be made to the untoward possibility than cannot, in the strictest logic, be refused it. From this obligation the prince derives a great advantage in preserving his power despite the people, without it being possible to say he usurped it; for, seeming to avail himself only of his rights, he finds it very easy to extend them, and to prevent, under the pretext of keeping the peace, assemblies that are destined to the re-establishment of order; with the result that he takes advantage of a silence he does not allow to be broken, or of irregularities he causes to be committed, to assume that he has the support of those whom fear prevents from speaking, and to punish those who dare to speak. Thus it was that the decemvirs, first elected for one year and then kept on in office for a second, tried to perpetuate their power by forbidding the comitia to assemble; and by this easy method every government in the world, once clothed with the public power, sooner or later usurps the sovereign authority.

The periodical assemblies of which I have already spoken are designed to prevent or postpone this calamity, above all when they need no formal summoning; for in that case, the prince cannot stop them without openly declaring himself a law-breaker and an enemy of the State.

The opening of these assemblies, whose sole object is the maintenance of the social treaty, should always take the form of putting two propositions that may not be suppressed, which should be voted on separately.

The first is: "Does it please the Sovereign to preserve the present form of government?"

The second is: "Does it please the people to leave its administration in the hands of those who are actually in charge of it?"

I am here assuming what I think I have shown; that there is in the State no fundamental law that cannot be revoked, not excluding the social compact itself; for if all the citizens assembled of one accord to break the compact, it is impossible to doubt that it would be very legitimately broken. Grotius even thinks that each man can renounce his membership of his own State, and recover his natural liberty and his goods on leaving the country. It would be indeed absurd if all the citizens in assembly could not do what each can do by himself.

Revolutionary Documents

As the 18th Century drew to a close, two major political documents appeared, containing principles of freedom, citizenship and sovereignty which had been debated and propagandized during the Enlightenment. In *The Declaration of Independence* (1776) and *The Declaration of the Rights of Man and Citizen* (1789), these general principles were related concretely to specific situations, such as rebellious colonies and rebellious citizens against their king. In reading these two declarations, note the rights which are safeguarded, and how both realities and ideologies are given proper attention. Each document attempted to establish a new way of life and, if at times they did not completely succeed, they were of tremendous influence on succeeding governments throughout the world. The third selection in this group is the *Bill of Rights,* the first ten amendments to the Constitution of the United States, which guaranteed the citizens of the new country specific rights which had been popularized by the political theorists of the 17th and 18th centuries.

THE DECLARATION OF INDEPENDENCE, 1776

In Congress, July 4, 1776: The unanimous Declaration of the thirteen united States of America

When in the Course of human events, it becomes necessary for one people to dissolve the political bands which have connected them with another, and to assume among the Powers of the earth, the separate and equal station to which the Laws of Nature and of Nature's God entitle them, a decent respect to the opinions of mankind requires that they should declare the causes which impel them to the separation.

We hold these truths to be self-evident, that all men are created equal, that they are endowed by their Creator with certain unalienable Rights, that among these are Life, Liberty and the pursuit of Happiness. That to secure these rights, Governments are instituted among Men, deriving their just powers from the consent of the governed, That whenever any Form of Government becomes destructive of these ends, it is the Right of the People to alter or to abolish it, and to institute new Government, laying its foundation on such principles and organizing its powers in such form, as to them shall seem most likely to effect their Safety and Happiness. Prudence, indeed, will dictate that Governments long established should not be changed for light and transient causes; and accordingly all experience hath shown, that mankind are more disposed to suffer, while evils are sufferable, than to right themselves by abolishing the forms to which they are accustomed. But when a long train of abuses and usurpations, pursuing invariably the same Object evinces a design to reduce them under absolute Despotism, it is their right, it is their duty, to throw off such Government, and to provide new Guards for their future security.—Such has been the patient sufferance of these Colonies; and such is now the necessity which constrains them to alter their former Systems of Government. The history of the present King of Great Britain is a history of repeated injuries and usurpations, all having in direct object the establishment of an absolute Tyranny over these States. To prove this, let Facts be submitted to a candid world.

He has refused his Assent to Laws, the most wholesome and necessary for the public good.

He has forbidden his Governors to pass Laws of immediate and pressing importance, unless suspended in their operation till his Assent should be obtained; and when so suspended he has utterly neglected to attend to them.

He has refused to pass other Laws for the accommodation of large districts of people, unless those people would relinquish the right of Representation in the Legislature, a right inestimable to them and formidable to tyrants only.

He has called together legislative bodies at places unusual, uncomfortable, and distant from the depository of their Public Records, for the sole purpose of fatiguing them into compliance with his measures.

He has dissolved Representative Houses repeatedly, for opposing with manly firmness his invasions on the rights of the people.

He has refused for a long time, after such dissolutions, to cause others to be elected; whereby the Legislative Powers, incapable of Annihilation, have returned to the People at large for their exercise; the State remaining in the mean time exposed to all the dangers of invasion from without, and convulsions within.

He has endeavoured to prevent the population of these States; for that purpose obstructing the Laws for Naturalization of Foreigners; refusing to pass others to encourage their migration hither, and raising the conditions of new Appropriations of Lands.

He has obstructed the Administration of Justice, by refusing his Assent to Laws for establishing Judiciary Powers.

He has made Judges dependent on his Will alone, for the tenure of their offices, and the amount and payment of their salaries.

He has erected a multitude of New Offices, and sent hither swarms of Officers to harrass our People, and eat out their substance.

He has kept among us, in times of peace, Standing Armies without the Consent of our legislature.

He has affected to render the Military independent of and superior to the Civil Power.

He has combined with others to subject us to a jurisdiction foreign to our constitution, and unacknowledged by our laws; giving his Assent to their acts of pretended Legislation:

For quartering large bodies of armed troops among us:

For protecting them, by a mock Trial, from Punishment for any Murders which they should commit on the Inhabitants of these States:

For cutting off our Trade with all parts of the world:

For imposing taxes on us without our Consent:

For depriving us in many cases, of the benefits of Trial by Jury:

For transporting us beyond Seas to be tried for pretended offences:

For abolishing the free System of English Laws in a neighbouring Province, establishing therein an Arbitrary government, and enlarging its Boundaries so as to render it at once an example and fit instrument for introducing the same absolute rule into these Colonies:

For taking away our Charters, abolishing our most valuable Laws, and altering fundamentally the Forms of our Governments:

For suspending our own Legislatures, and declaring themselves invested with Powers to legislate for us in all cases whatsoever.

He has abdicated Government here, by declaring us out of his Protection and waging War against us.

He has plundered our seas, ravaged our Coasts, burnt our towns, and destroyed the lives of our people.

He is at this time transporting large armies of foreign mercenaries to complete the works of death, desolation and tyranny, already begun with circumstances of Cruelty & perfidy scarcely paralleled in the most barbarous ages, and totally unworthy the Head of a civilized nation.

He has constrained our fellow Citizens taken Captive on the high Seas to bear Arms against their Country, to become the executioners of their friends and Brethren, or to fall themselves by their Hands.

He has excited domestic insurrections amongst us, and has endeavoured to bring on the inhabitants of our frontiers, the merciless Indian Savages, whose known rule of warfare, is an undistinguished destruction of all ages, sexes and conditions.

In every stage of these Oppressions We have Petitioned for Redress in the most humble terms: Our repeated Petitions have been answered only by repeated injury. A Prince, whose character is thus marked by every act which may define a Tyrant, is unfit to be a ruler of a free People.

Nor have We been wanting in attention to our British brethren. We have warned them from time to time of attempts by their legislature to extend an unwarrantable jurisdiction over us. We have reminded them of the circumstances of our emigration and settlement here. We have appealed to their native justice and magnanimity, and we have conjured them by the ties of our common kindred to disavow these usurpations, which, would inevitably interrupt our connections and correspondence. They too have been deaf to the voice of justice and of consanguinity. We must, therefore, acquiesce in the necessity, which denounces our Separation, and hold them, as we hold the rest of mankind. Enemies in War, in Peace Friends.

We, therefore, the Representatives of the united States of America, in General Congress, Assembled, appealing to the Supreme Judge of the world for the rectitude of our intentions, do, in the Name, and by Authority of the good People of these Colonies, solemnly publish and declare, That these United Colonies are, and of Right ought to be Free and Independent States; that they are Absolved from all Allegiance to the British Crown, and that all political connection between them and the State of Great Britain, is and ought to be totally dissolved; and that as Free and Independent States, they have full Power to levy War, conclude Peace, contract Alliances, establish Commerce, and to do all other Acts and Things which Independent States may of right do. And for the support of this Declaration, with a firm reliance on the Protection of Divine Providence, we mutually pledge to each other our Lives, our Fortunes and our sacred Honor.

DECLARATION OF THE RIGHTS OF MAN AND CITIZEN

27 August, 1789

The representatives of the French people, organized in National Assembly, considering that ignorance, forgetfulness, or contempt of the rights of man are the sole causes of public misfortunes and of the corruption of governments, have resolved to set forth in a solemn declaration the natural, inalienable, and sacred rights of man, in order that such declaration, continually before all members of the social body, may be a perpetual reminder of their rights and duties; in order that the acts of the legislative power and those of the executive power may constantly be compared with the aim of every political institution and may accordingly be more respected; in order that the demands of the citizens, founded henceforth upon simple and incontestable principles, may always be directed towards the maintenance of the Constitution and the welfare of all.

Accordingly, the National Assembly recognizes and proclaims, in the presence and under the auspices of the Supreme Being, the following rights of man and citizen.

1. Men are born and remain free and equal in rights; social distinctions may be based only upon general usefulness.

2. The aim of every political association is the preservation of the natural and inalienable rights of man; these rights are liberty, property, security, and resistance to oppression.

3. The source of all sovereignty resides essentially in the nation; no group, no individual may exercise authority not emanating expressly therefrom.

4. Liberty consists of the power to do whatever is not injurious to others; thus the enjoyment of the natural rights of every man has for its limits only those that assure other members of society the enjoyment of those same rights; such limits may be determined only by law.

5. The law has the right to forbid only actions which are injurious to society. Whatever is not forbidden by law may not be prevented, and no one may be constrained to do what it does not prescribe.

6. Law is the expression of the general will; all citizens have the right to concur personally, or through their representatives, in its formation; it must be the same for all, whether it protects or punishes. All citizens, being equal before it, are equally admissible to all public offices, positions, and employments, according to their capacity, and without other distinction than that of virtues and talents.

7. No man may be accused, arrested, or detained except in the cases determined by law, and according to the forms prescribed thereby. Whoever solicit, expedite, or execute arbitrary orders, or have them executed, must be punished; but every citizen summoned or apprehended in pursuance of the law must obey immediately; he renders himself culpable by resistance.

8. The law is to establish only penalties that are absolutely and obviously necessary; and no one may be punished except by virtue of a law established and promulgated prior to the offence and legally applied.

9. Since every man is presumed innocent until declared guilty, if arrest be deemed indispensable, all unnecessary severity for securing the person of the accused must be severely repressed by law.

10. No one is to be disquieted because of his opinions, even religious, provided their manifestation does not disturb the public order established by law.

11. Free communication of ideas and opinions is one of the most precious of the rights of man. Consequently, every citizen may speak, write, and print freely, subject to responsibility for the abuse of such liberty in the cases determined by law.

12. The guarantee of the rights of man and citizen necessitates a public force; such a force, therefore, is instituted for the advantage of all and not for the particular benefit of those to whom it is entrusted.

13. For the maintenance of the public force and for the expenses of administration a common tax is indispensable; it must be assessed equally on all citizens in proportion to their means.

14. Citizens have the right to ascertain, by themselves or through their representatives, the necessity of the public tax, to consent to it freely, to supervise its use, and to determine its quota, assessment, payment, and duration.

15. Society has the right to require of every public agent an accounting of his administration.

16. Every society in which the guarantee of rights is not assured or the separation of powers not determined has no constitution at all.

17. Since property is a sacred and inviolable right, no one may be deprived thereof unless a legally established public necessity obviously requires it, and upon condition of a just and previous indemnity.

THE BILL OF RIGHTS
(The ten original amendments to the Constitution of the United States)

Article I
RELIGIOUS ESTABLISHMENT PROHIBITED. FREEDOM OF SPEECH, OF THE PRESS, AND RIGHT TO PETITION

Congress shall make no law respecting an establishment of religion or prohibiting the free exercise thereof; or abridging the freedom of speech or of the press; or the right of the people peaceably to assemble and to petition the Government for a redress of grievances.

Article II
RIGHT TO KEEP AND BEAR ARMS

A well-regulated militia being necessary to the security of a free State, the right of the people to keep and bear arms shall not be infringed.

Article III
NO SOLDIER TO BE QUARTERED IN ANY HOUSE, UNLESS, ETC.

No soldier shall, in time of peace, be quartered in any house without the consent of the owner, nor in time of war but in a manner to be prescribed by law.

Article IV
RIGHT OF SEARCH AND SEIZURE REGULATED

The right of the people to be secure in their persons, houses, papers, and effects, against unreasonable searches and seizures shall not be violated, and no warrants shall issue but upon probable cause, supported by oath or affirmation, and particularly describing the place to be searched, and the persons or things to be seized.

Article V
PROVISIONS CONCERNING PROSECUTION, TRIAL AND PUNISHMENT. PRIVATE PROPERTY NOT TO BE TAKEN FOR PUBLIC USE WITHOUT COMPENSATION

No person shall be held to answer for a capital or other infamous crime unless on a presentment or indictment of a Grand Jury, except in cases arising in the land or naval forces, or in the militia, when in actual service, in time of war or public danger; nor shall any person be subject for the same offense to be twice put in jeopardy of life or limb; nor shall be compelled in any criminal case to be a witness against himself, nor be deprived of life, liberty, or property, without due process of law; nor shall private property be taken for public use without just compensation.

Article VI
RIGHT TO SPEEDY TRIAL, WITNESSES, ETC.

In all criminal prosecutions, the accused shall enjoy the right to a speedy and public trial, by an impartial jury of the State and district wherein the crime shall have been committed, which districts shall have been previously ascertained by law, and to be informed of the nature and cause of the accusation; to be confronted with the witnesses against him; to have compulsory process for obtaining witnesses in his favor, and to have the assistance of counsel for his defense.

Article VII
RIGHT OF TRIAL BY JURY

In suits at common law, where the value in controversy shall exceed twenty dollars, the right of trial by jury shall be preserved, and no fact tried by a jury shall be otherwise re-examined in any court of the United States than according to the rules of the common law.

Article VIII
EXCESSIVE BAIL OR FINES AND CRUEL PUNISHMENT PROHIBITED

Excessive bail shall not be required, nor excessive fines imposed, nor cruel and unusual punishments inflicted.

Article IX
RULE OF CONSTRUCTION OF CONSTITUTION

The enumeration in the Constitution of certain rights shall not be construed to deny or disparage others retained by the people.

Article X
RIGHTS OF STATES UNDER CONSTITUTION

The powers not delegated to the United States by the Constitution, nor prohibited by it to the States, are reserved to the States respectively, or to the people.

Edmund Burke

Edmund Burke (1729-1797) offered the most thoughtful critique of the French Revolution. Generally considered as a "conservative," Burke was appalled at the thoroughness with which the French were destroying their past institutions. This led him to write his *Reflections on the French Revolution* (1790). Prophesying anarchy and despotism for France, Burke advised his fellow Englishmen to allow the slow evolution of freedom. He viewed human society as an organism which grew slowly; it could not be successfully rearranged by human manipulation. Notice Burke's emphasis on history, tradition and constitutionalism, and his rejection of the abstract idea of "the rights of man."

REFLECTIONS ON THE FRENCH REVOLUTION

The ceremony of cashiering kings, of which these gentlemen talk so much at their ease, can rarely, if ever, be performed without force. It then becomes a case of war, and not of constitution. Laws are commanded to hold their tongues amongst arms; and tribunals fall to the ground with the peace they are no longer able to uphold. The Revolution of 1688 was obtained by a just war, in the only case in which any war, and much more a civil war, can be just. "Justa bella quibus *necessaria*." The question of dethroning, or, if these gentlemen like the phrase better, "cashiering kings," will always be, as it has always been, an extraordinary question of state, and wholly out of the law; a question (like all other questions of state) of dispositions, and of means, and of probable consequences, rather than of positive rights. As it was not made for common abuses, so it is not to be agitated by common minds. The speculative line of demarcation, where obedience ought to end, and resistance must begin, is faint, obscure, and not easily definable. It is not a single act, or a single event, which determines it. Governments must be abused and deranged indeed, before it can be thought of; and the prospect of the future must be as bad as the experience of the past. When things are in that lamentable condition, the nature of the disease is to indicate the remedy to those whom nature has qualified to administer in extremities this critical, ambiguous, bitter potion to a distempered state. Times, and occasions, and provacations, will teach their own lessons. The wise will determine from the gravity of the case; the irritable from sensibility to oppression; the high-minded from disdain and indignation at abusive power in unworthy hands; the brave and bold from

From Burke, *Reflections on the French Revolution*, edited by W. Alison Phillips, and Catherine Beatrice Phillips. Published by Cambridge: at the University Press, 1912. Used by permission.

the love of honourable danger in a generous cause: but, with or without right, a revolution will be the very last resource of the thinking and the good.

The third head of right, asserted by the pulpit of the Old Jewry, namely, the "right to form a government for ourselves," has, at least, as little countenance from any thing done at the Revolution, either in precedent or principle, as the two first of their claims. The Revolution was made to preserve our *ancient,* indisputable laws and liberties, and that *ancient* constitution of government which is our only security for law and liberty. If you are desirous of knowing the spirit of our constitution, and the policy which predominated in that great period which has secured it to this hour, pray look for both in our histories, in our records, in our acts of parliament, and journals of parliament, and not in the sermons of the Old Jewry, and the after-dinner toasts of the Revolution Society. In the former you will find other ideas and another language. Such a claim is as ill-suited to our temper and wishes as it is unsupported by any appearance of authority. The very idea of the fabrication of a new government is enough to fill us with disgust and horrour. We wished at the period of the Revolution, and do now wish, to derive all we possess as *an inheritance from our forefathers.* Upon that body and stock of inheritance we have taken care not to inoculate any scion alien to the nature of the original plant. All the reformations we have hitherto made have proceeded upon the principle of reference to antiquity; and I hope, nay I am persuaded, that all those which possibly may be made hereafter, will be carefully formed upon analogical precedent, authority, and example.

Our oldest reformation is that of Magna Charta. You will see that Sir Edward Coke, that great oracle of our law, and indeed all the great men who follow him, to Blackstone, are industrious to prove the pedigree of our liberties. They endeavour to prove, that the ancient charter, the Magna Charta of King John, was connected with another positive charter from Henry I and that both the one and the other were nothing more than a reaffirmance of the still more ancient standing law of the kingdom. In the matter of fact, for the greater part, these authors appear to be in the right; perhaps not always; but if the lawyers mistake in some particulars, it proves my position still the more strongly; because it demonstrates the powerful prepossession towards antiquity, with which the minds of all our lawyers and legislators, and of all the people whom they wish to influence, have

been always filled; and the stationary policy of this kingdom in considering their most sacred rights and franchises as an *inheritance.*

In the famous law of the 3d of Charles I called the *Petition of Right,* the parliament says to the king, "Your subjects have *inherited* this freedom," claiming their franchises not on abstract principles "as the rights of men," but as the rights of Englishmen, and as a patrimony derived from their forefathers. Selden, and the other profoundly learned men, who drew this petition of right, were as well acquainted, at least, with all the general theories concerning the "rights of men," as any of the discoursers in our pulpits, or on your tribune; full as well as Dr. Price, or as the Abbe Sieyes. But, for reasons worthy of that practical wisdom which superseded their theoretick science, they preferred this positive, recorded, *hereditary* title to all which can be dear to the man and the citizen, to that vague speculative right, which exposed their sure inheritance to be scrambled for and torn to pieces by every wild, litigious spirit.

The same policy pervades all the laws which have since been made for the preservation of our liberties. In the 1st of William and Mary, in the famous statute, called the Declaration of Right, the two houses utter not a syllable of "a right to frame a government for themselves." You will see, that their whole care was to secure the religion, laws, and liberties, that had been long possessed, and had been lately endangered. "Taking into their most serious consideration the *best* means for making such an establishment, that their religion, laws, and liberties, might not be in danger of being again subverted," they auspicate all their proceedings, by stating as some of those *best* means, "in the *first place*" to do as their *ancestors in like cases have usually* done for vindicating their *ancient* rights and liberties, to *declare"*;–and then they pray the king and queen, "that it may be *declared* and enacted, that *all and singular* the rights and liberties *asserted and declared* are the true *ancient* and indubitable rights and liberties of the people of this kingdom."

You will observe, that from Magna Charta to the Declaration of Right, it has been the uniform policy of our constitution to claim and assert our liberties, as an *entailed inheritance* derived to us from our forefathers, and to be transmitted to our posterity; as an estate specially belonging to the people of this kingdom, without any reference whatever to any other more general or prior right. By this means our constitution preserves an unity in so great a diversity of its parts. We have an inheritable crown; an inheritable peerage; and a house of commons and a people inheriting privileges, franchises, and liberties, from a long line of ancestors.

The policy appears to me to be the result of profound reflection; or rather the happy effect of following nature, which is wisdom without reflection, and above it. A spirit of innovation is generally the result of a selfish temper, and confined views. People will not look forward to posterity, who never look backward to their ancestors. Besides, the people of England well know, that the idea of inheritance furnishes a sure principle of conservation, and a sure principle of transmission; without at all excluding a principle of improvement. It leaves acquisition free; but it secures what it acquires. Whatever advantages are obtained by a state proceeding on these maxims, are locked fast as in a sort of family settlement; grasped as in a kind of mortmain for ever. By a constitutional policy working after the pattern of nature, we receive, we hold, we transmit our government and our privileges, in the same manner in which we enjoy and transmit our property and our lives. The institutions of policy, the goods of fortune, the gifts of Providence, are handed down to us, and from us, in the same course and order. Our political system is placed in a just correspondence and symmetry with the order of the world, and with the mode of existence decreed to a permanent body composed of transitory parts; wherein, by the disposition of a stupendous wisdom, moulding together the great mysterious incorporation of the human race, the whole, at one time, is never old, or middle-aged, or young, but, in a condition of unchangeable constancy, moves on through the varied tenour of perpetual decay, fall, renovation, and progression. Thus, by preserving the method of nature in the conduct of the state, in what we improve, we are never wholly new; in what we retain, we are never wholly obsolete. By adhering in this manner and on those principles to our forefathers, we are guided not by the superstition of antiquarians, but by the spirit of philosophick analogy. In this choice of inheritance we have given to our frame of polity the image of a relation in blood; binding up the constitution of our country with our dearest domestick ties; adopting our fundamental laws into the bosom of our family affections; keeping inseparable, and cherishing with the warmth of all their combined and mutually reflected charities, our state, our hearths, our sepulchres, and our altars.

Through the same plan of a conformity to nature in our artificial institutions, and by calling in the aid of her unerring and powerful instincts, to fortify the fallible and feeble contrivances of our reason, we have derived several other, and those no small benefits, from considering our liberties in the light of an inheritance. Always acting as if in the presence of canonized forefathers, the spirit of freedom, leading in itself to misrule and excess, is tempered with an awful gravity. This idea of a liberal descent inspires us with a sense of habitual native dignity, which prevents that upstart insolence almost inevitably adhering to and disgracing those who are the first acquirers of any distinction. By this means our liberty becomes a noble freedom. It carries an imposing and majestick aspect. It has a pedigree and illustrating ancestors. It has its bearings and its ensigns armorial. It has its gallery of portraits; its monumental inscriptions; its records, evidences, and titles. We procure reverence to our civil institutions on the principle upon which nature teaches us to revere individual men; on account of their age, and on account of those from whom they are descended. All your sophisters cannot produce any thing better adapted to preserve a rational and manly freedom than the course that we have pursued, who have chosen our nature rather than our speculations, our breasts rather than our inventions, for the great conservatories and magazines of our rights and privileges.

You might, if you pleased, have profited of our example, and have given to your recovered freedom a correspondent dignity. Your privileges, though discontinued, were not lost to memory. Your constitution, it is true, whilst you were out of possession, suffered waste and dilapidation; but you possessed in some parts the walls, and, in all, the foundations, of a noble and venerable castle. You might have repaired those walls; you might have built on those old foundations. Your constitution was suspended before it was perfected; but you had the elements of a constitution very nearly as good as could be wished. In your old states you possessed that variety of parts corresponding with the various descriptions of which your community was happily composed; you had all that combination, and all that opposition of interests, you had that action and counteraction which, in the natural and in the political world, from the reciprocal struggle of discordant powers, draws out the harmony of the universe. These opposed and conflicting interests, which you considered as so great a blemish in your old and in our present constitution, interpose a salutary check to all precipitate resolutions. They render deliberation a matter not of choice, but of necessity; they make all change a subject of *compromise,* which naturally begets moderation; they produce *temperaments,* preventing the sore evil of harsh, crude, unqualified reformations; and rendering all the headlong exertions of arbitrary power, in the few or in the many, for ever impracticable. Through that diversity of members and interests, general liberty had as many securities as there were separate views in the several orders; whilst by pressing down the whole by the weight of a real monarchy, the separate parts would have been prevented from warping, and starting from their allotted places.

You had all these advantages in your ancient states; but you chose to act as if you had never been moulded into civil society, and had every thing to begin anew. You began ill, because you began by despising every thing that belonged to you. You set up your trade without a capital. If the last generations of your country appeared without much lustre in your eyes, you might have passed them by, and derived your claims from a more early race of ancestors. Under a pious predilection for those ancestors, your imaginations would have realized in them a standard of virtue and wisdom, beyond the vulgar practice of the hour: and you would have risen with the example to whose imitation you aspired. Respecting your forefathers, you would have been taught to respect yourselves. You would not have chosen to consider the French as a people of yesterday, as a nation of low-born servile wretches until the emancipating year of 1789. In order to furnish, at the expence of your honour, an excuse to your apologists here for several enormities of yours, you would not have been content to be represented as a gang of Maroon slaves, suddenly broke loose from the house of bondage, and therefore to be pardoned for your abuse of the liberty to which you were not accustomed, and were ill fitted. Would it not, my worthy friend, have been wiser to have you thought, what I, for one, always thought you, a generous and gallant nation, long misled to your disadvantage by your high and romantick sentiments of fidelity, honour, and loyalty; that events had been unfavourable to you, but that you were not enslaved through any illiberal or servile disposition; that in your most devoted submission, you were actuated by a principle of publick spirit, and that it was your country you worshipped, in the person of your king? Had you made it to be understood, that in the delusion of this amiable errour you had gone further than your wise ancestors; that you were resolved to resume your ancient privileges, whilst you preserved the spirit of your ancient and your recent loyalty and honour; or if, diffident of yourselves, and not clearly discerning the almost obliterated constitution of your ancestors, you had looked to your neighbours in this land, who had kept alive the ancient principles and models of the old common law of Europe, meliorated and adapted to its present state—by following wise examples you would have given new examples of wisdom to the world. You would have rendered the cause of liberty venerable in the eyes of every worthy mind in every nation. You would have shamed despotism from the earth, by shewing that freedom was not only reconcilable, but, as when well disciplined it is, auxiliary to law. You would have had an unoppressive but a productive revenue. You would have had a flourishing commerce to feed it. You would have had a free constitution; a potent monarchy; a disciplined army; a reformed and venerated clergy; a mitigated but spirited nobility, to lead your virtue, not to overlay it; you would have had a liberal order of commons, to emulate and to recruit that nobility; you would have had a protected, satisfied, laborious, and obedient people, taught to seek and to recognise the happiness that is to be found by virtue in all conditions; in which consists the true moral equality of mankind, and not in that monstrous fiction, which, by inspiring false ideas and vain expectations into men destined to travel in the obscure walk of laborious life, serves only to aggravate and embitter that real inequality, which it never can remove; and which the order of civil life establishes as much for the benefit of those whom it must leave in an humble state, as those whom it is able to exalt to a condition more splendid, but not more happy. You had a smooth and easy career of felicity and glory laid open to you, beyond any thing recorded in the history of the world; but you have shewn that difficulty is good for man.

. . . .

I do not know under what description to class the present ruling authority in France. It affects to be pure democracy, though I think it in a direct train of becoming shortly a mischievous and ignoble oligarchy. But for the present I admit it to be a contrivance of the nature and effect of what it pretends to. I reprobate no form of government merely upon abstract principles. There may be situations in which the purely democratick form will become necessary. There may be some (very few, and very particularly circumstanced) where it would be clearly desirable. This I do not take to be the case of France, or of any other great country. Until now, we have seen no examples of considerable democracies. The ancients were better acquainted with them. Not being wholly unread in the authors, who had seen the most of those constitutions, and who best understood them, I cannot help concurring with their opinion, that an absolute democracy, no more than absolute monarchy, is to be reckoned among the legitimate forms of government. They think it rather the corruption and degeneracy, than the sound constitution of a republick. If I recollect rightly, Aristotle observes, that a democracy has many striking points of resemblance with a tyranny. Of this I am certain, that in a democracy, the majority of the citizens is capable of exercising the most cruel oppressions upon the minority, whenever strong divisions prevail in that kind of polity, as they often must; and that oppression of the minority will extend to far greater numbers, and will be carried on with much greater fury, than can almost ever be apprehended from the dominion of a single sceptre. In such a popular persecution, individual sufferers are in a much more deplorable condition than in any other. Under a cruel prince they have the balmy compassion of mankind to assuage the smart of their wounds; they have the plaudits of the people to animate their generous constancy under their sufferings: but those who are subjected to wrong under multitudes, are deprived of all external consolation. They seem deserted by mankind, overpowered by a conspiracy of their whole species.

Adam Smith

Adam Smith (1723-1790) is most famous for his work *An Inquiry into the Nature and Causes of the Wealth of Nations*, which appeared in the year 1776. The *Wealth of Nations* destroyed mercantilism, and, although written during the Enlightenment, was the manifesto of economic liberalism. Smith, a university professor and economist, stressed the fact that each individual should have the freedom to follow his own self-interest in business and trade. He argued for little government interference with business and a great deal of individual enterprise. His doctrine of *laissez-faire* had a great appeal to the businessmen and industrialists of the 19th century. The *Wealth of Nations* became their Bible and is one of the most influential works dealing with economics.

ADAM SMITH, AN INQUIRY INTO THE NATURE AND CAUSES OF THE WEALTH OF NATIONS[1]

INTRODUCTION

The annual labour of every nation is the fund which originally supplies it with all the necessaries and conveniences of life which it annually consumes, and which consist always either in the immediate produce of that labour, or in what is purchased with that produce from other nations.

According, therefore, as this produce, or what is purchased with it, bears a greater or smaller proportion to the number of those who are to consume it, the nation will be better or worse supplied with all the necessaries and conveniences for which it has occasion.

But this proportion must in every nation be regulated by two different circumstances: first, by the skill, dexterity, and judgment with which its labour is generally applied; and secondly, by the proportion between the number of those who are employed in useful labour, and that of those who are not so employed. Whatever be the soil, climate, or extent of territory of any particular nation, the abundance or scantiness of its annual supply must, in that particular situation, depend upon those two circumstances.

The abundance or scantiness of this supply, too, seems to depend more upon the former of those two circumstances than upon the latter. Among the savage nations of hunters and fishers, every individual who is able to work is less employed in useful labour, and endeavours to provide, as well as he can, the necessaries and conveniences of life, for himself, and such of his family or tribe as are either too old, or too young, or too infirm, to go a-hunting and fishing. Such nations, however, are so miserably poor, that, from mere want, they are frequently reduced, or at least think themselves reduced, to the necessity sometimes of abandoning, their infants, their old people, and those afflicted with lingering diseases, to perish with hunger, or to be devoured by wild beasts. Among civilised and thriving nations, on the contrary, though a great number of people do not labour at all, many of whom comsume the produce of ten times, frequently of a hundred times, more labour than the greater part of those who work; yet the produce of the whole labour of the society is so great, that all are often abundantly supplied; and a workman, even of the lowest and poorest order, if he is frugal and industrious, may enjoy a greater share of the necessaries and conveniences of life than it is possible for any savage to acquire.

The causes of this improvement in the productive powers of labour, and the order according to which its produce is naturally distributed among the different ranks and conditions of men in the society, make the subject of the first book of this inquiry. . . .

The greatest improvements in the productive powers of labour, and the greater part of the skill, dexterity, and judgment, with which it is anywhere directed, or applied, seem to have been the effects of the division of labour.

The effects of the division of labour, in the

1. Smith, Adam, *An Enquiry into the Nature and Causes of the Wealth of Nations.* London, 1870.

general business of society, will be more easily understood, by considering in what manner it operates in some particular manufactures. It is commonly supposed to be carried furthest in some very trifling ones; not perhaps that it really is carried further in them than in others of more importance: but in those trifling manufactures which are destined to supply the small wants of but a small number of people, the whole number of workmen must necessarily be small; and those employed in every different branch of the work can often be collected into the same workhouse, and placed at once under the view of the spectator. In those great manufactures, on the contrary, which are destined to supply the great wants of the great body of the people, every different branch of the work employs so great a number of workmen, that it is impossible to collect them all into the same workhouse. We can seldom see more, at one time, than those employed in one single branch. Though in such manufactures, therefore, the work may really be divided into a much greater number of parts, than in those of a more trifling nature, the division is not near so obvious, and has accordingly been much less observed.

To take an example, therefore, from a very trifling manufacture, but one in which the division of labour has been very often taken notice of, the trade of a pinmaker: a workman not educated to this business (which the division of labour has rendered a distinct trade) nor acquainted with the use of the machinery employed in it (to the invention of which the same division of labor has probably given occasion), could scarce, perhaps, with his utmost industry, make one pin in a day, and certainly could not make twenty. But in the way in which this business is now carried on, not only the whole work is a peculiar trade, but it is divided into a number of branches, of which the greater part are likewise peculiar trades. One man draws out the wire; another straights it; a third cuts it; a fourth points it; a fifth grinds it at the top for receiving the head; to make the head requires two or three distinct operations; to put it on is a peculiar business; to whiten the pins is another, it is even a trade by itself to put them into the paper; and the important business of making a pin is, in this manner, divided into about eighteen distinct operations, which, in some manufactories, are all performed by distinct hands, though in others the same man will sometimes perform two or three of them. I have seen a small manufactory of this kind, where ten men only were employed, and where some of them consequently performed two or three distinct operations. But though they were very poor, and therefore but indifferently accommodated with the necessary machinery, they could, when they exerted themselves, make among them about twelve pounds of pins in a day. There are in a pound upwards of four thousand pins of a middling size. Those ten persons, therefore, could make among them upwards of forty-eight thousand pins in a day. Each person, therefore, making a tenth part of forty-eight thousand pins, might be considered as making four thousand eight hundred pins in a day. But if they had all wrought separately and independently, and without any of them having been educated to this particular business, they certainly could not each of them have made twenty, perhaps not one pin in a day; that is, certainly, not the two hundred and fortieth, perhaps not the four thousand eight hundredth, part of what they are at present capable of performing, in consequence of a proper division and combination of their different operations.

In every other art and manufacture, the effects of the division of labour are similar to what they are in this very trifling one, though, in many of them, the labour can neither be so much subdivided, nor reduced to so great a simplicity of operation. The division of labour, however, so far as it can be introduced, occasions, in every art, a proportionable increase of the productive powers of labour. The separation of different trades and employments from one another, seems to have taken place in consequence of this advantage. This separation, too, is generally carried furthest in those countries which enjoy the highest degree of industry and improvement; what is the work of one man, in a rude state of society, being generally that of several in an improved one. In every improved society, the farmer is generally nothing but a farmer; the manufacturer, nothing but a manufacturer. The labour, too, which is necessary to produce any one complete manufacture, is almost always divided among a great number of hands. How many different trades are employed in each branch of the linen and woolen manufactures, from the growers of the flax and the wool, to the bleachers and smoothers of the linen, or to the dyers and dressers of the cloth! The nature of agriculture, indeed, does not admit of so many subdivisions of labour, nor of so complete a separation of one business from another, as manufacturers. It is impossible to separate so entirely the business of the grazier from that of the corn-farmer, as the trade of the carpenter is commonly separated from that of the smith. The spinner is almost always a distinct person from the weaver; but the ploughman, the harrower, the sower of the seed, and the reaper of the corn, are often the same. The occasions for those different sorts of labour returning with the different seasons of the year, it is impossible that one man should be constantly employed in any one of them. This impossibility of making so complete and entire a separation of all the different branches of labour employed in agriculture, is perhaps the reason why the improvement of the productive powers of labour, in this art, does not always keep pace with their improvement in manufactures. The most opulent nations, indeed, generally excel all their neighbours in agriculture as well as in manufactures; but they are commonly more distinguished by their superiority in the latter than in the former . . . .

This great increase in the quantity of work, which, in consequence of the division of labour, the same number of people are capable of performing is owing to three different circumstances; first, to the increase of dexterity in every particular workman; secondly, to the saving of the time which is commonly lost in passing from one species of work to another; and, lastly, to the invention of a great number of machines which facilitate and abridge labour, and enable one man to do the work of many . . . .

It is the great multiplication of the productions of all the different arts, in consequence of the division of labour, which occasions, in a well-governed society, that universal opulence which extends itself to the lowest ranks of the people. Every workman has a great quantity of his own work to dispose of beyond what he himself has occasion for; and every other workman being exactly in the same situation, he is enabled to exchange a great quantity of his own goods for a great quantity, or what comes to the same thing, for the price of a great quantity of theirs. He supplies them abundantly with what they have occasion for, and they accommodate him as amply with what he has occassion for, and general plenty diffuses itself through all the different ranks of the society.

Observe the accommodation of the most common artificer or day-labourer in a civilised and thriving country, and you will perceive that the number of people, of whose industry a part, though but a small part, has been employed in procuring him this accommodation, exceeds all computation. The woolen coat, for example, which covers the day-labourer, as coarse and rough as it may appear is the produce of the joint labour of a great multitude of workmen. The shepherd, the sorter of the wool, the wool-comber or carder, the dyer, the scribbler, the spinner, the weaver, the fuller, the dresser, with many others, must all join their different arts in order to complete even this homely production. How many merchants and carriers, besides, must have been employed in transporting the materials from some of those workmen to others who often live in a very distant part of the country? How much commerce and navigation in particular, how many ship-builders, sailors, sail-makers, rope-makers, must have been employed in order to bring together the different drugs made use of by the dyer, which often come from the remotest corners of the world?

. . . If we examine, I say, all these things, and consider what a variety of labour is employed about each of them, we shall be sensible that, without the assistance and co-operation of many thousands, the very meanest person in a civilized country could not be provided, even according to what we very falsely imagine the easy and simple manner in which he is commonly accommodated. Compared, indeed, with the more extravagant luxury of the great, his accommodation must no doubt appear extremely simple and easy; and yet it may be true, perhaps, that the accommodation of an European prince does not always so much exceed that of an industrious and frugal peasant, as the accommodation of the latter exceeds that of many an African king, the absolute masters of the lives and liberties of ten thousand naked savages.

Of the Principle Which Gives Occasion to the Division of Labour

This division of labour, from which so many advantages are derived, is not originally the effect of any human wisdom, which foresees and intends that general opulence to which it gives occasion. It is the necessary, though very slow and gradual, consequence of a certain propensity in human nature, which has in view no such extensive utility; the propensity to truck, barter, and exchange one thing for another.

Whether this propensity be one of those original principles in human nature, of which no further account can be given, or whether, as seems more probable, it be the necessary consequence of the faculties of reason and speech, it belongs not to our present subject to inquire. It is common to all men, and to be found in no other race of animals, which seem to know neither this nor any other species of contracts. Two greyhounds, in running down the same hare, have sometimes the appearance of acting in some sort of concert. Each turns her towards his companion, or endeavours to intercept her when his companion turns her toward himself. This, however, is not the effect of any contract, but of the accidental concurrence of their passions in the same object at that particular time. Nobody ever saw a dog make a fair and deliberate exchange of one bone for another with another dog. Nobody every saw one animal, by its gestures and natural cries, signify to another, this is mine, that yours; I am willing to give this for that. When an animal wants to obtain something either of a man, or of another animal, it has no other means of persuasion, but to gain the favour of those whose service it requires. A puppy fawns upon its dam, and a spaniel endeavours, by a thousand attractions, to engage the attention of its master who is at dinner, when it wants to be fed by him. Man sometimes uses the same arts with his brethren, and when he has no other means of engaging them to act according to his inclinations, endeavours by every servile and fawning attention to obtain their good will. He has not time, however, to do this upon every occasion. In civilised society he stands at all times in need of the co-operation and assistance of great multitudes, while his whole life is scarce sufficient to gain the friendship of a few persons. In almost every other race of animals, each individual, when it is grown up to maturity, is entirely independent, and in its natural state has occasion for the assistance of no other living creature. But man has almost constant occasion for the help of his brethren, and it is in vain for him to expect it from their benevolence only. He will be more likely to prevail if he can interest their self-love in his favour, and show them that it is for their own advantage to do for him what he requires of them. Whoever offers to another a bargain of any kind, proposes to do this. Give me that which I want, and you shall have this which you want, is the meaning of every such offer, and it is in this manner that we obtain from one another the far greater part of those good offices which we stand in need of. It is not from the benevolence of the butcher, the brewer, or the baker, that we expect our dinner, but from their regard to their own interest. We address ourselves, not to their humanity, but to their self-love, and never talk to them of our own necessities, but of their advantages. Nobody but a beggar chooses to depend chiefly upon the benevolence of his fellow-citizens. Even a beggar does not depend upon it entirely. The charity of well-disposed people, indeed, supplies him with the whole fund of his subsistence. But though this principle ultimately provides him with all the necessaries of life which he has occasion for, it neither does nor can provide him with them as he has occasion for them. The greater part of his occasional wants are supplied in the same manner as those of other people, by treaty, by barter, and by purchase. With the money which one man gives him he purchases food. The old clothes which another bestows upon him he exchanges for other clothes which suit him better, or for lodging, or for food, or for money, with which he can buy either food, clothes, or lodging, as he has occasion.

As it is by treaty, by barter, and by purchase, that we obtain from one another the greater part of those mutual good offices which we stand in need of, so it is this trucking disposition which originally gives occasion to the division of labour. In a tribe of hunters or shepherds, a particular person makes bows and arrows, for example, with more readiness and dexterity than any other. He frequently exchanges them for cattle or for venison, with his companions; and he finds at last that he can, in this manner, get more cattle and venison, than if he himself went to the field to catch them. From a regard to his own interest, therefore, the making of bows and arrows grows to be his chief business, and he becomes a sort of armourer. Another excels in making the frames and covers of their little huts or moveable houses. He is accustomed to be of use in this way to his neighbours, who reward him in the same manner with cattle and with venison, till at last he finds it his interest to dedicate himself entirely to this employment, and to become a sort of house-carpenter. In the same manner a third becomes a smith or a brazier; a fourth, a tanner or dresser of hides or skins, the principle part of the clothing of savages. And thus the certainty of being able to exchange all that surplus part of the produce of his own labour, which is over and above his own consumption, for such parts of the produce of other men's labour as he may have occasion for, encourages every man to apply himself to a particular occupation, and to cultivate and bring to perfection whatever talent of genius he may possess for that particular species of business.

The difference of natural talents in different men, is, in reality, much less than we are aware of; and the very different genius which appears to distinguish men of different professions, when grown up to maturity, is not upon many occasions so much the cause, as the effect of the division of labour. The difference between the most dissimilar characters, between a philosopher and a common street porter, for example, seems to arise not so much from nature as from habit, custom, and education. When they came into the world, and for the first six or eight years of their existence, they were perhaps, very much alike, and neither their parents nor playfellows could perceive any remarkable difference. About that age, or soon after, they come to be employed in very different occupations. The difference of talents comes then to be taken notice of, and widens by degrees till at last the vanity of the philosopher is willing to acknowledge scarce any resemblance. But without the disposition to truck, barter, and exchange, every man must have procured to himself every necessary and conveniency of life which he wanted. All must have had the same duties to perform, and the same work to do, and there could have been no such difference of employment as could alone give occasion to any great difference of talents.

As it is this disposition which forms that difference of talents, so remarkable among men of different professions, so it is this same disposition which renders that difference useful. Many tribes of animals, acknowledged to be all the same species, derive from nature a much more remarkable distinction of genius, than what, antecedent to custom and education, appears to take place among men. By nature a philosopher is not in genius and disposition half so different from a street porter, as a mastiff is from a greyhound, or a greyhound from a spaniel, or this last from a shepherd's dog. Those different tribes of animals, however, though all the same species, are of scarce any use to one another. The strength of the mastiff is not in the least supported either by the swiftness of the greyhound, or by the sagacity of the spaniel, or by the docility of the shepherd's dog. The effects of those different geniuses and talents, for want of the power or disposition to barter and exchange, cannot be brought into a common stock, and do not in the least contribute to the better accommodation and conveniency of the species. Each animal is still obliged to support and defend itself, separately and independently, and derives no sort of advantage from that variety of talents with which nature has distinguished its fellows. Among men, on the contrary, the most dissilimar geniuses are of use to one another; the different produces of their respective talents, by the general disposition to truck, barter, and exchange, being brought, as it were, into a common stock, where every man may purchase whatever part of the produce of other men's talent he has occasion for.

That the Division of Labour is Limited by the Extent of the Market

As it is the power of exchanging that gives occasion to the division of labour, so the extent of this division must always be limited by the extent of the market. When the market is very small, no person can have any encouragement to dedicate himself entirely to one employment, for want of the power to exchange all that surplus part of the produce of his own labour, which is over and above his own consumption, for such parts of the produce of other man's labour as he has occasion for.

There are some sorts of industry, even of the lowest kind, which can be carried on nowhere but in a great town. A porter for example can find employment and subsistence in no other place. A village is by much too narrow a sphere for him; even an ordinary market-town is scarce large enough to afford him constant occupation. In the lone houses and very small villages which are scattered about in so desert a country as the highlands of Scotland, every farmer must be butcher, baker, and brewer, for his own family. In such situations we can scarce expect to find even a smith, a carpenter, or a mason, within less than twenty miles of another of the same trade. The scattered families that live at eight or ten miles distance from the nearest of them, must learn to perform themselves a great number of little pieces of work, for which, in more populous countries, they would call in the assistance of those workmen. Country workmen are almost everywhere obliged to apply themselves to all the different branches of industry that have so much affinity to one another as to be employed about the same sort of materials. A country carpenter deals in every sort of work that is made of wood; a country smith in every sort of work that is made of iron. The former is not only a carpenter, but a joiner, a cabinet-maker, and even a carver in wood, as well as a wheel-wright, a ploughwright, a cart and wagon-maker. The employments of the latter are still more various. It is impossible that there should be such a trade as even that of a nailer in the remote and inland parts of the highlands of Scotland. Such a workman at the rate of a thousand nails a-day, and three hundred working days in the year, will make three hundred thousand nails in the year. But in such a situation it would be impossible to dispose of one thousand, that is, of one day's work in the year.

As by means of water-carriage, a more expensive market is opened to every sort of industry than what land-carriage alone can afford it, so it is upon the sea-coast, and along the banks of navigable rivers, that industry of every kind naturally begins to subdivide and improve itself, and it is frequently not till a long time after that those improvements extend themselves to the inland parts of the country. A broad-wheeled waggon, attended by two men and drawn by eight horses, in about six weeks' time, carries and brings back between London and Edinburgh near four top weight of goods. In about the same time a ship navigated by six or eight men, and sailing between the ports of London and Leith, frequently carries and brings back two hundred ton weight of goods. Six or eight men, therefore, by the help of a water-carrier, can carry and bring back in the same time, the same quantity of goods between London and Edinburgh as fifty broad-wheeled waggons, attended by a hundred men and drawn by four hundred horses. Upon two hundred tons of goods, therefore, carried by the cheapest land-carriage from London to Edinburgh, there must be charged the maintenance of a hundred men for three weeks, and both the maintenance and what is nearly equal to maintenance the wear and tear of four hundred horses, as well as of fifty great waggons. Whereas, upon the same quantity of goods carried by water, there is to be charged only the maintenance of six or eight men, and the wear and tear of a ship of two hundred tons burthen, together with the value of the superior risk, or the difference of the insurance between land and water-carriage. Were there no other communication between these two places, therefore, but by land-carriage, as no goods could be transported from the one to the other, except such whose price was very considerable in proportion to their weight, they could carry on but a small part of that commerce which at present subsists between them, and consequently could give but a small part of that encouragement which they at present mutually afford to each other's industry. There could be little or no commerce of any kind between the distant parts of the world. What goods could bear the expense of land-carriage between London and Calcutta? Or if there were any so precious as to be able to support this expense, with what safety could they be transported through the territories of so many barbarous nations? Those two cities, however, at present carry on a very considerable commerce with each

other, and by mutually affording a market, give a good deal of encouragement to each other's industry. . . .

Of Restraints Upon Importation From Foreign Countries of Such Goods As Can Be Produced At Home

By restraining, either by high duties, or by absolute prohibitions, the importations of such goods from foreign countries as can be produced at home, the monopoly of the home market is more or less secured to the domestic industry employed in producing them. Thus the prohibition of importing either live cattle or sale provisions from foreign countries, secures to the graziers of Great Britain the monopoly of the home market for butcher's meat. The high duties upon the importation of corn, which in times of moderate plenty, amount to a prohibition, give a like advantage to the growers of that commodity. The prohibition of the importation of foreign woollens is equally favourable to the woollen manufacturers. The silk manufacture, though altogether employed upon foreign materials, has lately obtained the same advantage. The linen manufacture has not yet obtained it, but is making great strides towards it. Many other sorts of manufactureres have, in the same manner obtained in Great Britain, either altogether, or very nearly, a monopoly against their countrymen. The variety of goods, of which the importation into Great Britain is prohibited, either absolutely, or under certain circumstances, greatly exceeds what can easily be suspected by those who are not well acquainted with the laws of the customs.

That this monopoly of the home market frequently gives great encouragement to that particular species of industry which enjoys it, and frequently turns towards that employment a greater share of both the labour and stock of the society than would otherwise have gone to it, cannot be doubted. But whether it tends either to increase the general industry or the society, or to give it the most advantageous direction, is not, perhaps, altogether so evident.

The general industry of the society can never exceed what the capital of the society can employ. As the number of workmen that can be kept in employment by any particular person must bear a certain proportion to his capital, so the number of those that can be continually employed by all the members of a great society must bear a certain proportion to the whole capital of the society, and never can exceed that proportion. No regulation of commerce can increase the quantity of industry in any society beyond what its capital can maintain. It can only divert a part of it into a direction into which it might not otherwise have gone; and it is by no means certain that this artificial direction is likely to be more advantageous to the society than that into which it would have gone of its own accord.

Every individual is continually exerting himself to find out the most advantageous employment for whatever capital he can command. It is his own advantage, indeed, and not that of the society, which he has in view. But the study of his own advantage naturally, or rather necessarily, leads him to prefer that employment which is most advantageous to the society. . . .

The produce of industry is what it adds to the subject or materials upon which it is employed. In proportion as the value of this produce is great or small, so will likewise be the profits of the employer. But it is only for the sake of profit that any man employs a capital in the support of industry; and he will always, therefore, endeavour to employ it in the support of that industry of which the produce is likely to be of the greatest value, or to exchange for the greatest quantity either of money or of other goods.

But the annual revenue of every society is always precisely equal to the exchangeable value of the whole annual produce of its industry, or rather is precisely the same thing with that exchangeable value. As every individual, therefore, endeavours as much as he can, both to employ his capital in the support of domestic industry, and so to direct that industry that its produce may be of the greatest value, every individual necessarily labours to render the annual revenue of the society as great as he can. He generally, indeed, neither intends to promote the public interest, nor knows how much he is promoting it. By preferring the support of domestic to that of foreign industry, he intends only his own security; and by directing that industry in such a manner as its produce may be of the greatest value, he intends only his own gain; and he is in this, as in many other cases, led by an invisible hand to promote an end which was no part of his intention. Nor is it always the worse for the society that it was no part of it. By pursuing his own interest, he frequently promotes that of the society more effectually than when he really intends to promote it. I have never known much good done by those who affected to trade for the public good. It is an affectation, indeed, not very common among merchants, and very few words need be employed in dissuading them from it.

What is the species of domestic industry which his capital can employ, and of which the produce is likely to be of the greatest value, every individual, it is evident, can in his local situation judge much better than any statesman or lawgiver can do for him. The statesman, who should attempt to direct private people in what manner they ought to employ their capitals, would not only load himself with a most unnecessary attention, but assume an authority which could safely be trusted, not only to no single person, but to no council or senate whatever, and which would nowhere be so dangerous as in the hands of a man who had folly and presumption enough to fancy himself fit to exercise it.

To give the monopoly of the home market to the produce of domestic industry, in any particular art or manufacture, is in some measure to direct private people in what manner they ought to employ their capitals, and must in almost all cases be either a useless or a hurtful regulation. If the produce of domestic can be brought there as cheap as that of foreign industry, the regulation is evidently useless. If it cannot, it must generally be hurtful. It is the maxim of every prudent master of a family, never to attempt to make at home what it will cost him more to make than to buy. The tailor does not attempt to make his own shoes, but buys them of the shoemaker. The shoemaker does not attempt to make his own clothes, but employs a tailor. The farmer attempts to make neither the one nor the other, but employs those different artificers. All of them find it for their interest to employ their whole industry in a way in which they have some advantage over their neighbours, and to purchase with part of its produce, or, what is the same thing, with he price of a part of it, whatever else they have occasion for.

What is prudence in the conduct of every private family, can scarcely be folly in that of a great kingdom. If a foreign country can supply us with a commodity cheaper than we ourselves can make it, better buy it of them with some part of the produce of our own industry, employed in a way in which we have some advantage. The general industry of the country being always in proportion to the capital which employs, it will not thereby be diminished,no more than that of the above-mentioned artificers; but only left to find out the way in which it can be employed with the greatest advantage. It is certainly not employed to the greatest advantage, when it is thus directed towards an object which it can buy cheaper than it can make. The value of its annual produce is certainly more or less diminished, when it is thus turned away from producing commodities evidently of more value than the commodity which it is directed to produce. According to the supposition, that commodity could be purchased from foreign countries cheaper than it can be made at home; it could therefore have been purchased with a part only of the commodities, or, what is the same thing, with a part only of the price of the commodities, which the industry employed by an equal capital would have produced at home, had it been left to follow its natural course. The industry of the country, therefore, is thus turned away from a more to a less advantageous employment; and the exchangeable value of its annual produce, instead of being increased, according to the intention of the law-giver, must necessarily be diminished by every such regulation.

By means of such regulations, indeed, a particular manufacture may sometimes be acquired sooner than it could have been otherwise, and after a certain time may be made at home as cheap, or cheaper, than in the foreign country. But though the industry of the society may be thus carried with advantage into a particular channel sooner than it could have been otherwise, it will by no means follow that the sum total, either of its industry, or of its revenue, can ever be augmented by any such regulation. The industry of the society can augment only in proportion as its capital augments, and its capital can augment only in proportion to what can be gradually saved out of its revenue. But the immediate effect of every such regulation is to diminish its revenue; and what diminishes its revenue is certainly not very likely to augment its capital faster than it would have augmented of its own accord, had both capital and industry been left to find out their natural employments.

Though, for want of such regulations, the society should never acquire the proposed manufacture, it would not upon that account necessarily be the poorer in any one period of its duration. In every period of its duration its whole capital and industry might still have been employed, though upon different objects, in the manner that was most advantageous at the time. In every period its revenue might have been the greatest which its capital could afford, and both capital and revenue might have been augmented with the greatest possible rapidity.

The natural advantages which one country has over another, in producing particular commodities, are sometimes so great, that it is acknowledged by all the world to be in vain to struggle with them. By means of glasses, hot-beds, and hot-walls, very good grapes can be raised in Scotland, and very good wine, too, can be made of them, at about thirty times the expense for which at least equally good can be brought from foreign countries. Would it be a reasonable law to prohibit the importation of all foreign wines, merely to encourage the making of claret and Burgundy in Scotland? But if there would be a manifest absurdity in turning towards any employment thirty times more of the capital and industry of the country than would be necessary to purchase from foreign countries an equal quantity of the commodities wanted, there must be an absurdity, though not altogether so glaring, yet exactly of the same kind, in turning towards any such employment a thirtieth, or even a three-hundredth part more of either. Whether the advantages which one country has over another be natural or acquired, is in this respect of no consequence. As long as the one country has those advantages, and the other wants them, it will always be more advantageous for the latter rather to buy of the former than to make. It is an acquired advantage only, which one artificer has over his neighbour, who exercises another trade; and yet they both find it more advantageous to buy of one another, than to make what does not belong to their particular trades. . . .

There seem, however, to be two cases, in which it will generally be advantageous to lay some burden upon foreign, for the encouragement of domestic industry.

The first is, when some particular sort of industry is necessary for the defence of the country. The defence of Great Britain, for example, depends very much upon the number of its sailors and shipping. The act of navigation, therefore, very properly endeavours to give the sailors and shipping of Great Britain the monopoly of the trade of their own country, in some cases, by absolute prohibitions, and in others, by heavy burdens upon the shipping of foreign countries. . . .

The second case, in which it will generally be advantageous to lay some burden upon foreign for the encouragement of domestic industry, is when some tax is imposed at home upon the produce of the latter. In this case, it seems reasonable that an equal tax should be imposed upon the like produce of the former. This would not give the monopoly of the home market to domestic industry, nor turn towards a particular employment a greater share of the stock and labour of the country, than what would naturally go to it. It would only hinder any part of what would naturally go to it from being turned away by the tax into a less natural direction, and would leave the competition between foreign and domestic industry, after the tax, as nearly as possible upon the same footing as before it. In Great Britain, when any such tax is laid upon the produce of domestic industry, it is usual, at the same time, in order to stop the clamorous complaints of our merchants and manufacturers, that they will be undersold at home, to lay a much heavier duty upon the importation of all foreign goods of the same kind. . . .

As there are two cases in which it will generally be advantageous to lay some burden upon foreign for the encouragement of domestic industry, so there are two others in which it may sometimes be a matter of deliberation, in the one, how far it is proper to continue the free importation of certain foreign goods; and, in the other, how far, or in what manner, it may be proper to restore that free importation, after it has been for some time interrupted.

The case in which it may sometimes be a matter of deliberation how far it is proper to continue the free importation of certain foreign goods, is when some foreign nation restrains, by high duties or prohibitions, the importation of some of our manufactures into their country. Revenge, in this case, naturally dictates retaliation, and that we should impose the like duties and prohibitions upon the importation of some or all of their manufactures into ours. Nations, accordingly, seldom fail to retaliate in this manner. The French have been particularly forward to favour their own manufactures, by restraining the importation of such foreign goods as could come into competition with them. . . .

There may be good policy in retaliations of this kind when there is a probability that they will procure the repeal of the high duties or prohibitions complained of. The recovery of a great foreign market will generally more than compensate the transitory inconveniency of paying dearer during a short time for some sorts of goods. To judge whether such retaliations are likely to produce such an effect, does not, perhaps, belong so much to the science of a legislator, whose deliberations ought to be governed by general principles, which are always the same, as to the skill of that insidious and crafty animal vulgarly called a statesman or politician, whose councils are directed by the momentary fluctuations of affairs. When there is no probability that any such repeal can be procured, it seems a bad method of compensating the injury done to certain classes of our people, to do another injury ourselves, not only to those classes, but to almost all the other classes of them. When our neighbours prohibit some manufacture of ours, we generally prohibit, not only the same, for that alone would seldom affect them considerably, but some other manufacture of theirs. This may, no doubt, give encouragement to some particular class of workmen among ourselves, and, by excluding some of their rivals, may enable them to raise their price in the home market. Those workmen, however, who suffered by our neighbours prohibition, will not be benefited by ours. On the contrary, they, and almost all the other classes of our citizens, will thereby be obliged to pay dearer than before for certain goods. Every such law, therefore, imposes a real tax upon the whole country, not in favour of that particular class of workmen who were injured by our neighbours' prhibitions, but of some other class.

The case in which it may sometimes be a matter of deliberation, how far, or in what manner, it is proper to restore the free importation of foreign goods, after it has been for some time interrupted, is when particular manufactures, by means of high duties or prohibitions upon all foreign goods which can come into competition with them, have been so far extended as to employ a great multitude of hands. Humanity may in this case require that the freedom of trade should be restored only by slow gradations, and with a good deal of reserve and circumspection. Were those high duties and prohibitions taken away all at once, cheaper foreign goods of the same kind might be poured so fast into the home market, as to deprive all at once many thousands of our people of their ordinary employment and means of subsistence. The disorder which this would occasion might no doubt be very considerable. . . .

To expect, indeed, that the freedom of trade should ever be entirely restored in Great Britain, is as absurd as to expect that an Oceana or Utopia should ever be established in it. Not only the prejudices of the public, but, what is much more unconquerable, the private interests of many individuals, irresistibly oppose it. Were the officers of the army to oppose, with the same zeal and unanimity, any reduction in the number of forces, with which master manufacturers set themselves against every law that is likely to increase the number of their rivals in the home market; were the former to animate the soldiers, in the same manner as the latter inflame their workmen, to attack with violence and outrage the proposers of any such regulation; to attempt to reduce the army would be as dangerous as it has now become to attempt to diminish, in any respect, the monopoly which our manufacturers have obtained against us. This monopoly has so much increased the number of some particular tribes of them, that like an overgrown standing army, they have become formidable to the government, and, upon many occasions, intimidate the legislature. The member of parliament who supports every proposal for strengthening this monopoly, is sure to acquire not only the reputation of understanding trade, but great popularity and influence with an order of men whose numbers and wealth render them of great importance. If he opposes them, on the contrary, and still more, if he has authority enough to be able to thwart them, neither the most acknowledged probity, nor the highest rank, nor the greatest public services, can protect him from the most infamous abuse and detraction, from personal insults, nor sometimes from real danger, arising from the insolent outrage of furious and disappointed monopolists.

The undertaker of a great manufacture, who, by the home markets being suddenly laid open to the competition of foreigners, should be obliged to abandon his trade, would no doubt suffer very considerably. That part of his capital which had usually been employed in purchasing materials, and in paying his workmen, might, without much difficulty, perhaps, find another employment; but that part of it which was fixed in workhouses, and in the instruments of trade, could scarce be disposed of without considerable loss. The equitable regard, therefore, to his interest, requires that changes of this kind should never be introduced suddenly, but slowly, gradually, and after a very long warning. The legislature, were it possible that its deliberations could be always directed, not by the clamorous importunity of partial interests, but by an extensive view of the general good, ought, upon this very account, perhaps, to be particularly careful, neither to establish any new monopolies of this kind, nor to extend further those which are already established. Every such regulation introduces some degree of real disorder into the constitution of the state, which it will be difficult afterwards to cure without occasioning another disorder.

THE
NINETEENTH
CENTURY

William Wordsworth

The Age of Romanticism is in part a reaction to the Age of Reason and the excesses of the revolutions at the end of the 18th century. The Romantic period has many characteristics but in particular the Romantics stressed nature, and exhibited a desire to escape from their immediate historical surroundings. This escape most often took the form of flights of fancy as expressed in literature, but occasionally an individual romantic went to the ultimate extreme of suicide. One particularly important group of romantic writers was the English poets who lived in the early years of the 19th century. The importance of nature to these poets is evident in the following selections. William Wordsworth (1770-1850) had a mystical admiration of nature as demonstrated in the first three poems in this group. He was, however, also deeply moved by the excesses of the Napoleonic conquests at the turn of the century. The next four poems express his feelings concerning these political events.

POEMS

THE TABLES TURNED

An Evening Scene on the Same Subject

Up! up! my Friend, and quit your books;
Or surely you'll grow double:
Up! up! my Friend, and clear your looks;
Why all this toil and trouble?

The sun, above the mountain's head,   5
A freshening lustre mellow
Through all the long green fields has spread,
His first sweet evening yellow.

Books! 'tis a dull and endless strife:
Come, hear the woodland linnet,   10
How sweet his music! on my life,
There's more of wisdom in it.

And hark! how blithe the throstle sings!
He, too, is no mean preacher:
Come forth into the light of things,   15
Let Nature be your teacher.

She has a world of ready wealth,
Our minds and hearts to bless—
Spontaneous wisdom breathed by health,
Truth breathed by cheerfulness.   20

One impulse from a vernal wood
May teach you more of man,
Of moral evil and of good,
Than all the sages can.

Sweet is the lore which Nature brings;   25
Our meddling intellect
Mis-shapes the beauteous forms of things:—
We murder to dissect.

Enough of Science and of Art;
Close up those barren leaves;   30
Come forth, and bring with you a heart
That watches and receives.

LINES

Composed a Few Miles Above Tintern Abbey, on Revisiting the Banks of the Wye During a Tour. July 13, 1798.

Five years have past; five summers, with the
    length
Of five long winters! and again I hear
These waters, rolling from their mountain-
    springs
With a soft inland murmur.[1] —Once again
Do I behold these steep and lofty cliffs,   5
That on a wild secluded scene impress
Thoughts of more deep seclusion; and con-
    nect
The landscape with the quiet of the sky.
The day is come when I again repose
Here, under this dark sycamore, and view   10
These plots of cottage-ground, these orchard-
    tufts
Which at this season, with their unripe fruits,
Are clad in one green hue, and lose themselves
'Mid groves and copses. Once again I see

From *Poems* by William Wordsworth, a selection edited by Edward Dowden. Copyright 1897 by Ginn & Company Boston, New York, Chicago and London.

1. The river is not affected by the tides a few miles above Tintern.

These hedge-rows, hardly hedge-rows, little
    lines   15
Of sportive wood run wild: these pastoral
    farms,
Green to the very door; and wreaths of smoke
Sent up, in silence, from among the trees!
With some uncertain notice, as might seem
Of vagrant dwellers in the houseless woods,   20
Or of some Hermit's cave, where by his fire
The Hermit sits alone.
                              These beauteous forms,
Through a long absence, have not been to me
As is a landscape to a blind man's eye:
But oft, in lonely rooms, and 'mid the din   25
Of towns and cities, I have owed to them
In hours of weariness, sensations sweet,
Felt in the blood, and felt along the heart;
And passing even into my purer mind,
With tranquil restoration:—feelings too   30
Of unremembered pleasure: such, perhaps,
As have no slight or trivial influence
On that best portion of a good man's life,
His little, nameless, unremembered, acts
Of kindness and of love. Nor less, I trust,   35
To them I may have owed another gift,
Of aspect more sublime; that blessed mood,
In which the burthen of the mystery,
In which the heavy and the weary weight
Of all this unintelligible world,   40
Is lightened:—that serene and blessed mood
In which the affections gently lead us on,—
Until, the breath of this corporeal frame
And even the motion of our human blood
Almost suspended, we are laid asleep   45
In body, and become a living soul:
While with an eye made quiet by the power
Of harmony, and the deep power of joy,
We see into the life of things.
                                                    If this
Be but a vain belief, yet oh! how oft—   50
In darkness and amid the many shapes
Of joyless daylight; when the fretful stir
Unprofitable, and the fever of the world,
Have hung upon the beatings of my heart—
How oft, in spirit, have I turned to thee,   55
O sylvan Wye! thou wanderer thro' the
    woods,
How often has my spirit turned to thee!
    And now, with gleams of half-extinguished
       thought,
With many recognitions dim and faint,
And somewhat of a sad perplexity,   60
The picture of the mind revives again:
While here I stand, not only with the sense

Of present pleasure, but with pleasing
    thoughts
That in this moment there is life and food
For future years. And so I dare to hope,   65
Though changed, no doubt, from what I was
    when first
I came among these hills; when like a roe
I bounded o'er the mountains, by the sides
Of the deep rivers, and the lonely streams,
Wherever nature led: more like a man   70
Flying from something that he dreads, than
    one
Who sought the thing he loved. For nature
    then
(The coarser pleasures of my boyish days,
And their glad animal movements all gone by)
To me was all in all.—I cannot paint   75
What then I was. The sounding cataract
Haunted me like a passion; the tall rock,
The mountain, and the deep and gloomy
    wood,
Their colours and their forms, were then to
    me
An appetite; a feeling and a love,   80
That had no need of a remoter charm,
By thought supplied, nor any interest
Unborrowed from the eye.—That time is past,
And all its aching joys are now no more,
And all its dizzy raptures. Not for this   85
Faint I, nor mourn, nor murmur; other gifts
Have followed; for such loss, I would believe,
Abundant recompence. For I have learned
To look on nature, not as in the hour
Of thoughtless youth; but hearing oftentimes 90
The still, sad music of humanity,
Nor harsh nor grating, though of ample power
To chasten and subdue. And I have felt
A presence that disturbes me with the joy
Of elevated thoughts; a sense sublime,   95
Of something far more deeply interfused,
Whose dwelling is the light of setting suns,
And the round ocean and the living air,
And the blue sky, and in the mind of man;
A motion and a spirit, that impels   100
All thinking things, all objects of all thought,
And rolls through all things. Therefore am I
    still
A lover of the meadows and the woods,
And mountains; and of all that we behold
From this green earth; of all the mighty world 105
Of eye, and ear,—both what they half create,
And what perceive; well pleased to recognise
In nature and the language of the sense,
The anchor of my purest thoughts, the nurse,

The guide, the guardian of my heart, and soul 110
Of all my moral being.
                              Nor perchance,
If I were not thus taught, should I the more
Suffer my genial spirits to decay:
For thou art with me here upon the banks
Of this fair river; thou my dearest Friend,   115
My dear, dear Friend; and in thy voice I catch
The language of my former heart, and read
My former pleasures in the shooting lights
Of thy wild eyes. Oh! yet a little while
May I behold in thee what I was once,   120
My dear, dear Sister! and this prayer I make,
Knowing that Nature never did betray
The heart that loved her; 'tis her privilege,
Through all the years of this our life, to lead
From joy to joy: for she can so inform   125
The mind that is within us, so impress
With quietness and beauty, and so feed
With lofty thoughts, that neither evil tongues,
Rash judgments, nor the sneers of selfish men,
Nor greetings where no kindness is, nor all   130
The dreary intercourse of daily life,
Shall e'er prevail against us, or disturb
Our cheerful faith, that all which we behold
Is full of blessings. Therefore let the moon
Shine on thee in thy solitary walk;   135
And let the misty mountain-winds be free
To blow against thee: and, in after years,
When these wild ecstasies shall be matured
Into a sober pleasure; when thy mind
Shall be a mansion for all lovely forms,   140
Thy memory be as a dwelling-place
For all sweet sounds and harmonies; oh! then,
If solitude, or fear, or pain, or grief,
Should be thy portion, with what healing
   thoughts
Of tender joy wilt thou remember me,   145
And these my exhortations! Nor, perchance—
If I should be where I no more can hear
Thy voice, nor catch from thy wild eyes these
   gleams
Of past existence—wilt thou then forget
That on the banks of this delightful stream   150
We stood together; and that I, so long
A worshipper of Nature, hither came
Unwearied in that service: rather say
With warmer love—oh! with far deeper zeal
Of holier love. Nor wilt thou then forget,   155
That after many wanderings, many years
Of absence, these steep woods and lofty cliffs,
And this green pastoral landscape, were to me
More dear, both for themselves and for thy
   sake!

"MY HEART LEAPS UP WHEN I BEHOLD."

My heart leaps up when I behold
   A rainbow in the sky:
So was it when my life began;
So is it now I am a man;
So be it when I shall grow old,   5
   Or let me die!
The Child is father of the Man;
And I could wish my days to be
Bound each to each by natural piety.

1801

I grieved for Buonaparté, with a vain
And an unthinking grief! The tenderest mood
Of that Man's mind—what can it be? what
   food
Fed his first hopes? what knowledge could *he*
   gain?
'Tis not in battles that from youth we train   5
The Governor who must be wise and good,
And temper with the sternness of the brain
Thoughts motherly, and meek as womanhood.
Wisdom doth live with children round her
   knees:
Books, leisure, perfect freedom, and the talk   10
Man holds with week-day man in the hourly
   walk
Of the mind's business; these are the degrees
By which true Sway doth mount; this is the
   stalk
True Power doth grow on; and her rights are
   these.

ON THE EXTINCTION OF THE
VENETIAN REPUBLIC

Once did She hold the gorgeous east in fee;
And was the safeguard of the west: the worth
Of Venice did not fall below her birth,
Venice, the eldest Child of Liberty.
She was a maiden City, bright and free;   5
No guile seduced, no force could violate;
And, when she took unto herself a Mate,
She must espouse the everlasting Sea.
And what if she had seen those glories fade,
Those titles vanish, and that strength decay;   10
Yet shall some tribute of regret be paid
When her long life hath reached its final day:
Men are we, and must grieve when even the
   Shade
Of that which once was great is passed
   away.

THOUGHT OF A BRITON ON THE SUBJUGATION OF SWITZERLAND

Two Voices are there; one is of the sea,
One of the mountains; each a mighty Voice:
In both from age to age thou didst rejoice,
They were thy chosen music, Liberty!
There came a Tyrant, and with holy glee   5
Thou fought'st against him; but hast vainly
    striven:
Thou from thy Alpine holds at length art
    driven,
Where not a torrent murmurs heard by thee.
Of one deep bliss thine ear hath been bereft:
Then cleave, O cleave to that which still is left; 10
For, high-souled Maid, what sorrow would it
    be
That Mountain floods should thunder as be-
    fore,
And Ocean bellow from his rocky shore,
And neither awful Voice he heard by thee.

NOVEMBER, 1806
(Defeat of Prussia)

Another year!—another deadly blow!
Another mighty Empire overthrown!
And We are left, or shall be left, alone;
The last that dare to struggle with the Foe.
'Tis well! from this day forward we shall know 5
That in ourselves our safety must be sought;
That by our own right hands it must be
    wrought;
That we must stand unpropped, or be laid low.
O dastard whom such foretaste doth not cheer!
We shall exult, if they who rule the land   10
Be men who hold its many blessings dear
Wise, upright, valiant; not a servile band,
Who are to judge of danger which they fear
And honour which they do not understand.

Samuel Taylor Coleridge

Samual Taylor Coleridge (1772-1834) is perhaps best known for his *Rime of the Ancient Mariner,* but in this selection, *Kubla Khan,* he exemplifies the Romantic poet's desire to escape from his own historical present by the vehicle of poetry.

KUBLA KHAN

In Xanadu did Kubla Khan
A stately pleasure-dome decree:
Where Alph, the sacred river, ran
Through caverns measureless to man
    Down to a sunless sea.
So twice five miles of fertile ground
With walls and towers were girdled round:
And there were gardens bright with sinuous
    rills,
Where blossomed many an incense-bearing
    tree;
And here were forests ancient as the hills,
Enfolding sunny spots of greenery.

But oh! that deep romantic chasm which
    slanted
Down the green hill athwart a cedarn cover!
A savage place! as holy and enchanted

As e'er beneath a waning moon was haunted
By woman wailing for her demon-lover!
And from this chasm, with ceaseless turmoil
    seething,
As if this earth in fast thick pants were breath-
    ing,
A mighty fountain momently was forced:
Amid whose swift half-intermitted burst
Huge fragments vaulted like rebounding hail,
Or chaffy grain beneath the thresher's flail:
And 'mid these dancing rocks at once and ever
It flung up momently the sacred river.

From *The Complete Poetical Works of Samuel Taylor Coleridge* including *Poems and Versions of Poems Now Published For the First Time* edited with textual and bibliographical notes by Ernest Hartley Coleridge Volume 1. Copyright 1912 by the Clarendon Press, Oxford.

Five miles meandering with a mazy motion
Through wood and dale the sacred river ran,
Then reached the caverns measureless to man,
And sank in tumult to a lifeless ocean:
And 'mid this tumult Kubla heard from far
Ancestral voices prophesying war!
  The shadow of the dome of pleasure
    Floated midway on the waves;
  Where was heard the mingled measure
    From the fountain and the caves.
It was a miracle of rare device,
A sunny pleasure-dome with caves of ice!

  A damsel with a dulcimer
  In a vision once I saw:
  It was an Abyssinian maid.

And on her dulcimer she played,
  Singing of Mount Abora.
  Could I revive within me
  Her symphony and song.
    To such a deep delight 'twould win me,
That with music loud and long,
I would build that dome in air,
That sunny dome! those caves of ice!
And all who heard should see them there,
And all should cry, Beware! Beware!
His flashing eyes, his floating hair!
Weave a circle round him thrice,
And close your eyes with holy dread,
For he on honey-dew hath fed,
And drunk the milk of Paradise.

Lord Byron

Another famous romantic poet was George Gordon, Lord Byron (1788-1824).
Lord Byron was both a poet who could express beautiful thoughts of nature and
an individual who reacted strongly against injustice and tyranny. He was involved
in several personal scandals, lived in exile for eight years and died while aiding
the Greeks in their war of independence. His long poem, *Childe Harold's
Pilgrimage* is another expression of the wanderings of the Romantic poet as well
as a description of the wonders of nature.

STANZAS
Composed During A Thunder-Storm

[This storm occurred on the night of October
11, 1809, when Byron's guides had lost the road to
Zitza in Albania.]

Chill and mirk is the nightly blast,
  Where Pindus' mountains rise,
And angry clouds are pouring fast
  The vengeance of the skies.

Our guides are gone, our hope is lost,
  And lightnings, as they play,
But show where rocks our paths have crost,
  Or gild the torrent's spray.

Is yon a cot I saw, though low?
  When lightning broke the gloom—   10
How welcome were its shade!—ah, no!
  'Tis but a Turkish tomb.

Through sounds of foaming waterfalls,
  I hear a voice exclaim—
My way-worn countryman, who calls
  On distant England's name.

A shot is fired—by foe or friend?
  Another—'T is to tell
The mountain-peasants to descend,
  And lead us where they dwell.   20

Oh! who in such a night will dare
  To tempt the wilderness?
And who 'mid thunder peals can hear
  Our signal of distress?

And who that heard our shouts would rise
  To try the dubious road;
Nor rather deem from nightly cries
  That outlaws were abroad?

Clouds burst, skies flash, oh, dreadful hour!
  More fiercely pours the storm!   30
Yet here one thought has still the power
  To keep my bosom warm.

From *The Complete Poetical Works of Lord Byron*, Student's
Cambridge Edition. Copyright 1905 by Houghton Mifflin Company,
Boston, New York, Chicago, Dallas, San Francisco.

While wand'ring through each broken path,
    O'er brake and craggy brow;
While elements exhaust their wrath,
    Sweet Florence, where art thou?

Not on the sea, not on the sea,
    Thy bark hath long been gone:
Oh, may the storm that pours on me,
    Bow down my head alone!   40

Full swiftly blew the swift Siroc,
    When last I press'd thy lip;
And long ere now, with foaming shock,
    Impell'd thy gallant ship.

Now thou art safe; nay, long ere now
    Hast trod the shore of Spain;
'T were hard if aught so fair as thou
    Should linger on the main.

And since I now remember thee
    In darkness and in dread,   50
As in those hours of revelry
    Which mirth and music sped;

Do thou, amid the fair white walls,
    If Cadiz yet be free,
At times from out her latticed halls
    Look o'er the dark blue sea;

Then think upon Calypso's isles,
    Endear'd by days gone by;
To others give a thousand smiles,
    To me a single sigh.   60

And when the admiring circle mark
    The paleness of thy face,
A half-form'd tear, a transient spark
    Of melancholy grace.

Again thou'lt smile, and blushing shun
    Some coxcomb's raillery;
Nor own for once thou thought'st on one,
    Who ever thinks on thee.

Though smile and sigh alike are vain,
    When sever'd hearts repine,   70
My spirit flies o'er mount and main,
    And mourns in search of thine.

STANZAS
Written in Passing the Ambracian Gulf

Through cloudless skies, in silvery sheen,
    Full beams the moon on Actium's coast;
And on these waves, for Egypt's queen,
    The ancient world was won and lost.

And now upon the scene I look,
    The azure grave of many a Roman;
Where stern Ambition once forsook
    His wavering crown to follow woman.

Florence! whom I will love as well
    As ever yet was said or sung
(Since Orpheus sang his spouse from hell),
    Whilst thou art fair and I am young.

Sweet Florence! those were pleasant times,
    When words were staked for ladies' eyes:
Had bards as many realms as rhymes,
    Thy charms might raise new Antonies.

Though Fate forbids such things to be,
    Yet, by thine eyes and ringlets curl'd!
I cannot lose a world for thee,
    But would not lose thee for a world.

CHILDE HAROLD'S PILGRIMAGE

XII

But soon he knew himself the most unfit
Of men to herd with Man, with whom he
    held   101
Little in common;—untaught to submit
His thoughts to others, though his soul was
    quell'd
In youth by his own thoughts; still uncom-
    pell'd,
He would not yield dominion of his mind
To spirits against whom his own rebell'd;
Proud though in desolation; which could
    find
A life within itself to breathe without man-
    kind.

XIII

Where rose the mountains, there to him were
    friends;
Where roll'd the ocean, thereon was his
    home;   110
Where a blue sky, and glowing clime, ex-
    tends,
He had the passion and the power to roam;
The desert, forest, cavern, breaker's foam,
Were unto him companionship; they spake
A mutual language, clearer than the tome
Of his land's tongue, which he would oft
    forsake
For Nature's pages glass'd by sunbeams on the
    lake.

XIV

Like the Chaldean he could watch the stars,
Till he had peopled them with beings bright
As their own beams; and earth, and earth-
    born jars,   120
And human frailties, were forgotten quite.
Could he have kept his spirit to that flight
He had been happy; but this clay will sink
Its spark immortal, envying it the light
To which it mounts, as if to break the link
That keeps us from yon heaven which woos
    us to its brink.

XV

But in Man's dwellings he became a thing
Restless and worn, and stern and weari-
    some,
Droop'd as a wild-born falcon with clipt
    wing,
To whom the boundless air alone were
    home.   130
Then came his fit again, which to o'ercome,
As eagerly the barr'd-up bird will beat
His breast and beak against his wiry dome
Till the blood tinge his plumage, so the
    heat
Of his impeded soul would through his bosom
    eat.

. . . .

LXVIII

Lake Leman woos me with its crystal face,
The mirror where the stars and mountains
    view
The stillness of their aspect in each trace
Its clear depth yields of their far height and
    hue.
There is too much of man here, to look
    through
With a fit mind the might which I behold;
But soon in me shall Loneliness renew
Thoughts hid, but not less cherish'd than of
    old,   651
Ere mingling with the herd had penn'd me in
    their fold.

LXIX

To fly from, need not be to hate, mankind:
All are not fit with them to stir and toil,

Nor is it discontent to keep the mind
Deep in its fountain, lest it overboil
In the hot throng, where we become the
    spoil
Of our infection, till too late and long
We may deplore and struggle with the coil,
In wretched interchange of wrong for
    wrong   660
Midst a contentious world, striving where
    none are strong.

LXX

There, in a moment, we may plunge our
    years
In fatal penitence, and in the blight
Of our own soul turn all our blood to tears,
And colour things to come with hues of
    Night;
The race of life becomes a hopeless flight
To those that walk in darkness: on the sea,
The boldest steer but where their ports
    invite,
But there are wanderers o'er Eternity
Whose bark drives on and on, and anchor'd
    ne'er shall be.   670

LXXI

Is it not better, then, to be alone,
And love Earth only for its earthly sake?
By the blue rushing of the arrowy Rhone,
Or the pure bosom of its nursing lake,
Which feeds it as a mother who doth make
A fair but froward infant her own care,
Kissing its cries away as these awake;—
Is it not better thus our lives to wear,
Than join the crushing crowd, doom'd to
    inflict or bear?

LXXII

I live not in myself, but I become   680
Portion of that around me; and to me
High mountains are a feeling, but the hum
Of human cities torture: I can see
Nothing to loathe in nature, save to be
A link reluctant in a fleshly chain,
Class'd among creatures, when the soul can
    can flee,
And with the sky, the peak, the heaving
    plain
Of ocean, or the stars, mingle, and not in vain.

LXXIII

And thus I am absorb'd, and this is life:
I look upon the peopled desert past,   690
As on a place of agony and strife,
Where, for some sin, to sorrow I was cast,
To act and suffer, but remount at last
With a fresh pinion; which I feel to spring,
Though young, yet waxing vigorous, as the
    blast
Which it would cope with, on delighted
    wing,
Spurning the clay-cold bonds which round
    our being cling.

LXXIV

And when at length the mind shall be all
    free
From what it hates in this degraded form,
Reft of its carnal life, save what shall be   700
Existent happier in the fly and worm,—
When elements to elements conform,
And dust is as it should be, shall I not
Feel all I see, less dazzling, but more warm?
The bodiless thought? the Spirit of each
    spot?
Of which, even now, I share at times the
    immortal lot?

. . . .

CLXXVII

Oh that the Desert were my dwelling place,
With one fair Spirit for my minister,
That I might all forget the human race,
And, hating no one, love but only her!
Ye Elements, in whose ennobling stir
I feel myself exalted, can ye not   1590
Accord me such a being? Do I err
In deeming such inhabit many a spot,
Though with them to converse can rarely be
    our lot?

CLXXVIII

There is a pleasure in the pathless woods,
There is a rapture on the lonely shore,
There is society where none intrudes,
By the deep Sea, and music in its roar:
I love not Man the less, but Nature more,
From these our interviews, in which I
    steal

From all I may be or have been before,
To mingle with the Universe, and feel
What I can ne'er express, yet can not all
    conceal.

CLXXIX

Roll on, thou deep and dark blue Ocean,
    roll!
Ten thousand fleets sweep over thee in
    vain;
Man marks the earth with ruin, his control
Stops with the shore; upon the watery
    plain
The wrecks are all thy deed, nor doth
    remain
A shadow of man's ravage, save his own,
When, for a moment, like a drop of rain,
He sinks into thy depths with bubbling
    groan,   1610
Without a grave, unknell'd, uncoffin'd, and
    unknown.

CLXXX

His steps are not upon thy paths, thy fields
Are not a spoil for him,—thou dost arise
And shake him from thee; the vile strength
    he wields
For earth's destruction thou dost all de-
    spise,
Spurning him from thy bosom to the skies,
And send'st him, shivering in thy playful
    spray
And howling, to his Gods, where haply lies
His petty hope in some near port or bay,
And dashest him again to earth:—there let
    him lay.   1620

CLXXXI

The armaments which thunderstrike the
    walls
Of rock-built cities, bidding nations quake
And monarchs tremble in their capitals,
The oak leviathans, whose huge ribs make
Their clay creator the vain title take
Of lord of thee and arbiter of war,—
These are thy toys, and, as the snowy flake,
They melt into thy yeast of waves, which
    mar
Alike the Armada's pride or spoils of Trafal-
    gar.

CLXXXII

Thy shores are empires, changed in all save
    thee—   1630
Assyria, Greece, Rome, Carthage, what are
    they?
Thy waters wash'd them power while they
    were free,
And many a tyrant since; their shores obey
The stranger, slave, or savage; their decay
Has dried up realms to deserts:—not so
    thou,
Unchangeable save to thy wild waves play;
Time writes no wrinkle on thine azure
    brow;
Such as creation's dawn beheld, thou rollest
    now.

CLXXXIII

Thou glorious mirror, where the Almighty's
    form
Glasses itself in tempests; in all time,
Calm or convulsed—in breeze, or gale, or
    storm,   1641
Icing the pole, or in the torrid clime
Dark-heaving;—boundless, endless, and sub-
    lime—
The image of Eternity—the throne
Of the Invisible; even from out thy slime
The monsters of the deep are made; each
    zone
Obeys thee; thou goest forth, dread, fathom-
    less, alone.

CLXXXIV

And I have loved thee, Ocean! and my joy
Of youthful sports was on thy breast to be
Borne, like thy bubbles, onward. From a
    boy   1650

I wanton'd with thy breaker—they to me
Were a delight; and if the freshening sea
Made them a terror—'twas a pleasing fear,
For I was as it were a child of thee,
And trusted to thy billows far and near,
And laid my hand upon thy mane—as I do
    here.

CLXXXV

My task is done—my song hath ceased—my
    theme
Has died into an echo; it is fit
The spell should break of this protracted
    dream.
The torch shall be extinguish'd which hath
    lit   1660
My midnight lamp—and what is writ, is
    writ,—
Would it were worthier! but I am not now
That which I have been—and my visions flit
Less palpably before me—and the glow
Which in my spirit dwelt is fluttering, faint,
    and low.

CLXXXVI

Farewell! a word that must be, and hath
    been—
A sound which makes us linger;—yet—fare-
    well!
Ye! who have traced the Pilgrim to the
    scene
Which is his last, if in your memories dwell
A thought which once was his, if on ye
    swell
A single recollection, not in vain
He wore his sandal-shoon and scallop-shell;
Farewell! with *him* alone may rest the pain,
If such there were—with *you*, the moral of his
    strain.

Percy Bysshe Shelley

Percy Bysshe Shelly (1792-1822) was also preoccupied with nature, but note that the poem *Death* represents another Romantic characteristic, interest in the somber or macabre.

AUTUMN: A DIRGE

I

The warm sun is failing, the bleak wind is
    wailing,
The bare boughs are sighing, the pale flowers
    are dying,
        And the year
On the earth her deathbed, in a shroud of
    leaves dead,
        Is lying.
    Come, months, come away,
    From November to May,
    In your saddest array;
    Follow the bier
    Of the dead cold year,
And like dim shadows watch by her sepul-
    chre.

II

The chill is falling, the nipt worm is crawling,
The rivers are swelling, the thunder is knelling
        For the year;
The blithe swallows are flown, and the lizards
    each gone
        To his dwelling;
    Come, months, come away;
    Put on white, black, and gray;
    Let your light sisters play—
    Ye, follow the bier
    Of the dead cold year
And make her grave green with tear on tear.

DEATH

I

Death is here and death is there,
Death is busy everywhere,
All around, within, beneath,
Above is death—and we are death.

II

Death has set his mark and seal
On all we are and all we feel
On all we know and all we fear,

III

First our pleasures die—and then
Our hopes, and then our fears—and when
These are dead, the debt is due,
Dust claims dust—and we die too.

IV

All things that we love and cherish,
Like ourselves must fade and perish,
Such is our rude mortal lot—
Love itself would, did they not.

SUMMER AND WINTER

It was a bright and cheerful afternoon,
Towards the end of the sunny month of June,
When the north wind congregates in crowds
The floating mountains of the silver clouds
From the horizon—and the stainless sky
Opens beyond them like eternity.
All things rejoiced beneath the sun; the
    weeds,
The river, and the corn-fields, and the reeds;
The willow leaves that glanced in the light
    breeze,
And the firm foliage of the larger trees.

It was a winter such as when birds die
In the deep forests; and the fishes lie
Stiffened in the translucent ice, which makes
Even the mud and slime of the warm lakes
A wrinkled clod as hard as brick; and when,
Among their children, comfortable men
Gather about great fires, and yet feel cold:
Alas then for the homeless beggar old!

From *The Poetical Works of Percy Bysshe Shelley* edited by Edward Dowden. Copyright 1913 by MacMillan and Co., Limited, St. Martin's Street, London.

John Keats

The final poet of this group is John Keats (1795-1821). *To Autumn* further expresses the Romantic view of nature; the *Ode on A Grecian Urn* illustrates a basic belief of Keats and other Romantics, that beauty and truth are one.

ODE ON A GRECIAN URN

I

Thou still unravish'd bride of quietness,
  Thou foster-child of Silence and slow Time,
Sylvan historian, who canst thus express
  A flowery tale more sweetly than our
    rhyme:
What leaf-fringed legend haunts about thy
  shape
  Of deities or mortals, or of both,
    In Tempe or the dales of Arcady?
What men or gods are these? what maidens
  loth?
What mad pursuit? What struggle to escape?
    What pipes and timbrels? What wild
    ecstasy?   10

II

Heard melodies are sweet but those unheard
  Are sweeter; therefore, ye soft pipes, play
    on;
Not to the sensual ear, but, more endear'd
  Pipe to the spirit ditties of no tone:—
Fair youth, beneath the trees, thou canst not
  leave
  Thy song, nor ever can those trees be bare;
    Bold Lover, never, never canst thou kiss,
Though winning near the goal—yet, do not
  grieve;
  She cannot fade, though thou hast not
    thy bliss,   19
  For ever wilt thou love, and she be fair!

III

Ah, happy, happy boughs! that cannot shed
  Your leaves, nor ever bid the Spring adieu;
And, happy melodist, unwearied,
  For ever piping songs for ever new;
More happy love! more happy, happy love!
  For ever warm and still to be enjoy'd,
    For ever panting, and for ever young;

All breathing human passion far above,
  That leaves a heart high-sorrowful and
    cloy'd,
    A burning forehead, and a parching
    tongue.   30

IV

Who are these coming to the sacrifice?
  To what green altar, O mysterious priest,
Lead'st thou that heifer lowing at the skies,
  And all her silken flanks with garlands
    drest?
What little town by river or sea shore,
  Or mountain-built with peaceful citadel,
    Is emptied of this folk, this pious morn?
And, little town, thy streets for evermore
  Will silent be; and not a soul to tell
    Why thou art desolate, can e'er return. 40

V

O Attic shape! Fair attitude! with brede
  Of marble men and maidens overwrought,
With forest branches and the trodden weed;
  Thou, silent form, dost tease us out of
    thought
As doth eternity! Cold Pastoral!
  When old age shall this generation waste,
    Thou shalt remain, in midst of other woe
  Than ours, a friend to man, to whom thou
    say'st,
'Beauty is truth, truth beauty,'—that is all
    Ye know on earth, and all ye need to
    know.   50

From *The Complete Poetical Works and Letters of John Keats*, Student's Cambridge Edition. Copyright 1899 by Houghton Mifflin Company, Boston, New York, Chicago, San Francisco.

TO AUTUMN

I

Season of mists and mellow fruitfulness,
    Close bosom-friend of the maturing sun;
Conspiring with him how to load and bless
    With fruit the vines that round the thatch-
        eaves run;
To bend with apples the moss'd cottage-trees,
    And fill all fruit with ripeness to the core;
        To swell the gourd, and plump the hazel
            shells
With a sweet kernel; to set budding more,
And still more, later flowers for the bees,
Until they think warm days will never cease,
    For summer has o'er-brimm'd their clammy
        cells.

II

Who hath not seen thee oft amid thy store?
    Sometimes whoever seeks abroad may find
Thee sitting careless on a granary floor,
    Thy hair soft-lifted by the winnowing
        wind;
Or on a half-reap'd furrow sound asleep,
    Drowsed with the fume of poppies, while
        thy hook
Spares the next swath and all its twined
        flowers:
And sometimes like a gleaner thou dost keep
    Steady thy ladeu head across a brook;
    Or by a cider-press, with patient look,
        Thou watchest the last oozings, hours
            by hours.

III

Where are the songs of Spring? Ay, where are
        they?
    Think not of them, thou hast thy music
        too,—
While barred clouds bloom the soft-dying day,
    And touch the stubble-plains with rosy
        hue;
Then in a wailful choir the small gnats mourn
    Among the river sallows, borne aloft
        Or sinking as the light wind lives or dies;
And full-grown lambs loud bleat from hilly
        bourn;
    Hedge-crickets sing; and now with treble
        soft
    The redbreast whistles from a garden-croft,
        And gathering swallows twitter in the
            skies.

John Stuart Mill

John Stuart Mill (1806-1873) was one of the foremost Liberal spokesmen of the 19th century. He was a child prodigy who was educated at home by his father and by Jeremy Bentham, the great Utilitarian. Before he was eight years old he had read most of Plato in the original. Although Mill wrote on many subjects, economics and politics were his major areas of concentration. A skeptic in regard to final truth, he was a champion of the liberal point of view. He rejected the idea that "the pursuit of pleasure and the avoidance of pain" were the major purposes of human existence. His essay *On Liberty,* from which the following selection is taken, was written in 1859. It is perhaps the best known defense of human freedom in Western literature. As you read these excerpts note in particular what Mill has to say about the tyranny of the majority, freedom of the press, and the limits to the authority of society over the individual.

ON LIBERTY

Introductory

The subject of this Essay is not the so-called Liberty of the Will, so unfortunately opposed to the misnamed doctrine of Philosophical Necessity; but Civil, or Social Liberty: the nature and limits of the power which can be legitimately exercised by society over the individual. A question seldom stated, and hardly ever discussed, in general terms, but which profoundly influences the practical controversies of the age by its latent presence, and is likely soon to make itself recognized as the vital question of the future. It is so far from being new, that, in a certain sense, it has divided mankind, almost from the remotest ages, but in the stage of progress into which the more civilized portions of the species have now entered, it presents itself under new conditions, and requires a different and more fundamental treatment.

The struggle between Liberty and Authority is the most conspicuous feature in the portions of history with which we are earliest familiar, particularly in that of Greece, Rome, and England. But in old times this contest was between subjects, or some classes of subjects, and the government. By liberty, was meant protection against the tyranny of the political rulers. The rulers were conceived (except in some of the popular governments of Greece) as in a necessarily antagonistic position to the people whom they ruled. They consisted of a governing One, or a governing tribe or caste, who derived their authority from inheritance or conquest; who, at all events, did not hold it at the pleasure of the governed, and whose supremacy men did not venture, perhaps did not desire, to contest, whatever precautions might be taken against its oppressive exercise. Their power was regarded as necessary, but also as highly dangerous; as a weapon which they would attempt to use against their subjects, no less than against external enemies. To prevent the weaker members of the community from being preyed upon by innumerable vultures, it was needful that there should be an animal of prey stronger than the rest, commissioned to keep them down. But as the king of the vultures would be no less bent upon preying upon the flock than any of the minor harpies, it was indispensable to be in a perpetual attitude of defence against his beak and claws. The aim, therefore, of patriots, was to set limits to the power which the ruler should be suffered to exercise over the community; and this limitation was what they meant by liberty. It was attempted in two ways. First, by obtaining a recognition of certain immunities, called political liberties or rights, which it was to be regarded as a breach of duty in the ruler to infringe, and which, if he did infringe, specific resistance, or general rebellion, was held to be justifiable. A second, and generally a later expedient, was the establishment of constitutional checks; by which the consent of the

From *Autobiography Essay on Liberty* by John Stuart Mill. A Harvard Classics edited by Charles W. Eliot LL.D. Copyright 1909 by P. F. Collier and Son, New York.

community, or of a body of some sort supposed to represent its interests, was made a necessary condition to some of the more important acts of the governing power. To the first of these modes of limitation, the ruling power, in most European countries, was compelled, more or less, to submit. It was not so with the second; and to attain this, or when already in some degree possessed, to attain it more completely, became everywhere the principal object of the lovers of liberty. And so long as mankind were content to combat one enemy by another, and to be ruled by a master, on condition of being guaranteed more or less efficaciously against his tyranny, they did not carry their aspirations beyond this point.

A time, however, came in the progress of human affairs, when men ceased to think it a necessity of nature that their governors should be an independent power, opposed in interest to themselves. It appeared to them much better that the various magistrates of the State should be their tenants or delegates, revocable at their pleasure. In that way alone, it seemed, could they have complete security that the powers of government would never be abused to their disadvantage. By degrees, this new demand for elective and temporary rulers became the prominent object of the exertions of the popular party, wherever any such party existed; and superseded, to a considerable extent, the previous efforts to limit the power of rulers. As the struggle proceeded for making the ruling power emanate from the periodical choice of the ruled, some persons began to think that too much importance had been attached to the limitation of the power itself. *That* (it might seem) was a resource against rulers whose interests were habitually opposed to those of the people. What was now wanted was, that the rulers should be identified with the people; that their interest and will should be the interest and ill of the nation. The nation did not need to be protected against its own will. There was no fear of its tyrannizing over itself. Let the rulers be effectually responsible to it, promptly removable by it, and it could afford to trust them with power of which it could itself dictate the use to be made. Their power was but the nation's own power, concentrated, and in a form convenient for exercise. This mode of thought, or rather perhaps of feeling, was common among the last generation of European liberalism, in the Continental section of which, it still apparently predominates. Those who admit any limit to what a government may do, except in the case of such governments as they think ought not to exist, stand out as brilliant exceptions among the political thinkers of the Continent. A similar tone of sentiment might by this time have been prevalent in our own country, if the circumstances which for a time encouraged it had continued unaltered.

But, in political and philosophical theories, as well as in persons, success discloses faults and infirmities which failure might have concealed from observation. The notion, that the people have no need to limit their power over themselves, might seem axiomatic, when popular government was a thing only dreamed about, or read of as having existed at some distant period of the past. Neither was that notion necessarily disturbed by such temporary aberrations as those of the French Revolution, the worst of which were the work of an usurping few, and which, in any case, belonged, not to the permanent working of popular institutions, but to a sudden and convulsive outbreak against monarchical and aristocratic despotism. In time, however, a democratic republic came to occupy a large portion of the earth's surface, and made itself felt as one of the most powerful members of the community of nations; and elective and responsible government became subject to the observations and criticisms which wait upon a great existing fact. It was now perceived that such phrases as "self-government," and "the power of the people over themselves," do not express the true state of the case. The "people" who exercise the power, are not always the same people with those over whom it is exercised, and the "self-government" spoken of, is not the government of each by himself, but of each by all the rest. The will of the people, moreover, practically means, the will of the most numerous or the most active *part* of the people; the majority, or those who succeed in making themselves accepted as the majority: the people, consequently *may* desire to oppress a part of their number; and precautions are as much needed against this, as against any other abuse of power. The limitation, therefore, of the power of government over individuals, loses none of its importance when the holders of power are regularly accountable to the community, that is, to the strongest party therein. This view of things, recommending itself equally to the intelligence of thinkers and to the inclination of those important classes in European society to whose real or supposed interests democracy is adverse, has had no difficulty in establishing itself; and in political speculations "the tyranny of the majority" is now generally included among the evils against which society requires to be on its guard.

Like other tyrannies, the tyranny of the majority was at first, and is still vulgarly, held in dread, chiefly as operating through the acts of the public authorities. But reflecting persons perceived that when society is itself the tyrant—society collectively, over the separate individuals who compose it—its means of tyrannizing are not restricted to the acts which it may do by the hands of its political functionaries. Society can and does execute its own mandates: and if it issues wrong mandates instead of right, or any mandates at all in things with which it ought not to meddle, it practises a social tyranny more formidable than many kinds of political oppression, since, though not usually upheld by such extreme penalties, it leaves fewer means of escape, penetrating much more deeply into the details of life, and enslaving the soul itself. Protection, therefore, against the tyranny of the magistrate is not enough; there needs protection also against the tyranny of the prevailing opinion and feeling; against the tendency of society to impose, by other means than civil penalties, its own ideas and practices as rules of conduct on those who dissent from them; to fetter the development, and, if possible, prevent the formation, of any individuality not in harmony with its ways, and compel all characters to fashion themselves upon the model of its own. There is a limit to the legitimate interference of collective opinion with individual independence; and to find that limit, and maintain it against encroachment, is as indispensable to a good condition of human affairs, as protection against political despotism.

But though this proposition is not likely to be contested in general terms, the practical question, where to place the limit—how to make the fitting adjustment between individual independence and social control—is a subject on which nearly everything remains to be done. All that makes existence valuable to any one, depends on the enforcement of restraints upon the actions of other people. Some rules of conduct, therefore, must be imposed, by law in the first place, and by opinion on many things which are not fit subjects for the operation of law. What these rules should be, is the principal question in human affairs; but if we except a few of the most obvious cases, it is one of those which least progress has been made in resolving. No two ages, and scarcely any two countries, have decided it alike; and the decision of one age or country is a wonder to another. Yet the people of any given age and country no more suspect any difficulty in it, than if it were a subject on which mankind had always been agreed. The

rules which obtain among themselves appear to them self-evident and self-justifying. This all but universal illusion is one of the examples of the magical influence of custom, which is not only, as the proverb says a second nature, but is continually mistaken for the first. The effect of custom, in preventing any misgiving respecting the rules of conduct which mankind impose on one another, is all the more complete because the subject is one on which it is not generally considered necessary that reasons should be given, either by one person to others, or by each to himself. People are accustomed to believe and have been encouraged in the belief by some who aspire to the character of philosophers, that their feelings, on subjects of this nature, are better than reasons, and render reasons unnecessary. The practical principle which guides them to their opinions on the regulation of human conduct, is the feeling in each person's mind that everybody should be required to act as he, and those with whom he sympathizes, would like them to act. No one, indeed, acknowledges to himself that his standard of judgment is his own liking; but an opinion on a point of conduct, not supported by reasons, can only count as one person's preference; and if the reasons, when given, are a mere appeal to a similar preference felt by other people, it is still only many people's liking instead of one. To an ordinary man, however, his own preference, thus supported, is not only a perfectly satisfactory reason, but the only one he generally has for any of his notions of morality, taste, or propriety, which are not expressly written in his religious creed; and his chief guide in the interpretation even of that. Men's opinions, accordingly, on what is laudable or blamable, are affected by all the multifarious causes which influence their wishes in regard to the conduct of others, and which are as numerous as those which determine their wishes on any other subject. Sometimes their reason—at other times their prejudices or superstitions: often their social affections, not seldom their antisocial ones, their envy or jealousy, their arrogance or contemptuousness: but most commonly, their desires or fears for themselves—their legitimate or illegitimate self-interest. Wherever there is an ascendant class, a large portion of the morality of the country emanates from its class interests, and its feelings of class superiority. The morality between Spartans and Helots, between planters and negroes, between princes and subjects, between nobles and roturiers, between men and women, has been for the most part the creation of these class interests and feelings: and the sentiments thus generated, react in turn upon the moral feelings of the members of the ascendant class, in their relations among themselves. Where, on the other hand, a class, formerly ascendant, has lost its ascendency, or where its ascendency is unpopular, the prevailing moral sentiments frequently bear the impress of an impatient dislike of superiority. Another grand determining principle of the rules of conduct, both in act and forbearance which have been enforced by law or opinion, has been the servility of mankind towards the supposed preferences or aversions of their temporal masters, or of their gods. This servility though essentially selfish, is not hypocrisy; it gives rise to perfectly genuine sentiments of abhorrence; it made men burn magicians and heretics. Among so many baser influences, the general and obvious interests of society have of course had a share, and a large one, in the direction of the moral sentiments: less, however, as a matter of reason, and on their own account, than as a consequence of the sympathies and antipathies which had little or nothing to do with the interests of society, have made themselves felt in the establishment of moralities with quite as great force.

The likings and dislikings of society, or of some powerful portion of it, are thus the main thing which has practically determined the rules laid down for general observance, under the penalties of law or opinion. And in general, those who have been in advance of society in thought and feeling, have left this condition of things unassailed in principle, however they may have come into conflict with it in some of its details. They have occupied themselves rather in inquiring what things society ought to like or dislike, than in questioning whether its likings or dislikings should be a law to individuals. They preferred endeavouring to alter the feelings of mankind on the particular points on which they were themselves heretical, rather than make common cause in defence of freedom, with heretics generally. The only case in which the higher ground has been taken on principle and maintained with consistency, by any but an individual here and there, is that of religious belief: a case instructive in many ways, and not least so as forming a most striking instance of the fallibility of what is called the moral sense: for the *odium theologicum*, in a sincere bigot, is one of the most unequivocal cases of moral feeling. Those who first broke the yoke of what called itself the Universal Church, were in general as little willing to permit difference of religious opinion as that church itself. But when the heat of the conflict was over,

without giving a complete victory to any party, and each church or sect was reduced to limit its hopes to retaining possession of the ground it already occupied; minorities, seeing that they had no chance of becoming majorities, were under the necessity of pleading to those whom they could not convert, for permission to differ. It is accordingly on this battle-field, almost solely, that the rights of the individual society have been asserted on broad grounds of principle, and the claim of society to exercise authority over dissentients openly controverted. The great writers to whom the world owes what religious liberty it possesses, have mostly asserted freedom of conscience as an indefeasible right, and denied absolutely that a human being is accountable to others for his religious belief. Yet so natural to mankind is tolerance in whatever they really care about, that religious freedom has hardly anywhere been practically realized, except where religious indifference, which dislikes to have its peace disturbed by theological quarrels, has added its weight to the scale. In the minds of almost all religious persons, even in the most tolerant countries, the duty of toleration is admitted with tacit reserves. One person will bear with dissent in matters of church government, but not of dogma; another can tolerate everybody, short of a Papist or an Unitarian; another, every one who believes in revealed religion; a few extend their charity a little further, but stop at the belief in a God and in a future state. Wherever the sentiment of the majority is still genuine and intense, it is found to have abated little of its claim to be obeyed.

In England, from the peculiar circumstances of our political history, though the yoke of opinion is perhaps heavier, that of law is lighter, than in most other countries of Europe; and there is considerable jealousy of direct interference, by the legislative or the executive power with private conduct; not so much from any just regard for the independence of the individual, as from the still subsisting habit of looking on the government as representing an opposite interest to the public. The majority have not yet learnt to feel the power of the government their power, or its opinions their opinions. When they do so, individual liberty will probably be as much opposed to invasion from the government, as it already is from public opinion. But, as yet, there is a considerable amount of feeling ready to be called forth against any attempt of the law to control individuals in things in which they have not hitherto been accustomed to be controlled by it; and this with very little discrimination as to whether the matter is, or is not, within the legitimate sphere of legal control; insomuch that the feeling, highly salutary on the whole, is perhaps quite as often misplaced as well grounded in the particular instances of its application.

There is, in fact, no recognized principle by which the propriety or impropriety of government interference is customarily tested. People decide according to their personal preferences. Some, whenever they see any good to be done, or evil to be remedied, would willingly instigate the government to undertake the business; while others prefer to bear almost any amount of social evil, rather than add one to the departments of human interests amenable to governmental control. And men range themselves on one or the other side in any particular case, according to this general direction of their sentiments; or according to the degree of interest which they feel in the particular thing which it is proposed that the government should do; or according to the belief they entertain that the government would, or would not, do it in the manner they prefer; but very rarely on account of any opinion to which they consistently adhere, as to what things are fit to be done by a government. And it seems to me that, in consequence of this absence of rule or principle, one side is at present as often wrong as the other; the interference of government is, with about equal frequency, improperly invoked and improperly condemned.

The object of this Essay is to assert one very simple principle, as entitled to govern absolutely the dealings of society with the individual in the way of compulsion and control, whether the means used be physical force in the form of legal penalties, or the moral coercion of public opinion. That principle is, that the sole end for which mankind are warranted, individually or collectively in interfering with the liberty of action of any of their number, is self-protection. That the only purpose for which power can be rightfully exercised over any member of a civilized community, against his will, is to prevent harm to others. His own good, either physical or moral, is not a sufficient warrant. He cannot rightfully be compelled to do or forbear because it will be better for him to do so, because it will make him happier, because, in the opinions of others, to do so would be wise, or even right. These are good reasons for remonstrating with him, or reasoning with him, or persuading him, or entreating him, but not for compelling him, or visiting him with any evil, in case he do otherwise. To justify that, the conduct from which it is desired to deter him must be calculated to produce evil to some one else. The only part of the conduct of any one, for which he is amenable to society, is that which concerns others. In the part which merely concerns himself, his independence is, of right, absolute. Over himself, over his own body and mind, the individual is sovereign.

It is, perhaps, hardly necessary to say that this doctrine is meant to apply only to human beings in the maturity of their faculties. We are not speaking of children, or of young persons below the age which the law may fix as that of manhood or womanhood. Those who are still in a state to require being taken care of by others, must be protected against their own actions as well as against external injury. For the same reason, we may leave out of consideration those backward states of society in which the race itself may be considered as in its nonage. The early difficulties in the way of spontaneous progress are so great, that there is seldom any choice of means for overcoming them; and a ruler full of the spirit of improvement is warranted in the use of any expedients that will attain an end, perhaps otherwise unattainable. Despotism is a legitimate mode of government in dealing with barbarians, provided the end be their improvement, and the means justified by actually effecting that end. Liberty, as a principle, has no application to any state of things anterior to the time when mankind have become capable of being improved by free and equal discussion. Until then, there is nothing for them but implicit obedience to an Akbar or a Charlemagne, if they are so fortunate as to find one. But as soon as mankind have attained the capacity of being guided to their own improvement by conviction or persuasion (a period long since reached in all nations with whom we need here concern ourselves), compulsion, either in the direct form or in that of pains and penalties for non-compliance, is no longer admissible as a means to their own good, and justifiable only for the security of others.

It is proper to state that I forego any advantage which could be derived to my argument from the idea of abstract right as a thing independent of utility. I regard utility as the ultimate appeal on all ethical questions; but it must be utility in the largest sense, grounded on the permanent interests of man as a progressive being. Those interests, I contend, authorize the subjection of individual spontaneity to external control, only in respect to those actions of each, which concern the interest of other people. If any one does an act hurtful to others, there is a *primâ facie* case for punishing him, by law, or, where legal penalties are not safely applicable, by general disapprobation. There are also many positive acts for the benefit of others, which he may rightfully be compelled to perform; such as, to give evidence in a court of justice; to bear his fair share in the common defence, or in any other joint work necessary to the interest of the society of which he enjoys the protection; and to perform certain acts of individual beneficence, such as saving a fellow-creature's life, or interposing to protect the defenceless against ill-usage, things which whenever it is obviously a man's duty to do, he may rightfully be made responsible to society for not doing.

Of the Liberty of Thought and Discussion

The time, it is to be hoped, is gone by when any defence would be necessary of the "liberty of the press" as one of the securities against corrupt or tyrannical government. No argument, we may suppose, can now be needed, against permitting a legislature or an executive, not identified in interest with the people, to prescribe opinions to them, and determine what doctrines or what arguments they shall be allowed to hear. This aspect of the question, besides, has been so often and so triumphantly enforced by preceding writers, that it needs not be specially insisted on in this place. Though the law of England, on the subject of the press, is as servile to this day as it was in the time of the Tudors, there is little danger of its being actually put in force against political discussion, except during some temporary panic, when fear of insurrection drives ministers and judges from their propriety; and, speaking generally, it is not, in constitutional countries, to be apprehended that the government, whether completely responsible to the people or not, will often attempt to control the expression of opinion, except when in doing so it makes itself the organ of the general intolerance of the public. Let us suppose, therefore, that the government is entirely at one with the people, and never thinks of exerting any power of coercion unless in agreement with what it conceives to be their voice. But I deny the right of the people to exercise such coercion, either by themselves or by their government. The power itself is illegitimate. The best government has no more title to it than the worst. It is as noxious, or more noxious, when exerted in accordance with public opinion, than when in opposition to it. If all mankind minus one, were of one opinion, and only one person were of the contrary opinion, mankind would be no more justified in silencing that one person, than he, if he had the power, would be justified in silencing mankind. Were an opinion a personal possession of no value except to the owner; if to be obstructed in the enjoyment of it were simply a private injury, it would make some difference whether the injury was inflicted only on a few persons or on many. But the peculiar evil of silencing the expression of an opinion is, that it is robbing the human race; posterity as well as the existing generation; those who dissent from the opinion, still more than those who hold it. If the opinion is right, they are deprived of the opportunity of exchanging error for truth: if wrong, they lose, what is almost as great a benefit, the clearer perception and livelier impression of truth, produced by its collision with error. . . .

We have now recognized the necessity to the mental well-being of mankind (on which all their other well-being depends) of freedom of opinion, and freedom of the expression of opinion, on four distinct grounds; which we will now briefly recapitulate.

First, if any opinion is compelled to silence, that opinion may, for aught we can certainly know, be true. To deny this is to assume our own infallibility.

Secondly, though the silenced opinion be an error, it may, and very commonly does, contain a portion of truth; and since the general or prevailing opinion on any object is rarely or never the whole truth, it is only by the collision of adverse opinions that the remainder of the truth has any chance of being supplied.

Thirdly, even if the received opinion be not only true, but the whole truth; unless it is suffered to be, and actually is, vigorously and earnestly contested, it will, by most of those who receive it, be held in the manner of a prejudice, with little comprehension of feeling of its rational grounds. And not only this, but, fourthly, the meaning of the doctrine itself will be in danger of being lost, or enfeebled, and deprived of its vital effect on the character and conduct: the dogma becoming a mere formal profession, inefficacious for good, but cumbering the ground, and preventing the growth of any real and heartfelt conviction, from reason or personal experience.

Before quitting the subject of freedom of opinion, it is fit to take notice of those who say, that the free expression of all opinions should be permitted, on condition that the manner be temperate, and do not pass the bounds of fair discussion. Much might be said on the impossibility of fixing where these supposed bounds are to be placed; for if the test be offence to those whose opinion is attacked, I think experience testifies that this offence is given whenever the attack is telling and powerful, and that every opponent who pushes them hard, and whom they find it difficult to answer, appears to them, if he shows any strong feeling on the subject, an intemperate opponent. But this, though an important consideration in a practical point of view, merges in a more fundamental objection. Undoubtedly the manner of asserting an opinion, even though it be a true one, may be very objectionable, and may justly incur severe censure. But the principal offences of the kind are such as it is mostly impossible, unless by accidental self-betrayal, to bring home to conviction. The gravest of them is, to argue sophistically, to suppress facts or arguments, to misstate the elements of the case, or misrepresent the opposite opinion. But all this, even to the most aggravated degree, is so continually done in perfect good faith, by persons who are not considered, and in many other respects may not deserve to be considered, ignorant or incompetent, that it is rarely possible on adequate grounds conscientiously to stamp the misrepresentation as morally culpable; and still less could law presume to interfere with this kind of controversial misconduct. With regard to what is commonly meant by intemperate discussion, namely, invective, sarcasm, personality, and the like, the denunciation of these weapons would deserve more sympathy if it were ever proposed to interdict them equally to both sides; but it is only desired to restrain the employment of them against the prevailing opinion: against the unprevailing they may not only be used without general disapproval, but will be likely to obtain for him who uses them the praise of honest zeal and righteous indignation. Yet whatever mischief arises from their use, is greatest when they are employed against the comparatively defenceless; and whatever unfair advantage can be derived by any opinion from this mode of asserting it, accrues almost exclusively to received opinions. The worst offence of this kind which can be committed by a polemic, is to stimatize those who hold the contrary opinion as bad and immoral men. To calumny of this sort, those who hold any unpopular opinion are peculairly exposed, because they are in general few and uninfluential, and nobody but themselves feels much interest in seeing justice done them; but this weapon is, from the nature of the case, denied to

those who attack a prevailing opinion: they can neither use it with safety to themselves, nor if they could, would it do anything but recoil on their own cause. In general, opinions contrary to those commonly received can only obtain a hearing by studied moderation of language, and the most cautious avoidance of unnecessary offence, from which they hardly ever deviate even in a slight degree without losing ground: while unmeasured vituperation employed on the side of the prevailing opinion, really does deter people from professing contrary opinions, and from listening to those who profess them. For the interest, therefore, of truth and justice, it is far more important to restrain this employment of vituperative language than the other; and, for example, if it were necessary to choose, there would be much more need to discourage offensive attacks on infidelity, than on religion. It is, however, obvious that law and authority have no business with restraining either, while opinion ought, in every instance, to determine its verdict by the circumstances of the individual case; condemning every one, on whichever side of the argument he places himself, in whose mode of advocacy either want of candor, or malignity, bigotry or intolerance of feeling manifest themselves, but not inferring these vices from the side which a person takes, though it be the contrary side of the question to our own; and giving merited honor to every one, whatever opinion he may hold, who has calmness to see and honesty to state what his opponents and their opinions really are, exaggerating nothing to their discredit, keeping nothing back which tells, or can be supposed to tell, in their favor. This is the real morality of public discussion; and if often violated, I am happy to think that there are many controversialists who to a great extent observe it, and a still greater number who conscientiously strive towards it. . . . .

Of the Limits to the Authority of Society Over the Individual

What, then, is the rightful limit to the sovereignty of the individual over himself? Where does the authority of society begin? How much of human life should be assigned to individuality, and how much to society?

Each will receive its proper share, if each has that which more particularly concerns it. To individuality should belong the part of life in which it is chiefly the individual that is interested; to society, the part which chiefly interests society.

Though society is not founded on a contract, and though no good purpose is answered by inventing a contract in order to deduce social obligations from it, every one who receives the protection of society owes a return for the benefit, and the fact of living in society renders it indispensable that each should be bound to observe a certain line of conduct towards the rest. This conduct consists, first, in not injuring the interests of one another; or rather certain interests, which, either by express legal provision or by tacit understanding, ought to be considered as rights; and secondly, in each person's bearing his share (to be fixed on some equitable principle) of the labors and sacrifices incurred for defending the society or its members from injury and molestation. These conditions society is justified in enforcing, at all costs to those who endeavor to withhold fulfilment. Nor is this all that society may do. The acts of an individual may be hurtful to others, or wanting in due consideration for their welfare, without going the length of violating any of their constituted rights. The offender may then be justly punished by opinion, though not by law. As soon as any part of a person's conduct affects prejudicially the interests of others, society has jurisdiction over it, and the question whether the general welfare will or will not be promoted by interfering with it, becomes open to discussion. But there is no room for entertaining any such question when a person's conduct affects the interests of no persons besides himself, or needs not affect them unless they like (all the persons concerned being of full age, and the ordinary amount of understanding). In all such cases there should be perfect freedom, legal and social, to do the action and stand the consequences.

It would be a great misunderstanding of this doctrine, to suppose that it is one of selfish indifference, which pretends that human beings have no business with each other's conduct in life, and that they should not concern themselves about the well-doing or well-being of one another, unless their own interest is involved. Instead of any diminution, there is need of a great increase of disinterested exertion to promote the good of others. But disinterested benevolence can find other instruments to persuade people to their good, than whips and scourges, either of the literal or the metaphorical sort. I am the last person to undervalue the self-regarding virtues; they are only second in importance, if even second, to the social. It is equally the business of education to cultivate both. But even education works by conviction and persuasion as well as by compulsion, and it is by the former only that, when the period of education is past, the self-regarding virtues should be inculcated. Human beings owe to each other help to distinguish the better from the worse, and encouragement to choose the former and avoid the latter. They should be forever stimulating each other to increased exercise of their higher faculties, and increased direction of their feelings and aims towards wise instead of foolish, elevating instead of degrading, objects and contemplations. But neither one person, nor any number of persons, is warranted in saying to another human creature of ripe years, that he shall not do with his life for his own benefit what he chooses to do with it. He is the person most interested in his own well-being, the interest which any other person, except in cases of strong personal attachment, can have in it, is trifling, compared with that which he himself has; the interest which society has in him individually (except as to his conduct to others) is fractional, and altogether indirect: while, with respect to his own feelings and circumstances, the most ordinary man or woman has means of knowledge immeasurably surpassing those that can be possessed by any one else. The interference of society to overrule his judgment and purposes in what only regards himself, must be grounded on general presumptions; which may be altogether wrong, and even if right, are as likely as not to be misapplied to individual cases, by persons no better acquainted with the circumstances of such cases than those are who look at them merely from without. In this department, therefore, of human affairs, Individuality has its proper field of action. In the conduct of human beings towards one another, it is necessary that general rules should for the most part be observed, in order that people may know what they have to expect; but in each person's own concerns, his individual spontaneity is entitled to free exercise. Considerations to aid his judgment, exhortations to strengthen his will, may be offered to him, even obtruded on him, by others; but he, himself, is the final judge. All errors which he is likely to commit against advice and warning, are far outweighed by the evil of allowing others to constrain him to what they deem his good.

I do not mean that the feelings with which a person is regarded by others, ought not to be in any way affected by his self-regarding qualities or deficiencies. This is neither possible nor desirable. If he is eminent in any of the qualities which conduce to his own good, he is, so far, a proper object of admiration. He is so much the nearer to the ideal perfection of human nature. If he is grossly deficient in these qualities, a sentiment the opposite of admiration will follow. There is a degree of folly, and a degree of what may be called (though the phrase is not unobjectionable) lowness or depravation of taste, which, though it cannot justify doing harm to the person who manifests it, renders him necessarily and properly a subject of distaste, or, in extreme cases, even of contempt: a person could not have the opposite qualities in due strength without entertaining these feelings. Though doing no wrong to any one, a person may so act as to compel us to judge him, and feel to him, as a fool, or as a being of an inferior order: and since this judgment and feeling are a fact which he would prefer to avoid, it is doing him a service to warn him of it beforehand, as of any other disagreeable consequence to which he exposes himself. It would be well, indeed, if this good office were much more freely rendered than the common notions of politeness at present permit, and if one person could honestly point out to another that he thinks him in fault, without being considered unmannerly or presuming. We have a right, also, in various ways, to act upon our unfavorable opinion of any one, not to the oppression of his individuality, but in the exercise of ours. We are not bound, for example, to seek his society; we have a right to avoid it (though not to parade the avoidance) for we have a right to choose the society most acceptable to us. We have a right, and it may be our duty, to caution others against him, if we think his example or conversation likely to have a pernicious effect on those with whom he associates. We may give others a preference over him in optional good offices, except those which tend to his improvement. In these various modes a person may suffer very severe penalties at the hands of others, for faults which directly concern only himself; but he suffers these penalties only in so far as they are the natural, and, as it were, the spontaneous consequences of the faults themselves, not because they are purposely inflicted on him for the sake of punishment. A person who shows rashness, obstinacy, self-conceit—who cannot live within moderate means—who cannot restrain himself from hurtful indulgences—who pursues animal pleasures at the expense of those of feeling and intellect—must expect to be lowered in the opinion of others, and to have a less share of their favorable sentiments, but of this he has no right to complain, unless he has merited their favor by special excellence in his social relations, and has thus established a title to their good offices, which is not affected by his demerits towards himself.

What I contend for is, that the inconveniences which are strictly inseparable from the unfavorable judgment of others, are the only ones to which a person should ever be subjected for that portion of his conduct and character which concerns his own good, but which does not affect the interests of others in their relations with him. Acts injurious to others require a totally different treatment. Encroachment on their rights; infliction on them of any loss or damage not justified by his own rights; falsehood or duplicity in dealing with them; unfair or ungenerous use of advantages over them; even selfish abstinence from defending them against injury—these are fit objects of moral reprobation, and, in grave cases, of moral retribution and punishment. And not only these acts, but the dispositions which lead to them, are properly immoral, and fit subjects of disapprobation which may rise to abhorrence. Cruelty of disposition; malice and ill-nature; that most anti-social and odious of all passions, envy; dissimulation and insincerity; irascibility on insufficient cause, and resentment disproportioned to the provocation; the love of domineering over others; the desire to engross more than one's share of advantages (the πλεονεξια of the Greeks); the pride which derives gratification from the abasement of others; the egotism which thinks self and its concerns more important than everything else, and decides all doubtful questions in his own favor;—these are moral vices, and constitute a bad and odious moral character: unlike the self-regarding faults previously mentioned, which are not properly immoralities, and to whatever pitch they may be carried, do not constitute wickedness. They may be proofs of any amount of folly, or want of personal dignity and self-respect; but they are only a subject of moral reprobation when they involve a breach of duty to others, for whose sake the individual is bound to have care for himself. What are called duties to ourselves are not socially obligatory, unless circumstances render them at the same time duties to others. The term duty to oneself, when it means anything more than prudence, means self-respect or self-development; and for none of these is any one accountable to his fellow-creatures, because for none of them is it for the good of mankind that he be held accountable to them. . . .

Applications

The principles asserted in these pages must be more generally admitted as the basis for discussion of details, before a consistent application of them to all the various departments of government and morals can be attempted with any prospect of advantage. The few observations I propose to make on questions of detail, are designed to illustrate the principles, rather than to follow them out to their consequences. I offer, not so much applications, as specimens of application; which may serve to bring into greater clearness the meaning and limits of the two maxims which together form the entire doctrine of this Essay and to assist the judgment in holding the balance between them, in the cases where it appears doubtful which of them is applicable to the case.

The maxims are, first, that the individual is not accountable to society for his actions, in so far as these concern the interests of no person but himself. Advice, instruction, persuasion, and avoidance by other people, if thought necessary by them for their own good, are the only measures by which society can justifiably express its dislike or disapprobation of his conduct. Secondly, that for such actions as are prejudicial to the interests of others, the individual is accountable, and may be subjected either to social or to legal punishments, if society is of opinion that the one or the other is requisite for its protection.

In the first place, it must by no means be supposed, because damage, or probability of damage, to the interests of others, can alone justify the interference of society, that therefore it always does justify such interference. In many cases, an individual, in pursuing a legitimate object, necessarily and therefore legitimately causes pain or loss to others, or intercepts a good which they had a reasonable hope of obtaining. Such oppositions of interest between individuals often arise from bad social institutions, but are unavoidable while those institutions last; and some would be unavoidable under any institutions. Whoever succeeds in an overcrowded profession, or in a competitive examination; whoever is preferred to another in any contest for an object which both desire, reaps benefit from the loss of others, from their wasted exertion and their disappointment. But it is, by common admission, better for the general interest of mankind, that persons should pursue their objects undeterred by this sort of consequences. In other words, society admits no right, either legal or moral, in the disappointed competitors, to immunity from this kind of suffering; and feels called on to interfere, only when means of success have been employed which it is contrary to the general interest to permit—namely, fraud or treachery, and force.

Again, trade is a social act. Whoever undertakes to sell any description of goods to the public, does what affects the interest of other persons, and of society in general; and thus his conduct, in principle, comes within the jurisdiction of society: accordingly, it was once held to be the duty of governments, in all cases which were considered of importance, to fix prices, and regulate the processes of manufacture. But it is now recognized, though not till after a long struggle, that both the cheapness and the good quality of commodities are most effectually provided for by leaving the producers and sellers perfectly free, under the sole check of equal freedom to the buyers for supplying themselves elsewhere. This is the so-called doctrine of Free Trade, which rests on grounds different from, though equally solid with, the principle of individual liberty asserted in this Essay. Restrictions on trade, or on production for purposes of trade, are indeed restraints; and all restraint, *quâ* restraint, is an evil: but the restraints in question affect only that part of conduct which society is competent to restrain, and are wrong solely because they do not really produce the results which it is desired to produce by them. As the principle of individual liberty is not involved in the doctrine of Free Trade so neither is it in most of the questions which arise respecting the limits of that doctrine: as for example, what amount of public control is admissible for the prevention of fraud by adulteration; how far sanitary precautions, or arrangements to protect work-people employed in dangerous occupations, should be enforced on employers. Such questions involve considerations of liberty, only in so far as leaving people to themselves is always better, *cateris paribus,* than controlling them: but that they may be legitimately controlled for these ends, is in principle undeniable. On the other hand, there are questions relating to interference with trade which are essentially questions of liberty; such as the Maine Law, already touched upon; the prohibition of the importation of opium into China; the restriction of the sale of poisons; all cases, in short, where the object of the interference is to make it impossible or difficult to obtain a particular commodity. These interferences are objectionable, not as infringements on the liberty of the producer or seller, but on that of the buyer.

One of these examples, that of the sale of poisons, opens a new question; the proper limits of what may be called the functions of police; how far liberty may legitimately be invaded for the prevention of crime, or of accident. It is one of the undisputed functions of government to take precautions against crime before it has been committed, as well as to detect and punish it afterwards. The preventive function of government, however, is far more liable to be abused, to the prejudice of liberty, than the punitory function; for there is hardly any part of the legitimate freedom of action of a human being which would not admit of being represented, and fairly too, as increasing the facilities for some form or other of delinquency. Nevertheless, if a public authority, or even a private person, sees any one evidently preparing to commit a crime, they are not bound to look on inactive until the crime is committed, but may interfere to prevent it. If poisons were never bought or used for any purpose except the commission of murder, it would be right to prohibit their manufacture and sale. They may, however, be wanted not only for innocent but for useful purposes, and restrictions cannot be imposed in the one case without operating in the other. Again, it is a proper office of public authority to guard against accidents. If either a public officer or any one else saw a person attempting to cross a bridge which had been ascertained to be unsafe, and there were no time to warn him of his danger, they might seize him and turn him back without any real infringement of his liberty; for liberty consists in doing what one desires, and he does not desire to fall into the river. Nevertheless, when there is not a certainty, but only a danger of mischief, no one but the person himself can judge of the sufficiency of the motive which may prompt him to incur the risk: in this case, therefore, (unless he is a child, or delirious, or in some state of excitement or absorption incompatible with the full use of the reflecting faculty,) he ought, I conceive, to be only warned of the danger; not forcibly prevented from exposing himself to it. Similar considerations, applied to such a question as the sale of poisons, may enable us to decide which among the possible modes of regulation are or are not contrary to principle. Such a precaution, for example, as that of labelling the drug with some word expressive of its dangerous character, may be enforced without violation of liberty: the buyer cannot wish not to know that the thing he possesses has poisonous qualities. But to require in all cases the certificate of a medical practitioner, would make it sometimes impossible, always expensive, to obtain the article for legitimate uses. The only mode apparent to me, in which difficulties may be thrown in the way of crime committed through this means, without any infringement,

worth taking into account, upon the liberty of those who desire the poisonous substance for other purposes, consists in providing what, in the apt language of Bentham, is called "preappointed evidence." This provision is familiar to every one in the case of contracts. It is usual and right that the law, when a contract is entered into, should require as the condition of its enforcing performance that certain formalities should be observed, such as signatures, attestation of witnesses, and the like, in order that in case of subsequent dispute, there may be evidence to prove that the contract was really entered into, and that there was nothing in the circumstances to render it legally invalid: the effect being, to throw great obstacles in the way of fictitious contracts, or contracts made in circumstances which, if known, would destroy their validity. Precautions of a similar nature might be enforced in the sale of articles adapted to be instruments of crime. The seller, for example, might be required to enter in a register the exact time of the transaction, the name and address of the buyer, the precise quality and quantity sold; to ask the purpose for which it was wanted, and record the answer he received. When there was no medical prescription, the presence of some third person might be required, to bring home the fact to the purchaser, in case there should afterwards be reason to believe that the article had been applied to criminal purposes. Such regulations would in general be no material impediment to obtaining the article, but a very considerable one to making an improper use of it without detection.

The right inherent in society, to ward off crimes against itself by antecedent precautions, suggests the obvious limitations to the maxim, that purely self-regarding misconduct cannot properly be meddled with in the way of prevention or punishment. Drunkennesses, for example, in ordinary cases, is not a fit subject for legislative interference; but I should deem it perfectly legitimate that a person, who had once been convicted of any act of violence to others under the influence of drink, should be placed under a special legal restriction, personal to himself; that if he were afterwards found drunk, he should be liable to a penalty, and that if when in that state he committed another offence, the punishment to which he would be liable for that other offence should be increased in severity. The making himself drunk, in a person whom drunkenness excites to do harm to others, is a crime against others. So, again, idleness, except in a person receiving support from the public, or except when it constitutes a breach of contract, cannot without tyranny be made a subject of legal punishment; but if either from idleness or from any other avoidable cause, a man fails to perform his legal duties to others, as for instance to support his children, it is no tyranny to force him to fulfil that obligation, by compulsory labor, if no other means are available.

Again, there are many acts which, being directly injurious only to the agents themselves, ought not to be legally interdicted, but which, if done publicly, are a violation of good manners, and coming thus within the category of offences against others, may rightfully be prohibited. Of this kind are offences against decency; on which it is unnecessary to dwell, the rather as they are only connected indirectly with our subject, the objection to publicity being equally strong in the case of many actions not in themselves condemnable, nor supposed to be so. . . .

G. W. F. Hegel

Georg Wilhelm Friedrich Hegel (1770-1831) was perhaps the most influential thinker of the nineteenth century. By the end of the century his major ideas had found wide acceptance in many fields of thought. It was Hegel who best formulated the idea of a universal history, the concept that there was a great process at work in history, a great Idea becoming reality, despite the apparent confusion of events. In other words, Hegel built a rational philosophy of history, teleological in nature, and offered it as a secular substitute for the old Christian explanation of human affairs. He postulated the existence of a *Weltgeist* (World Spirit), which embodies itself in the *Volksgeist* (cultural spirit of a people), which in turn determines the shape of the political institutions, mores and culture of that particular nation. The *Weltgeist* uses nations for its own purpose; such a nation would thus be a world-historical-state and its citizens a world-historical-people. Such a state and people would thus advance the will of the *Weltgeist*. In time, however, this triumphant nation will elicit conflict (either internal or external) and a new world-historical-state will emerge, incorporating the best features of the old. Thus the workings of the dialectic—thesis, antithesis and synthesis—which Marx would later use for his own purposes. The process, according to Hegel, would continue, until freedom would inevitably emerge. Hegel, then, secularized the Christian dream of salvation and the millennium, finding salvation in freedom and the end of history in the state rather than in the church.

LECTURES ON THE PHILOSOPHY OF HISTORY

Introduction

A World-historical individual is not so unwise as to indulge a variety of wishes to divide his regards. He is devoted to the One Aim, regardless of all else. It is even possible that such men may treat other great, even sacred interests, inconsiderately; conduct which is indeed obnoxious to moral reprehension. But so mighty a form must trample down many an innocent flower—crush to pieces many an object in its path.

The special interest of passion is thus inseparable from the active development of a general principle: for it is from the special and determinate and from its negation, that the Universal results. Particularity contends with its like, and some loss is involved in the issue. *It* is not the general idea that is implicated in opposition and combat, and that is exposed to danger. It remains in the background,

From *Lectures on the Philosophy of History* by G. W. F. Hegel translated from the third German edition by J. Sibree. Copyright 1872 by Bell & Daldy York Street, Covent Garden London.

untouched and uninjured. This may be called the *cunning of reason,*—that it sets the passions to work for itself, while that which develops its existence through such impulsion pays the penalty, and suffers loss. For it is *phenomenal* being that is so treated, and of this, part is of no value, part is positive and real. The particular is for the most part of too trifling value as compared with the general: individuals are sacrificed and abandoned. The Idea pays the penalty of determinate existence and of corruptibility, not from itself, but from the passions of individuals.

But though we might tolerate the idea that individuals, their desires and the gratification of them, are thus sacrificed, and their happiness given up to the empire of chance, to which it belongs; and that as a general rule, individuals come under the category of means to an ulterior end,—there is one aspect of human individuality which we should hesitate to regard in that subordinate light, even in relation to the highest; since it is absolutely no subordinate element, but exists in those individuals as inherently eternal and divine. I mean *morality, ethics, religion.* Even when speaking of the realization of the great ideal aim by means of individuals, the *subjective* element in them—their interest and that of their cravings and impulses, their views and judgments, though exhibited as the merely formal side of their existence,—was spoken of as having an infinite right to be consulted. The first idea that presents itself in speaking of *means* is that of something external to the object, and having no share in the object itself. But merely natural things—even the commonest lifeless objects—used as means, must be of such a kind as adapts them to their purpose; they must possess something in common with it. Human beings least of all, sustain the bare external relation of mere means to the great ideal aim. Not only do they in the very act of realising it, make it the occasion of satisfying personal desires, whose purport is diverse from that aim—but they share in that ideal aim itself; and are for that very reason objects of their own existence; not *formally* merely, as the world of living beings generally is,—whose individual life is essentially subordinate to that of man, and is properly used *up* as an instrument. Men, on the contrary, are objects of existence to themselves, as regards the intrinsic import of the aim in question. To this order belongs that in them which we would exclude from the category of mere means, Morality, Ethics, Religion. That is to say, man is an object of existence in himself only in virtue of the Divine that is in him,—that which was designated at the outset as *Reason;* which, in view of its activity and power of self-determination, was called *Freedom.* And we affirm—without entering at present on the proof of the assertion—that Religion, Morality,&c. have their foundation and source in that principle, and so are essentially elevated above all alien necessity and chance. And here we must remark that individuals, to the extent of their freedom, are responsible for the depravation and enfeeblement of morals and religion. This is the seal of the absolute and sublime destiny of man—that he knows what is good and what is evil; that is, his destiny, his very ability to will either good or evil,—in one word, that he is the subject of moral imputation, imputation not only of evil, but of good; and not only concerning this or that particular matter, and all that happens *ab extrâ,* but *also* the good and evil attaching to his individual freedom. The brute alone is simply innocent. It would, however, demand an extensive explanation—as extensive as the analysis of moral freedom itself—to preclude or obviate all the misunderstandings which the statement that what is called innocence imports the entire unconsciousness of evil—is wont to occasion.

In comtemplating the fate which virtue, morality, even piety experience in history, we must not fall into the Litany of Lamentations, that the good and pious often—or for the most part—fare ill in the world, while the evil-disposed and wicked prosper. The term *prosperity* is used in a variety of meanings—riches, outward honour, and the like. But in speaking of something which in and for itself constitutes an aim of existence, that so-called well or ill-faring of these or those isolated individuals cannot be regarded as an essential element in the rational order of the universe. With more justice than happiness,—or a fortunate environment for individuals,—it is demanded of the grand aim of the world's existence, that it should foster, nay involve the execution and ratification of good, moral, righteous purposes. What makes men morally discontented (a discontent, by the bye, on which they somewhat pride themselves), is that they do not find the present adapted to the realization of aims which they hold to be right and just (more especially in modern times, ideals of political constitutions); they contrast unfavourably things as they *are,* with their idea of things as they *ought* to be. In this case it is not private interest nor passion that desires gratification, but Reason, Justice, Liberty; and equipped with this title, the demand in question assumes a lofty bearing, and readily adopts a position not merely of discontent, but of open revolt against the actual condition of the world. To estimate such a feeling and such views aright, the demands insisted upon, and the very dogmatic opinions asserted, must be examined. At no time so much as in our own, have such general principles and notions been advanced, or with greater assurance. If in days gone by, history seems to present itself as a struggle of passions; in our time—though displays of passion are not wanting—it exhibits partly a predominance of the struggle of notions assuming the authority of principles; partly that of passions and interests essentially subjective, but under the mask of such higher sanctions. The pretensions thus contended for as legitimate in the name of that which has been stated as the ultimate aim of Reason, pass accordingly, for absolute aims,—to the same extent as Religion, Morals, Ethics. Nothing, as before remarked, is now more common than the complaint that the *ideals* which imagination sets up are not realized—that these glorious dreams are destroyed by cold actuality. These Ideals—which in the voyage of life founder on the rocks of hard reality—may be in the first instance only subjective, and belong to the idiosyncrasy of the individual, imagining himself the highest and wisest. Such do not properly belong to this category. For the fancies which the individual in his isolation indulges, cannot be the model for universal reality; just as *universal* law is not designed for the units of the mass. These as such may, in fact, find their interests decidedly thrust into the background. But by the term "Ideal," we also understand the ideal of Reason, of the Good, of the True. Poets, as *e.g.* Schiller, have painted such ideals touchingly and with strong emotion, and with the deeply melancholy conviction that they could not be realized. In affirming, on the contrary, that the Universal Reason *does* realize itself, we have indeed nothing to do with the individual empirically regarded. That admits of degrees of better and worse, since here chance and speciality have received authority from the Idea to exercise their monstrous power. Much, therefore, in particular aspects of the grand phenomenon might be found fault with. This subjective fault-finding,—which, however, only keeps in view the individual and its deficiency, without taking notice of Reason pervading the whole,—is easy; and inasmuch as asserts an excellent intention with regard to the good and the whole, and seems to result from a kindly heart, it feels authorized to give itself airs and assume great consequence. It is easier to discover a deficiency in individuals, in states, and in Providence, than to see

their real import and value. For in this merely negative fault-finding a proud position is taken,—one which overlooks the object, without having entered into it,—without having comprehended its positive aspect. Age generally makes men more tolerant; youth is always discontented. The tolerance of age is the result of the ripeness of judgment which, not merely as the result of indifference, is satisfied even with what is inferior; but, more deeply taught by the grave experience of life, has been led to perceive the substantial, solid worth of the object in question. The insight then to which—in contradistinction from those ideals—philosophy is to lead us, is, that the real world is as it ought to be—that the truly good—the universal divine reason—is not a mere abstraction, but a vital principle capable of realising itself. This *Good,* this *Reason,* in its most concrete form, is God. God governs the world; the actual working of his government—the carrying out of his plan—is the History of the World. This plan philosophy strives to comprehend; for only that which has been developed as the result of it, possesses *bona fide* reality. That which does not accord with it, is negative, worthless existence. Before the pure light of this divine Idea—which is no mere Ideal—the phantom of a world whose events are an incoherent concourse of fortuitous circumstances, utterly vanishes. Philosophy wishes to discover the substantial purport, the real side of the divine idea, and to justify the so much despised Reality of things; for Reason is the comprehension of the Divine work. But as to what concerns the perversion, corruption, and ruin of religious, ethical and moral purposes, and states of society generally, it must be affirmed, that in their *essence* these are infinite and eternal; but that the forms they assume may be of a limited order, and consequently belong to the domain of mere nature, and be subject to the sway of chance. They are therefore perishable, and exposed to decay and corruption. Religion and morality—in the same way as inherently universal essences—have the peculiarity of being present in the individual soul, in the full extent of their Idea, and therefore truly and really; although they may not manifest themselves in it *in extenso,* and are not applied to fully developed relations. The religion, the morality of a limited sphere of life—that of a shepherd or a peasant, *e.g.*—in its intensive concentration and limitation to a few perfectly simple relations of life,—has infinite worth; the same worth as the religion and morality of extensive knowledge, and of an existence rich in the compass of its relations and actions. This inner focus—this simple region of the claims of subjective freedom,—the home of volition, resolution, and action,—the abstract sphere of conscience,—that which comprises the responsibility and moral value of the individual, remains untouched; and is quite shut out from the noisy din of the World's History—including not merely external and temporal changes, but also those entailed by the absolute necessity inseparable from the realization of the Idea of Freedom itself. But as a general truth this must be regarded as settled, that whatever in the world possesses claims as noble and glorious, has nevertheless a higher existence above it. The claim of the World-Spirit rises above all special claims.

These observations may suffice in reference to the means which the World-Spirit uses for realizing its Idea. Stated simply and abstractly, this mediation involves the activity of personal existences in whom Reason is present as their absolute, substantial being; but a basis, in the first instance, still obscure and unknown to them. But the subject becomes more complicated and difficult when we regard individuals not merely in their aspect of activity, but more concretely, in conjunction with a particular manifestation of that activity in their religion and morality,—forms of existence which are intimately connected with Reason, and share in its absolute claims. Here the relation of mere means to an end disappears, and the chief bearings of this seeming difficulty in reference to the absolute aim of Spirit, have been briefly considered.

The third point to be analysed is, therefore—what is the object to be realized by these means; *i.e.* what is the form it assumes in the realm of reality. We have spoken of *means;* but in the carrying out of a subjective, limited aim, we have also to take into consideration the element of a *material,* either already present or which has to be procured. Thus the question would arise: What is the material in which the Ideal of Reason is wrought out? The primary answer would be,—Personality itself—human desires—Subjectivity generally. In human knowledge and volition, as its material element, Reason attains positive existence. We have considered subjective volition where it has an object which is the truth and essence of a reality, viz. where it constitutes a great world-historical passion. As a subjective will, occupied with limited passions, it is dependent, and can gratify its desires only within the limits of this dependence. But the subjective will has also a substantial life—a reality,—in which it moves in the region of *essential*

being, and has the essential itself as the object of its existence. This essential being is the union of the *subjective* with the *rational* Will: it is the moral Whole, the *State,* which is that form of reality in which the individual has and enjoys his freedom; but on the condition of his recognizing, believing in and willing that which is common to the Whole. And this must not be understood as if the subjective will of the social unit attained its gratification and enjoyment through that common Will; as if this were a means provided for its benefit; as if the individual, in his relations to other individuals, thus limited his freedom, in order that this universal limitation—the mutual constraint of all—might secure a small space of liberty for each. Rather, we affirm, are Law, Morality, Government, and they alone, the positive reality and completion of Freedom. Freedom of a low and limited order, is mere caprice; which finds its exercise in the sphere of particular and limited desires.

Subjective volition—Passion—is that which sets men in activity, that which effects "practical" realization. The Idea is the inner spring of action; the State is the actually existing, realized moral life. For it is the Unity of the universal, essential Will, with that of the individual; and this is "Morality." The Individual living in this unity has a moral life; possesses a value that consists in this substantiality alone. Sophocles in his Antigone, says, "The divine commands are not of yesterday, nor of to-day; no, they have an infinite existence, and no one could say whence they came." The laws of morality are not accidental, but are the essentially Rational. It is the very object of the State that what is essential in the practical activity of men, and in their dispositions, should be duly recognized; that it should have a manifest existence, and maintain its position. It is the absolute interest of Reason that this moral Whole should exist; and herein lies the justification and merit of heroes who have founded states,—however rude these may have been. In the history of the World, only those peoples can come under our notice which form a state. For it must be understood that this latter is the realization of Freedom, *i.e.* of the absolute final aim, and that it exists for its own sake. It must further be understood that all the worth which the human being possesses—all spiritual reality, he possesses only through the State. For his spiritual reality consists in this, that his own essence—Reason—is objectively present to him, that it possesses objective immediate existence for him. Thus only is he fully conscious; thus only is he a partaker of morality—of a just and moral social and political life. For Truth is the Unity of the universal and subjective Will; and the Universal is to be found in the State, in its laws, its universal and rational arrangements. The State is the Divine Idea as it exists on Earth. We have in it, therefore, the object of History in a more definite shape than before; that in which Freedom obtains objectivity, and lives in the enjoyment of this objectivity. For Law is the objectivity of Spirit; volition in its true form. Only that will which obeys law, is free; for it obeys itself—it is independent and so free. When the State or our country constitutes a community of existence; when the subjective will of man submits to laws,—the contradiction between Liberty and Necessity vanishes. The Rational has necessary existence, as being the reality and substance of things, and we are free in recognizing it as law, and following it as the substance of our own being. The objective and the subjective will are then reconciled, and present one identical homogeneous whole. For the morality (Sittlichkeit) of the State is not of that ethical (moralische) reflective kind, in which one's own conviction bears sway; this latter is rather the peculiarity of the modern time, while the true antique morality is based on the principle of abiding by one's duty [to the state at large]. An Athenian citizen did what was required of him, as it were from instinct: but if I reflect on the object of my activity, I must have the consciousness that my will has been called into exercise. But morality is Duty—substantial Right—a "*second* nature" as it has been justly called; for the *first* nature of man is his primary merely animal existence.

The development *in extenso* of the Idea of the State belongs to the Philosophy of Jurisprudence; but it must be observed that in the theories of our time various errors are current respecting it, which pass for established truths, and have become fixed prejudices. We will mention only a few of them, giving prominence to such as have a reference to the object of our history.

The error which first meets us is the direct contradictory of our principle that the state presents the realization of Freedom; the opinion, viz., that man is free by *nature*, but that in *society*, in the State—to which nevertheless he is irresistibly impelled—he must limit this natural freedom. That man is free by Nature is quite correct in one sense; viz., that he is so according to the Idea of Humanity; but we imply thereby that he is such only in virtue of his destiny—that he has an undeveloped power to become such; for the "Nature" of an object is exactly synonymous with

its "Idea." But the view in question imports more than this. When man is spoken of as "free by Nature," the mode of his existence as well as his destiny is implied. His merely natural and primary condition is intended. In this sense a "state of Nature" is assumed in which mankind at large are in the possession of their natural rights with the unconstrained exercise and enjoyment of their freedom. This assumption is not indeed raised to the dignity of the historical fact; it would indeed be difficult, were the attempt seriously made, to point out any such condition as actually existing, or as having ever occurred. Examples of a savage state of life can be pointed out, but they are marked by brutal passions and deeds of violence; while, however rude and simple their conditions, they involve social arrangements which (to use the common phrase) *restrain* freedom. That assumption is one of those nebulous images which theory produces; an idea which it cannot avoid originating, but which it fathers upon real existence, without sufficient historical justification.

What we find such a state of Nature to be in actual experience, answers exactly to the Idea of a *merely* natural condition. Freedom as the *ideal* of that which is original and natural, does not exist *as original and natural.* Rather must it be first sought out and won; and that by an incalculable medial discipline of the intellectual and moral powers. The state of Nature is, therefore, predominantly that of injustice and violence, of untamed natural impulses, of inhuman deeds and feelings. Limitation is certainly produced by Society and the State, but it is a limitation of the mere brute emotions and rude instincts; as also, in a more advanced stage of culture, of the premeditated self-will of caprice and passion. This kind of constraint is part of the instrumentality by which only, the consciousness of Freedom and the desire for its attainment, in its true—that is Rational and Ideal form—can be obtained. To the Ideal of Freedom, Law and Morality are indispensably requisite; and they are in and for themselves, universal existences, objects and aims; which are discovered only by the activity of thought, separating itself from the merely sensuous, and developing itself, in opposition thereto; and which must on the other hand, be introduced into and incorporated with the originally sensuous will, and that contrarily to its natural inclination. The perpetually recurring misapprehension of Freedom consists in regarding that term only in its *formal*, subjective sense, abstracted from its essential objects and aims; thus a constraint put upon impulse, desire, passion—pertaining to the particular individual as such a limitation of caprice and self-will is regarded as a fettering of Freedom. We should on the contrary look upon such limitation as the indispensable proviso of emancipation. Society and the State are the very conditions in which Freedom is realized.

We must notice a second view, contravening the principle of the development of moral relations into a legal form. The *patriarchal* condition is regarded—either in reference to the entire race of man, or to some branches of it—as exclusively that condition of things, in which the legal element is combined with a due recognition of the moral and emotional parts of our nature; and in which justice as united with these, truly and really influences the intercourse of the social units. The basis of the patriarchal condition is the family relation; which develops the *primary* form of conscious morality, succeeded by that of the State as its *second* phase. The patriarchal condition is one of transition, in which the family has already advanced to the position of a race or people; where the union, therefore, has already ceased to be simply a bond of love and confidence, and has become one of plighted service. We must first examine the ethical principle of the Family. The Family may be reckoned as virtually a single person; since its members have either mutually surrendered their individual personality, (and consequently their legal position towards each other, with the rest of their particular interests and desires) as in the case of the Parents; or have not yet attained such an an independent personality,—(the Children,—who are primarily in that merely natural condition already mentioned. They live, therefore, in a unity of feeling love, confidence, and faith in each other. And in a relation of mutual love, the one individual has the consciousness of himself in the consciousness of the other; he lives out of self; and in this mutual self-renunciation each regains the life that had been virtually transferred to the other; gains, in fact, that other's existence and his own, as involved with that other. The farther interests connected with the necessities and external concerns of life, as well as the development that has to take place within their circle, *i.e.* of the children, constitute a common object for the members of the Family. The Spirit of the Family—the Penates—form one substantial being, as much as the Spirit of a People in the State; and morality in both cases consists in a feeling, a consciousness, and a will, not limited to individual personality and interest, but embracing the common interests of the members generally. But this unity is in the case of the Family essentially one of *feeling;* not advancing beyond the limits of the merely *natural.* The piety of the Family relation should be respected in the highest degree by the State; by its means the State obtains as its members individuals who are already moral (for as mere *persons* they are not) and in uniting to form a state bring with them that sound basis of a political edifice—the capacity of feeling one with a Whole. But the expansion of the Family to a patriarchal unity carries us beyond the ties of blood-relationship—the simply natural elements of that basis; and outside of these limits the members of the community must enter upon the position of independent personality. A review of the patriarchal condition, *in extenso,* would lead us to give special attention to the Theocratical Constitution. The head of the patriarchal clan is also its priest. If the Family in its general relations, is not yet separated from civic society and the state, the seapration of religion from it has also not yet taken place; and so much the less since the piety of the hearth is itself a profoundly subjective state of feeling.

We have considered two aspects of Freedom,—the objective and the subjective; if, therefore, Freedom is asserted to consist in the individuals of a State all agreeing in its arrangements, it is evident that only the subjective aspect is regarded. The natural inference from this principle is, that no law can be valid without the approval of all. This difficulty is attempted to be obviated by the decision that the minority must yield to the majority; the majority therefore bear the sway. But long ago J.J. Rousseau remarked, that in that case there would be no longer freedom, for the will of the *minority* would cease to be respected. At the Polish Diet each single member had to give his consent before any political step could be taken; and this kind of freedom it was that ruined the State. Besides, it is a dangerous and false prejudice, that the People *alone* have reason and insight, and know what justice is; for each popular faction may represent itself as the People, and the question as to what constitutes the State is one of advanced science, and not of popular decision.

If the principle of regard for the individual will is recognized as the only basis of political liberty, viz., that nothing should be done by or for the State to which all the members of the body politic have not given their sanction, we have, properly speaking, no *Constitution.* The only arrangement that would be necessary, would be, first, a centre having no *will* of its own, but which should take into consideration what appeared to be the necessities of the State; and, secondly, a contrivance for calling the members of the State together, for taking the votes, and for performing the arithmetical operations of reckoning and comparing the number of votes for the different propositions, and thereby deciding upon them. The State is an *abstraction,* having even its generic existence in its citizens; but it is an actuality, and its simply generic existence must embody itself in individual will and activity.

Karl Marx

Karl Marx (1818-1883), a German economist and philosopher, and his life long friend Friedrich Engels (1820-1895), members of the International Communist League, were commissioned in 1847 to draw up the party platform of the organization. This document, published in January 1848 just before the revolutions swept over Europe, was titled *The Manifesto of the Communist Party.* It embodied the major thoughts of Karl Marx. In this *Manifesto,* which marks a division point between Utopian Socialism and Marxian Socialism, Marx expresses his hatred of the middle class or bourgeoisie, his desire to help the proletariat, his belief in the inevitability of Socialism and his faith in the economic interpretation of history. Marx calls for a revolution to bring forth the type of society he feels is necessary to free the proletariat from exploitation by the capitalists. Note as you read the *Manifesto* how Marx and Engels fit their theories into their own period in history, and how the theory of evolution tended to enhance many of their ideas, especially the dialectic. Also note that many of the ideas expressed here by Marx have been accepted by nations of the world, in particular by the Union of Soviet Socialist Republics.

MANIFESTO OF THE COMMUNIST PARTY

A spectre is haunting Europe—the spectre of Communism. All the powers of old Europe have entered into a holy alliance to exorcise this spectre; Pope and Czar, Metternich and Guizot, French Radicals and German police-spies.

Where is the party in opposition that has not been decried as communistic by its opponents in power? Where the Opposition that has not hurled back the branding reproach of Communism, against the more advanced opposition parties as well as against its reactionary adversaries?

Two things result from this fact.

1. Communism is already acknowledged by all European Powers to be itself a Power.

2. It is high time that Communists should openly, in the face of the whole world, publish their views, their aims, their tendencies, and meet this nursery tale of the Spectre of Communism with a Manifesto of the party itself.

To this end, Communists of various nationalities have assenbled in London, and sketched the following manifesto, to be published in the English, French, German, Italian, Flemish and Danish languages.

Bourgeois and Proletarians

The history of all hitherto existing society is the history of class struggles.

Freeman and slave, patrician and plebeian, lord and serf, guildmaster and journeyman, in a word, oppressor and oppressed, stood in constant opposition to one another, carried on an uninterrupted, now hidden, now open fight, a fight that each time ended, either in a revolutionary re-constitution of society at large, or in the common ruin of the contending classes.

In the earlier epochs of history, we find almost everywhere a complicated arrangement of society

Marx, Karl and Friederich Engels, *Manifesto of the Communist Party,* trans. by Samuel Moore (New York 1888).

into various orders, a manifold graduation of social rank. In ancient Rome we have patricians, knights, plebeians, slaves; in the Middle Ages, feudal lords, vassals, guildmasters, journeymen, apprentices, serfs; in almost all of these classes, again, subordinate gradations.

The modern bourgeois society that has sprouted from the ruins of feudal society, has not done away with class antagonisms. It has but established new classes, new conditions of oppression, new forms of struggle in place of the old ones.

Our epoch, the epoch of the bourgeoisie, possesses, however, this distinctive feature: it has simplified the class antagonisms. Society as a whole is more and more splitting up into two great hostile camps, into two great classes directly facing each other: Bourgeoisie and Proletariat.

From the serfs of the Middle Ages sprang the chartered burghers of the earliest towns. From these burgesses the first elements of the bourgeoisie were developed.

The discovery of America, the rounding of the Cape, opened up fresh ground for the rising bourgeoisie. The East-Indian and Chinese markets, the colonization of America, trade with the colonies, the increase in the means of exchange and in commodities generally, gave to commerce, to navigation, to industry, an impulse never before known, and thereby, to the revolutionary element in the tottering feudal society, a rapid development.

The feudal system of industry, under which industrial production was monopolized by close guilds, now no longer sufficed for the growing wants of the new markets. The manufacturing system took its place. The guildmasters were pushed on one side by the manufacturing middle-class; division of labor between the different corporate guilds vanished in the face of division of labor in each single workshop.

Meantime the markets kept ever growing, the demand, ever rising. Even manufacture no longer sufficed. Thereupon, steam and machinery revolutionized industrial production. The place of manufacture was taken by the giant, Modern Industry, the place of the industrial middle-class, by industrial millionaires, the leaders of whole industrial armies, the modern bourgeois.

Modern industry has established the world-market, for which the discovery of America paved the way. This market has given an immense development to commerce, to navigation, to communication by land. This development has, in its turn, reacted on the extension of industry; and in proportion as industry, commerce, navigation, railways extended, in the same proportion the bourgeoisie developed, increased its capital, and pushed into the background every class handed down from the Middle Ages.

We see, therefore, how the modern bourgeoisie is itself the product of a long course of development, of a series of revolutions in the modes of production and of exchange.

Each step in the development of the bourgeoisie was accompanied by a corresponding political advance of that class. An oppressed class under the sway of the feudal nobility, an armed and self-governing association in the medieval commune, here independent urban republic (as in Italy and Germany), there taxable "third estate" of the monarchy (as in France), afterwards, in the period of manufacture proper, serving either the semi-feudal or the absolute monarchy as a counterpoise against the nobility, and, in fact, corner stone of the great monarchies in general, the bourgeoisie has at last, since the establishment of Modern Industry and of the world-market, conquered for itself, in the modern representative State, exclusive political sway. The executive of the Modern State is but a committee for managing the common affairs of the whole bourgeoisie.

The bourgeoisie, historically, has played a most revolutionary part.

The bourgeoisie, wherever it has got the upper hand, has put an end to all feudal, patriarchal, idyllic relations. It has pitilessly torn asunder the motley feudal ties that bound man to his "natural superiors," and has left remaining no other nexus between man and man than naked self-interest, than callous "cash payment." It has drowned the most heavenly ecstasies of religious fervor, of chivalrous enthusiasm, of philistine sentimentalism, in the icy water of egotistical calculation. It has resolved personal worth into exchange value, and in place of the numberless indefeasible chartered freedoms, has set up that single, unconscionable freedom—Free Trade. In one word, for exploitation, veiled by religious and political illusions, it has substituted naked, shameless, direct, brutal exploitation.

The bourgeoisie has stripped of its halo every occupation hitherto honored and looked up to with reverent awe. It has converted the physician, the lawyer, the priest, the poet, the man of science, into its paid wage-laborers.

The bourgeoisie has torn away from the family its sentimental veil, and has reduced the family relation to a mere money relation.

The bourgeoisie has disclosed how it came to pass that the brutal display of vigor in the Middle Ages, which Reactionists so much admire, found its fitting complement in the most slothful indolence. It has been the first to show what man's activity can bring about. It has accomplished wonders far surpassing Egyptian pyramids, Roman aqueducts, and Gothic cathedrals; it has conducted expeditions that put in the shade all former Exoduses of nations and crusades.

The bourgeoisie cannot exist without constantly revolutionizing the instruments of production, and thereby the relations of production, and with them the whole relations of society. Conservation of the old modes of production in unaltered form, was, on the contrary, the first condition of existence for all earlier industrial classes. Constant revolutionizing of production, uninterrupted disturbance of all social conditions, everlasting uncertainty and agitation distinguish the bourgeois epoch from all earlier ones. All fixed, fast-frozen relations, with their train of ancient and venerable prejudices and opinions, are swept away, all new-formed ones become antiquated before they can ossify. All that is solid melts into air, all that is holy is profaned, and man is at last compelled to face with sober senses, his real conditions of life, and his relations with his kind.

The need of a constantly expanding market for its products chases the bourgeoisie over the whole surface of the globe. It must nestle everywhere, settle everywhere, establish connections everywhere.

The bourgeoisie has through its exploitation of the world-market given a cosmopolitan character to production and consumption in every country. To the great chagrin of Reactionists, it has drawn from under the feet of industry the national ground on which it stood. All old-established national industries have been destroyed or are daily being destroyed. They are dislodged by new industries, whose introduction becomes a life and death question for all civilized nations, by industries that no longer work up indigenous raw material, but raw material drawn from the remotest zones; industries whose products are consumed, not only at home, but in every quarter of the globe. In place of the old wants, satisfied by the productions of the country, we find new wants, requiring for their satisfaction the products of distant lands and climes. In place of the old local and national seclusion and self-sufficiency, we have intercourse in every direction, universal interdependence of nations. And as in material, so also in intellectual production. The intellectual creations of individual nations become common property. National onesidedness and narrow-mindedness become more and more impossible, and from the numerous national and local literatures there arises a world-literature.

The bourgeoisie, by the rapid improvement of all instruments of production, by the immensely facilitated means of communication, draws all, even the most barbarian, nations into civilization. The cheap prices of its commodities are the heavy artillery with which it batters down all Chinese walls, with which it forces the barbarians' intensely obstinate hatred of foreigners to capitulate. It compels all nations, on pain of extinction, to adopt the bourgeois mode of production; it compels them to introduce what it calls civilization into their midst, i.e., to become bourgeois themselves. In a word, it creates a world after its own image.

The bourgeoisie has subjected the country to the rule of the towns. It has created enormous cities, has greatly increased the urban population as compared with the rural, and has thus rescued a considerable part of the population from the idiocy of rural life. Just as it has made the country dependent on the towns, so it has made barbarian and semi-barbarian countries dependent on the civilized ones, nations of peasants on nations of bourgeois, the East on the West.

The bourgeoisie keeps more and more doing away with the scattered state of the population, of the means of production, nd of property. It has agglomerated population, centralized means of production, and has concentrated property in a few hands. The necessary consequence of this was political centralization. Independent, or but loosely connected provinces, with separate interests, laws, governments, and systems of taxation, became lumped together in one nation, with one government, one code of laws, one national class-interest, one frontier and one customs-tariff.

The bourgeoisie, during its rule of scarce one hundred years, has created more massive and more colossal productive forces than have all preceding generations together. Subjection of Nature's forces to man, machinery, application of chemistry to industry and agriculture, steam-navigation, railways, electric telegraphs, clearing of whole continents for cultivation, canalization of rivers, whole populations conjured out of the ground—what earlier century had even a presentiment that such productive forces slumbered in the lap of social labor?

We see then: the means of production and of

exchange on whose foundation the bourgeoisie built itself up, were generated in feudal society. At a certain state in the development of these means of production and of exchange, the conditions under which feudal society produced and exchanged, the feudal organization of agriculture and manufacturing industry, in one word, the feudal relations of property became no longer compatible with the already developed productive forces; they became so many fetters. They had to burst asunder; they were burst asunder.

Into their places stepped free competition, accompanied by a social and political constitution adapted to it, and by the economical and political sway of the bourgeois class.

A similar movement is going on before our own eyes. Modern bourgeois society with its relations of production, of exchange and of property, a society that has conjured up such gigantic means of production and of exchange, is like the sorcerer, who is no longer able to control the powers of the nether world whom he has called up by his spells. For many a decade past the history of industry and commerce is but the history of the revolt of modern productive forces against modern conditions of production, against the property relations that are the conditions for the existence of the bourgeoisie and of its rule. It is enough to mention the commercial crises that by their periodical return put on its trial, each time more threateningly, the existence of the entire bourgeois society. In these crises a great part not only of the existing products, but also of the previously created productive forces, are periodically destroyed. In these crises there breaks out an epidemic that, in all earlier epochs, would have seemed an absurdity—the epidemic of over-production. Society suddenly finds itself put back into a state of momentary barbarism; it appears as if a famine, a universal war of devastation had cut off the supply of every means of subsistence; industry and commerce seem to be destroyed; and why? Because there is too much civilization, too much means of subsistence, too much industry, too much commerce. The productive forces at the disposal of society no longer tend to further the development of the conditions of bourgeois property; on the contrary, they have become too powerful for these conditions, by which they are fettered, and so soon as they overcome these fetters, they bring disorder into the whole of bourgeois society, endanger the existence of bourgeois property. The conditions of bourgeois society are too narrow to comprise the wealth created by

them. And how does the bourgeoisie get over these crises? On the one hand by enforced destruction of a mass of productive forces; on the other, by the conquest of new markets, and by the more thorough exploitation of the old ones. That is to say, by paving the way for more extensive and more destructive crises, and by diminishing the means whereby crises are prevented.

The weapons with which the bourgeoisie felled feudalism to the ground are now turned against the bourgeoisie itself.

But not only has the bourgeoisie forged the weapons that bring death to itself; it has also called into existence the men who are to wield those weapons—the modern working-class—the proletarians.

In proportion as the bourgeoisie, i.e., capital, is developed, in the same proportion is the proletariat, the modern working-class, developed, a class of laborers, who live only so long as they find work, and who find work only so long as their labor increases capital. These laborers, who must sell themselves piecemeal, are a commodity, like every other article of commerce, and are consequently exposed to all the vicissitudes of competition, to all the fluctuations of the market.

Owing to the extensive use of machinery and to division of labor, the work of the proletarians has lost all individual charater, and, consequently, all charm for the workman. He becomes an appendage of the machine, and it is only the most simple, most monotonous, and most easily acquired knack that is required of him. Hence, the cost of production of a workman is restricted, almost entirely, to the means of subsistence that he requires for his maintenance, and for the propagation of his race. But the price of a commodity, and also of labor, is equal to its cost of production. In proportion, therefore, as the repulsiveness of the work increases, the wage decreases. Nay more, in proportion as the use of machinery and division of labor increases, in the same proportion the burden of toil also increases, whether by prolongation of the working hours, by increase of the work enacted in a given time, or by increased speed of the machinery, etc.

Modern industry has converted the little workshop of the patriarchal master into the great factory of the industrial capitalist. Masses of laborers, crowded into the factory, are organized like soldiers. As privates of the industrial army they are placed under the command of a perfect hierarchy of officers and sergeants. Not only are they the slaves of the bourgeois class, and of the bourgeois State, they are daily and hourly enslaved by the machine, by the over-looker, and, above all, by the individual bourgeois manufacturer himself. The more openly this despotism proclaims gain to be its end and aim, the more petty, the more hateful and the more embittering it is.

The less the skill and exertion or strength implied in manual labor, in other words, the more modern industry becomes developed, the more is the labor of men superseded by that of women. Differences of age and sex have no longer any distinctive social validity for the working class. All are instruments of labor, more or less expensive to use, according to their age and sex.

No sooner is the exploitation of the laborer by the manufacturer, so far at an end, that he receives his wages in cash, than he is set upon by the other portions of the bourgeoisie, the landlord, the shopkeeper, the pawnbroker, etc.

The lower strata of the middle class—the small tradespeople, shopkeepers, and retired tradesmen generally, the handicraftsmen and peasants—all these sink gradually into the proletariat, partly because their diminutive capital does not suffice for the scale on which Modern Industry is carried on, and is swamped in the competition with the large capitalists, partly because their specialized skill is rendered worthless by new methods of production. Thus the proletariat is recruited from all classes of the population.

The proletariat goes through various stages of development. With its birth begins its struggle with the bourgeoisie. At first the contest is carried on by individual laborers, then by the workpeople of a factory, then by the operatives of one trade, in one locality, against the individual bourgeois who directly exploits them. They direct their attacks not against the bourgeois conditions of production, but against the instruments of production themselves; they destroy imported wares that compete with their labor, they smash to pieces machinery, they set factories ablaze, they seek to restore by force the vanished status of the workman of the Middle Ages.

At this stage the laborers still form an incoherent mass scattered over the whole country, and broken up by their mutual competition. If anywhere they unite to form more compact bodies, this is not yet the consequence of their own active union, but of the union of the bourgeoisie, which class, in order to attain its own political ends, is compelled to set the whole proletariat in motion, and is moreover yet, for a time, able to do so. At this stage, therefore, the proletarians do not fight their enemies, but the enemies of their enemies, the remnants of absolute monarchy, the landowners, the non-industrial bourgeois, the petty bourgeoisie. Thus the whole historical movement is concentrated in the hands of the bourgeoisie; every victory so obtained is a victory for the bourgeoisie.

But with the development of industry the proletariat not only increases in number, it becomes concentrated in greater masses, its strength grows, and it feels that strength more. The various interests and conditions of life within the ranks of the proletariat are more and more equalized, in proportion as machinery obliterates all distinctions of labor, and nearly everywhere reduces wages to the same low level. The growing competition among the bourgeois, and the resulting commercial crises, make the wages of the workers ever more fluctuating. The unceasing improvement of machinery, ever more rapidly developing, makes their livelihood more and more precarious; the collisions between individual workmen and individual bourgeois take more and more the character of collisions between two classes. Thereupon the workers begin to form combinations (Trades' Unions) against the bourgeois; they club together in order to keep up the rate of wages; they found permanent associations in order to make provision beforehand for these occasional revolts. Here and there the contest breaks out into riots.

Now and then the workers are victorious, but only for a time. The real fruit of their battles lies, not in the immediate result, but in the ever expanding union of the workers. This union is helped on by the improved means of communication that are created by modern industry, and that place the workers of different localities in contact with one another. It was just this contact that was needed to centralize the numerous local struggles, all of the same character, into one national struggle between classes. But every class struggle is a political struggle. And that union, to attain which the burghers of the Middle Ages, with their miserable highways, required centuries, the modern proletarians, thanks to railways, achieve in a few years.

This organization of the proletarians into a class, and consequently into a political party, is continually being upset again by the competition between the workers themselves. But it ever rises up again, stronger, firmer, mightier. It compels legislative recognition of particular interests of the workers, by taking advantage of the divisions among the bourgeoisie itself. Thus the ten-hour bill in England was carried.

Altogether collisions between the classes of the old society further, in many ways, the course of development of the proletariat. The bourgeoisie finds itself involved in a constant battle. At first with the aristocracy; later on, with those portions of the bourgeoisie itself, whose interests have become antagonistic to the progress of industry; at all times, with the bourgeoisie of foreign countries. In all these battles it sees itself compelled to appeal to the proletariat, to ask for its help, and thus, to drag it into the political arena. The bourgeoisie itself, therefore, supplies the proletariat with its own elements of political and general education, in other words, it furnishes the proletariat with weapons for fighting the bourgeoisie.

· Further, as we have already seen, entire sections of the ruling classes are, by the advance of industry, precipitated into the proletariat, or are at least threatened in their conditions of existence. These also supply the proletariat with fresh elements of enlightenment and progress.

Finally, in times when the class-struggle nears the decisive hour, the process of dissolution going on within the ruling class, in fact, within the whole range of old society, assumes such a violent, glaring character, that a small section of the ruling class cuts itself adrift, and joins the revolutionary class, the class that holds the future in its hands. Just as, therefore, at an earlier period, a section of the nobility went over to the bourgeoisie, so now a portion of the bourgeoisie goes over to the proletariat, and in particular, a portion of the bourgeois ideologists, who have raised themselves to the level of comprehending theoretically the historical movements as a whole.

Of all the classes that stand face to face with the bourgeoisie today, the proletariat alone is a really revolutionary class. The other classes decay and finally disappear in the face of modern industry; the proletariat is its special and essential product.

The lower middle class, the small manufacturer, the shopkeeper, the artisan, the peasant, all these fight against the bourgeoisie, to save from extinction their existence as fractions of the middle class. They are, therefore, not revolutionary, but conservative. Nay more, they are reactionary, for they try to roll back the wheel of history. If by chance they are revolutionary, they are so, only in view of their impending transfer into the proletariat, they thus defend not their present, but their future interests, they desert their own standpoint to place themselves at that of the proletariat.

The "dangerous class," the social scum, that passively rotting mass thrown off by the lowest layers of old society, may, here and there, be swept into the movement by a proletarian revolution; its conditions of life, however, prepare it far more for the part of a bribed tool of reactionary intrigue.

In the conditions of the proletariat, those of old society at large are already virtually swamped. The proletarian is without property; his relation to his wife and children has no longer anything in common with the bourgeois family-relations; modern industrial labor, modern subjection to capital, the same in England as in France, in America as in Germany, has stripped him of every trace of national character. Law, morality, religion, are to him so many bourgeois prejudices, behind which lurk in ambush just as many bourgeois interests.

All the preceding classes that got the upper hand, sought to fortify their already acquired status by subjecting society at large to their conditions of appropriation. The proletarians cannot become masters of the productive forces of society, except by abolishing their own previous mode of appropriation, and thereby also every other previous mode of appropriation. They have nothing of their own to secure and to fortify; their mission is to destroy all previous securities for, and insurances of, individual property.

All previous historical movements were movements of minorities, or in the interest of minorities. The proletarian movement is the self-conscious, independent movement of the immense majority, in the interest of the immense majority. The proletariat, the lowest stratum of our present society, cannot stir, cannot raise itself up, without the whole superincumbent strata of official society being sprung into the air.

Though not in substance, yet in form, the struggle of the proletariat with the bourgeoisie is at first a national struggle. The proletariat of each country must, of course, first of all settle matters with its own bourgeoisie.

In depicting the most general phases of the development of the proletariat, we traced the more or less veiled civil war, raging within existing society, up to the point where that war breaks out into open revolution, and where the violent overthrow of the bourgeoisie lays the foundation for the sway of the proletariat.

Hitherto, every form of society has been based, as we have already seen, on the antagonism of oppressing and oppressed classes. But in order to oppress a class, certain conditions must be assured to it under which it can, at least, continue its slavish existence. The serf, in the period of serfdom, raised himself to membership in the commune, just as the petty bourgeois, under the yoke of feudal absolutism, managed to develop into a bourgeois. The modern laborer, on the contrary, instead of rising with the progress of industry, sinks deeper and deeper below the conditions of existence of his own class. He becomes a pauper, and pauperism develops more rapidly than population and wealth. And here it becomes evident, that the bourgeoisie is unfit any longer to be the ruling class in society, and to impose its conditions of existence upon society as an over-riding law. It is unfit to rule, because it is incompetent to assure an existence to its slave within his slavery, because it cannot help letting him sink into such a state that it has to feed him, instead of being fed by him. Society can no longer live under this bourgeoisie, in other words, its existence is no longer compatible with society.

The essential condition for the existence, and for the sway of the bourgeois class, is the formation and augmentation of capital; the condition for capital is wage-labor. Wage-labor rests exclusively on competition between the laborers. The advance of industry, whose involuntary promoter is the bourgeoisie, replaces the isolation of the laborers, due to competition, by their revolutionary combination, due to association. The development of Modern Industry, therefore, cuts from under its feet the very foundation on which the bourgeoisie produces and appropriates products. What the bourgeoisie therefore produces, above all, are its own grave-diggers. Its fall and the victory of the proletariat are equally inevitable.

Proletarians and Communists

In what relation do the Communists stand to the proletarians as a whole?

The Communists do not form a separate party opposed to other working class parties.

They have no interests separate and apart from those of the proletariat as a whole.

They do not set up any sectarian principles of their own, by which to shape and mould the proletarian movement.

The Communists are distinguished from the other working class parties by this only: 1. In the national struggles of the proletarians of the different countries, they point out and bring to the front the common interests of the entire proletariat independently of all nationality. 2. In the various stages of development which the struggle of the working class against the bourgeoisie has to pass through, they always and everywhere represent the interests of the movement as a whole.

The Communists, therefore, are on the one hand, practically, the most advanced and resolute section of the working class parties of every country, that section which pushes forward all others; on the other hand, theoretically, they have over the great mass of the proletariat the advantage of clearly understanding the line of march, the conditions, and the ultimate general results of the proletarian movement.

The immediate aim of the Communists is the same as that of all the other proletarian parties: formation of the proletariat into a class, overthrow of the bourgeois supremacy, conquest of political power by the proletariat.

The theoretical conclusions of the Communists are in no way based on ideas or principles that have been invented, or discovered, by this or that would-be universal reformer.

They merely express, in general terms, actual relations springing from an existing class struggle, from a historical movement going on under our very eyes. The abolition of existing property relations is not at all a distinctive feature of Communism.

All property relations in the past have continually been subject to historical change consequent upon the change in historical conditions.

The French Revolution, for example, abolished feudal property in favor of bourgeois property.

The distinguishing feature of Communism is not the abolition of property generally, but the abolition of bourgeois property. But modern bourgeois private property is the final and most complete expression of the system of producing and appropriating products, that is based on class antagonism, on the exploitation of the many by the few.

In this sense, the theory of the Communists may be summed up in the single sentence: Abolition of private property.

We Communists have been reproached with the desire of abolishing the right of personally acquiring property as the fruit of a man's own labor, which property is alleged to be the ground work of all personal freedom, activity and independence.

Hard-won, self-acquainted, self-earned property! Do you mean the property of the petty artisan and of the small peasant, a form of property that preceded the bourgeois form? There is no need to abolish that; the development of industry has to a great extent already destroyed it, and is still destroying it daily.

Or do you mean modern bourgeois private property?

But does wage-labor create any property for the laborer? Not a bit. It creates capital, i.e., that kind of property which exploits wage-laborer, and which cannot increase except upon condition of getting a new supply of wage-labor for fresh exploitation. Property, in its present form, is based on the antagonism of capital and wage-labor. Let us examine both sides of this antagonism.

To be a capitalist, is to have not only a purely personal, but a social status in production. Capital is a collective product, and only by the united action of many members, nay, in the last resort, only by the united action of all members of society, can it be set in motion.

Capital is therefore not a personal, it is a social power.

When, therefore, capital is converted into common property, into the property of all members of society, personal property is not thereby transformed into social property. It is only the social character of the property that is changed. It loses its class-character.

Let us now take wage-labor.

The average price of wage-labor is the minimum wage, i.e., that quantum of the means of subsistence, which is absolutely requisite to keep the laborer in bare existence as a laborer. What, therefore, the wage-laborer appropriates by means of his labor, merely suffices to prolong and reproduce a bare existence. We by no means intend to abolish this personal appropriation of the products of labor, an appropriation that is made for the maintenance and reproduction of human life, and that leaves no surplus wherewith to command the labor of others. All that we want to do away with is the miserable character of this appropriation, under which the laborer lives merely toclass requires it.

In bourgeois society, living labor is but a means to increase accumulated labor. In communist society, accumulated labor is but a means to widen, to enrich, to promote the existence of the laborer.

In bourgeois society, therefore, the past dominates the present; in communist society, the present dominates the past. In bourgeois society capital is independent and has individuality, while the living person is dependent and has no individuality.

And the abolition of this state of things is called by the bourgeois, abolition of individuality and freedom! And rightly so. The abolition of bourgeois individuality, bourgeois independence, and bourgeois freedom is undoubtedly aimed at.

By freedom is meant, under the present bourgeois conditions of production, free trade, free selling and buying.

But if selling and buying disappears, free selling and buying disappears also. This talk about free selling and buying, and all the other "brave words" of our bourgeoisie about freedom in general, have a meaning, if any, only in contrast with restricted selling and buying, with the fettered traders of the Middle Ages, but have no meaning when opposed to the Communistic abolition of buying and selling, of the bourgeois conditions of production, nd of the bourgeoisie itself.

You are horrified at our intending to do away with private property. But in your existing society, private property is already done away with for nine-tenths of the population; its existence for the few is solely due to its non-existence in the hands of those nine-tenths. You reproach us, therefore, with intending to do away with a form of property, the necessary condition for whose existence is, the non-existence of any property for the immense majority of society.

In one word, you reproach us with intending to do away with your property. Precisely so; that is just what we intend.

From the moment when labor can no longer be converted into capital, money, or rent, into a social power capable of being monopolized, i.e., from the moment when individual property can no longer be transformed into bourgeois property, into capital, from that moment, you say, individuality vanishes.

You must, therefore, confess that by "individual" you mean no other person than the bourgeois, than the middle-class owner of property. This person must, indeed, be swept out of the way, and made impossible.

Communism deprives no man of the power to appropriate the products of society: all that it does is to deprive him of the power to subjugate the labor of others by means of such appropriation.

It has been objected, that upon the abolition of private property all work will cease, and universal laziness will overtake us.

According to this, bourgeois society ought long ago to have gone to the dogs through sheer idleness; for those of its members who work, acquire nothing, and those who acquire anything, do not work. The whole of this objection is but another expression of the tautology: that there can no longer be any wage-labor when there is no longer any capital.

All objections urged against the Communistic mode of producing and appropriating material products, have, in the same way, been urged against the Communistic modes of producing and appropriating intellectual products. Just as, to the bourgeois, the disappearance of class property is the disappearance of production itself, so the disappearance of class culture is to him identical with the disappearance of all culture.

That culture, the loss of which he laments, is, for the enormous majority, a mere training to act as a machine.

But don't wrangle with us so long as you apply, to our intended abolition of bourgeois property, the standard of your bourgeois notions of freedom, culture, law, etc. Your very ideas are but the outgrowth of the conditions of your bourgeois production and bourgeois property, just as your jurisprudence is but the will of your class made into a law for all, a will, whose essential character and direction are determined by the economic conditions of existence of your class.

The selfish misconception that induces you to transform into eternal laws of nature and of reason, the social forms springing from your present mode of production and form of property—historical relations that rise and disappear in the progress of production—this misconception you share with every ruling class that has preceded you. What you see clearly in the case of ancient property, what you admit in the case of feudal property, you are of course forbidden to admit in the case of your own bourgeois form of property.

Abolition of the family! Even the most radical flare up at this infamous proposal of the Communists.

On what foundation is the present family, the bourgeois family, based? On capital, on private gain. In its completely developed form this family exists only among the bourgeoisie. But this state of things finds its complement in the practical absence of the family among the proletarians, and in public prostitution.

The bourgeois family will vanish as a matter of course when its complement vanishes, and both will vanish with the vanishing of capital.

Do you charge us with wanting to stop the exploitation of children by their parents? To this crime we plead guilty.

But, you will say, we destroy the most hallowed of relations, when we replace home education by social.

And your education! Is not that also social, and determined by the social conditions under which you educate, by the intervention, direct or indirect, of society by means of schools, etc.? The Communists have not invented the intervention of society in education; they do but seek to alter the character of that intervention, and to rescue education from the influence of the ruling class.

The bourgeois clap-trap about the family and education, about the hallowed co-relation of parent and child, becomes all the more disgusting, the more, by the action of Modern Industry, all family ties among the proletarians are torn asunder, and their children transformed into simple articles of commerce and instruments of labor.

But you Communists would introduce community of women, screams the whole bourgeoisie in chorus.

The bourgeois sees in his wife a mere instrument of production. He hears that the instruments of production are to be exploited in common, and, naturally, can come to no other conclusion, than that the lot of being common to all will likewise fall to the women.

He has not even a suspicion that the real point aimed at is to do away with the status of women as mere instruments of production.

For the rest, nothing is more ridiculous than the virtuous indignation of our bourgeois at the community of women which, they pretend is to be openly and officially established by the Communists. The Communists have no need to introduce community of women; it has existed almost from time immemorial.

Our bourgeois, not content with having the wives and daughters of their proletarians at their disposal, not to speak of common prostitutes, take the greatest pleasure in seducing each other's wives.

Bourgeois marriage is in reality a system of wives in common and thus, at the most, what the Communists might possibly be reproached with is that they desire to introduce, in substitution for a hypocritically concealed, an openly legalized community of women. For the rest, it is self-evident, that the abolition of the present system of production must bring with it the abolition of the community of women springing from that system, i.e., of prostitution both public and private.

The Communists are further reproached with desiring to abolish countries and nationalities.

The working men have no country. We cannot take from them what they have not got. Since the proletariat must first of all acquire political supremacy, must rise to be the leading class of the nation, must constitute itself the nation, it is, so far, itself national, though not in the bourgeois sense of the word.

National differences, and antagonisms between peoples, are daily more and more vanishing, owing to the development of the bourgeoisie, to freedom of commerce, to the world-market, to uniformity in the mode of production and in the conditions of life corresponding thereto.

The supremacy of the proletariat will cause them to vanish still faster. United action, of the leading civilized countries at least, is one of the first conditions for the emancipation of the proletariat.

In proportion as the exploitation of one individual by another is put an end to, the exploitation of one nation by another will also be put an end to. In proportion as the antagonism between classes within the nation vanishes, the hostility of one nation to another will come to an end.

The charges against Communism made from a religious, a philosophical, and generally, from an ideological standpoint, are not deserving of serious examination.

Does it require deep intuition to comprehend that man's ideas, views, and conceptions, in one word, man's consciousness, changes with every change in the conditions of his material existence, in his social relations and in his social life?

What else does the history of ideas prove, than that intellectual production changes in character in proportion as material production is changed? The ruling ideas of each age have ever been the ideas of its ruling class.

When people speak of ideas that revolutionize society, they do but express the fact, that within the old society, the elements of a new one have been created, and that the dissolution of the old ideas keeps even pace with the dissolution of the old conditions of existence.

When the ancient world was in its last throes, the ancient religions were overcome by Christianity. When Christian ideas succumbed in the 18th century to rationalist ideas, feudal society fought its death-battle with the then revolutionary bourgeoisie. The ideas of religious liberty and freedom of conscience, merely gave expression to the sway of free competition within the domain of knowledge.

"Undoubtedly," it will be said, "religious, moral, philosophical and juridical ideas have been modified in the course of historical development. But religion, morality, philosophy, political science, and law, constantly survived this change.

"There are, besides, eternal truths, such as Freedom, Justice, etc., that are common to all states of society. But Communism abolishes eternal truths, it abolishes all religion, and all morality, instead of constituting them on a new basis; it therefore acts in contradiction to all past historical experience."

What does this accusation reduce itself to? The history of all past society has consisted in the development of class antagonisms, antagonisms that assume different forms at different epochs.

But whatever form they may have taken, one fact is common to all past ages, viz., the exploitation of one part of society by the other. No wonder, then, that the social consciousness of past ages, despite all the multiplicity and variety it displays, moves within certain common forms, or general ideas, which cannot completely vanish except with the total disappearance of class antagonisms.

The Communist revolution is the most radical rupture with traditional property-relations; no wonder that its development involves the most radical rupture with traditional ideas.

But let us have done with the bourgeois objections to Communism.

We have seen above, that the first step in the revolution by the working class, is to raise the proletariat to the position of ruling class, to win the battle of democracy.

The proletariat will use its political supremacy, to wrest, by degrees, all capital from the bourgeoisie, to centralize all instruments of production in the hands of the State, i.e., of the proletariat organized as the ruling class; and to increase the total of productive forces as rapidly as possible.

Of course, in the beginning, this cannot be effected except by means of despotic inroads on the rights of property, and on the conditions of bourgeois production; by means of measures, therefore, which appear economically insufficient and untenable, but which, in the course of the movement, outstrip themselves, necessitate further inroads upon the old social order, and are unavoidable as a means of entirely revolutionizing the mode of production.

These measures will of course be different in different countries.

Nevertheless in the most advanced countries the following will be pretty generally applicable:

1. Abolition of property in land and application of all rents of land to public purposes.

2. A heavy progressive or graduated income tax.

3. Abolition of all right of inheritance.

4. Confiscation of the property of all emigrants and rebels.

5. Centralization of credit in the hands of the state, by means of a national bank with State capital and an exclusive monopoly.

6. Centralization of the means of communication and transport in the hands of the State.

7. Extension of factories and instruments of production owned by the State; the bringing into

cultivation of waste lands, and the improvement of the soil generally in accordance with a common plan.

8. Equal liability of all to labor. Establishment of industrial armies, especially for agriculture.

9. Combination of agriculture with manufacturing industries; gradual abolition of the distinction between town and country, by a more equable distribution of population over the country.

10. Free education for all children in public schools. Abolition of children's factory labor in its present form. Combination of education with industrial production, etc., etc.

When, in the course of development, class distinctions have disappeared, and all production has been concentrated in the hands of a vast association of the whole nation, the public power will lose its political character. Political power, properly so called, is merely the organized power of one class for oppressing another. If the proletariat during its contest with the bourgeoisie is compelled, by the force of circumstances, to organize itself as a class, if, by means of a revolution, it makes itself the ruling class, and, as such, sweeps away by force the old conditions of production, then it will, along with these conditions, have swept away the conditions for the existence of class antagonisms, and of classes generally, and will thereby have abolished its own supremacy as a class.

In place of the old bourgeois society, with its classes and class antagonisms, we shall have an association, in which the free development of each is the condition for the free development of all.

. . . .

Position of the Communists in Relation to the Various Existing Opposition Parties

The Communists fight for the attainment of the immediate aims, for the enforcement of the monetary interests of the working class; but in the movement of the present, they also represent and take care of the future of that movement. In France the Communists ally themselves with the Social-Democrats, against the conservative and radical bourgeoisie, reserving, however, the right to take up a critical position in regard to phrases and illusions traditionally handed down from the great Revolution.

. . . .

In Germany they fight with the bourgeoisie whenever it acts in a revolutionary way, against the absolute monarchy, the feudal squirearchy, and the petty bourgeoisie.

But they never cease, for a single instant, to instill into the working class the clearest possible recognition of the hostile antagonism between bourgeoisie and proletariat, in order that the German workers may straightway use, as so many weapons against the bourgeoisie, the social and political conditions that the bourgeoisie must necessarily introduce along with its supremacy, and in order that, after the fall of the reactionary classes in Germany, the fight against the bourgeoisie itself may immediately begin.

The Communists turn their attention chiefly to Germany, because that country is on the eve of a bourgeois revolution, that is bound to be carried out under more advanced conditions of European civilization, and with a more developed proletariat, than that of England was in the seventeenth, and of France in the eighteenth century, and because the bourgeois revolution in Germany will be but the prelude to an immediately following proletarian revolution.

In short, the Communists everywhere support every revolutionary movement against the existing social and political order of things.

In all these movements they bring to the front, as the leading question in each, the property question, no matter what its degree of development at the time.

Finally, they labor everywhere for the union and agreement of the democratic parties of all countries.

The Communists disdain to conceal their views and aims. They openly declare that their ends can be attained only by the forcible overthrow of all existing social conditions. Let the ruling classes tremble at a Communistic revolution. The proletarians have nothing to lose but their chains. They have a world to win.

Working men of all countries, unite!

Charles Darwin

Charles Darwin (1809-1882) was the author of one of the most influential works of modern time, *The Origin of Species*. While a student at Cambridge, Darwin was appointed as naturalist on a scientific expedition around the world aboard the H.M.S. Beagle. The journey took five years and gave Darwin the opportunity to collect a tremendous amount of information dealing with plant and animal life—information which was eventually published in 1859 in *The Origin of Species*. In this work Darwin put forth his hypothesis of natural selection, meaning that in the struggle for existence the stronger of the species will eventually win out and reproduce an even stronger species. The idea of evolution was extremely old but Darwin, because of his immense scientific research gave it added notoriety and influence as well as scientific respectability. Note in the first selection, from *The Origin of Species*, how Darwin defends the term natural selection and links it with the idea of survival of the fittest. He also is anxious to soothe, if possible, those who may object to his theories because of religious beliefs. *The Descent of Man*, from which the second selection is taken, was published in 1871—twelve years after *The Origin of Species*. In this work Darwin carries his ideas further and applies them to man. Imagine the shock to members of "high society" to find that, at least according to Darwin, they had descended from some lower form of animal—a "hairy, tailed quadruped." At the conclusion of this work, Darwin again shows his concern with those who will judge his work as highly irreligious and tries to soften any objections. Needless to say he was unsuccessful.

THE ORIGIN OF SPECIES

CHAPTER IV

Natural Selection; or the Survival of the Fittest

Natural Selection—its power compared with man's selection—its power on characters of trifling importance—its power at all ages and on both sexes—Sexual selection—On the generality of intercrosses between individuals of the same species—Circumstances favourable and unfavourable to the results of Natural Selection, namely, intercrossing, isolation, number of individuals—Slow action—Extinction caused by Natural Selection—Divergence of Character, related to the diversity of inhabitants of any small area, and to naturalisation—Action of Natural Selection, through divergence of Character and Extinction, on the descendants from a common parent—Explains the grouping of all organic beings—Advance in organisation—Low forms preserved—Convergence of Character—Indefinite multiplication of species—Summary.

How will the struggle for existence, briefly discussed in the last chapter, act in regard to variation? Can the principle of selection, which we have seen is so potent in the hands of man, apply under nature? I think we shall see that it can act most efficiently. Let the endless number of slight variations and individual differences occurring in our domestic productions, and, in a lesser degree, in those under nature, be borne in mind; as well as the strength of the hereditary tendency. Under domestication, it may be truly said that the whole organisation becomes in some degree plastic. But the variability, which we almost universally meet with in our domestic productions, is not directly produced, as Hooker and Asa Gray have well remarked, by man; he can neither originate varieties, nor prevent their occurrence; he can only preserve and accumulate such as do occur. Unintentionally he exposes organic beings to new and changing conditions of life, and variability ensues; but similar changes of conditions might and do occur under nature. Let it also be borne in mind how infinitely complex and close-fitting are the mutual relations of all organic beings to each other

From *The Origin of Species* by Charles Darwin with introductions and notes, Vol. 22. The Harvard Classics edited by Charles W. Eliot LL. D. Copyright 1901 by P. F. Collier & Son.

and to their physical conditions of life; and consequently what infinitely varied diversities of structure might be of use to each being under changing conditions of life. Can it, then, be thought improbable, seeing that variations useful to man have undoubtedly occurred, that other variations useful in some way to each being in the great and complex battle of life, should occur in the course of many successive generations? If such do occur, can we doubt (remembering that many more individuals are born than can possibly survive) that individuals having any advantage, however slight, over others, would have the best chance of surviving and or procreating their kind? On the other hand, we may feel sure that any variation in the least degree injurious would be rigidly destroyed. This preservation of favourable individual differences and variations, and the destruction of those which are injurious, I have called Natural Selection, or the Survival of the Fittest. Variations neither useful nor injurious would not be affected by natural selection, and would be left either a fluctuating element, as perhaps we see in certain polymorphic species, or would ultimately become fixed, owing to the nature of the organism and the nature of the conditions.

Several writers have misapprehended or objected to the term Natural Selection. Some have even imagined that natural selection induces invariability, whereas it implies only the preservation of such variations as arise and are beneficial to the being under its conditions of life. No one objects to agriculturists speaking of the potent effects of man's selection; and in this case the individual differences given by nature, which man for some object selects, must of necessity first occur. Others have objected that the term selection implies conscious choice in the animals which become modified; and it has even been urged that, as plants have no volition, natural selection is not applicable to them! In the literal sense of the word, no doubt, natural selection is a false term; but who ever objected to chemists speaking of the elective affinities of the various elements?—and yet an acid cannot strictly be said to elect the base with which it in preference combines. It has been said the I speak of natural selection as an active power of Deity; but who objects to an author speaking of the attraction of gravity as ruling the movements of the planets? Every one knows what is meant and is implied by such metaphorical expressions; and they are almost necessary for brevity. So again it is difficult to avoid personifying the word Nature; but I mean by Nature, only the aggregate action

and product of many natural laws, and by laws the sequence of events as ascertained by us. With a little familiarity such superficial objections will be forgotten.

We shall best understand the probable course of natural selection by taking the case of a country undergoing some slight physical change, for instance, of climate. The proportional numbers of its inhabitants will almost immediately undergo a change, and some species will probably become extinct. We may conclude, from what we have seen of the intimate and complex manner in which the inhabitants of each country are bound together, that any change in the numerical proportions of the inhabitants, independently of the change of climate itself, would seriously affect the others. If the country were open on its borders, new forms would certainly immigrate, and this would likewise seriously disturb the relations of some of the former inhabitants. Let it be remembered how powerful the influence of a single introduced tree or mammal has been shown to be. But in the case of an island, or of a country partly surrounded by barriers, into which new and better adapted forms could not freely enter, we should then have places in the economy of nature which would assuredly be better filled up if some of the original inhabitants were in some manner modified; for, had the area been open to immigration, these same places would have been seized on by intruders. In such cases, slight modifications, which in any way favoured the individuals of any species, by better adapting them to their altered conditions, would tend to be preserved; and natural selection would have free scope for the work of improvement.

We have good reason to believe, as shown in the first chapter, that changes in the conditions of life give a tendency to increased variability; and in the foregoing cases the conditions have changed, and this would manifestly be favourable to natural selection, by affording a better chance of the occurrence of profitable variations. Unless such occur, natural selection can do nothing. Under the term of "variations," it must never be forgotten that mere individual differences are included. As man can produce a great result with his domestic animals and plants by adding up in any given direction individual differences, so could natural selection, but far more easily from having incomparably longer time for action. Nor do I believe that any great physical change, as of climate, or any unusual degree of isolation to check immigration, is necessary in order that new and unoccupied places should be left, for natural selection to fill up by improving some of the varying inhabitants. For as all the inhabitants of each country are struggling together with nicely balanced forces, extremely slight modifications in the structure or habits of one species would often give it an advantage over others; and still further modifications of the same kind would often still further increase the advantage, as long as the species continued under the same conditions of life and profited by similar means of subsistence and defence. No country can be named in which all the native inhabitants are now so perfectly adapted to each other and to the physical conditions under which they live, that none of them could be still better adapted or improved; for in all countries, the natives have been so far conquered by naturalised productions, that they have allowed some foreigners to take firm possession of the land. And as foreigners have thus, in every country beaten some of the natives, we may safely conclude that the natives might have been modified with advantage, so as to have better resisted the intruders.

As man can produce, and certainly has produced, a great result by his methodical and unconscious means of selection, what may not natural selection effect? Man can act only on external and visible characters: Nature, if I may be allowed to personify the natural preservation or survival of the fittest, cares nothing for appearances, except in so far as they are useful to any being. She can act on every internal organ, on every shade of constitutional difference, on the whole machinery of life. Man selects only for his own good: Nature only for that of the being which she tends. Every selected character is fully exercised by her, as is implied by the fact of their selection. Man keeps the natives of many climates in the same country; he seldom exercises each selected character in some peculiar and fitting manner; he feeds a long and a short beaked pigeon on the same food; he does not exercise a long-backed or long-legged quadruped in any peculiar manner; he exposes sheep with long and short wool to the same climate. He does not allow the most vigorous males to struggle for the females. He does not rigidly destroy all inferior animals, but protects during each varying season, as far as lies in his power, all his productions. He often begins his selection by some half-monstrous form; or at least by some modification prominent enough to catch the eye or to be plainly useful to him. Under nature, the slightest differences of structure or constitution may well turn the nicely-balanced scale in the struggle for life, and so be preserved.

How fleeting are the wishes and efforts of man! how short his time! and consequently how poor will be his results, compared with those accumulated by Nature during whole geological periods? Can we wonder, then, that Nature's productions should be far "truer" in character than man's productions; that they should be infinitely better adapted to the most complex conditions of life, and should plainly bear the stamp of far higher workmanship? . . .

I have now recapitulated the facts and considerations which have thoroughly convinced me that species have been modified, during a long course of descent. This has been effected chiefly through the natural selection of numerous successive, slight, favourable variations; aided in an important manner by the inherited effects of the use and disuse of parts; and in an unimportant manner, that is in relation to adaptive structures, whether past or present, by the direct action of external conditions, and by variations which seem to us in our ignorance to arise spontaneously. It appears that I formerly underrated the frequency and value of these latter forms of variation, as leading to permanent modifications of structure independently of natural selection. But as my conclusions have lately been much misrepresented, and it has been stated that I attribute the modification of species exclusively to natural selection, I may be permitted to remark that in the first edition of this work, and subsequently, I placed in a most conspicuous position—namely, at the close of the Introduction—the following words: "I am convinced that natural selection has been the main but not the exclusive means of modification." This has been of no avail. Great is the power of steady misrepresentation; but the history of science shows that fortunately this power does not long endure.

It can hardly be supposed that a false theory would explain, in so satisfactory a manner as does the theory of natural selection, the several large classes of facts above specified. It has recently been objected that this is an unsafe method of arguing, but it is a method used in judging of the common events of life, and has often been used by the greatest natural philosophers. The undulatory theory of light has thus been arrived at; and the belief in the revolution of the earth on its axis was until lately supported by hardly any direct evidence. It is no valid objection that science as yet throws no light on the far higher problem of the essence or origin of life. Who can explain what is the essence of the attraction of gravity? No one now objects to following out the results consequent on this unknown element of attraction; notwithstanding that Leibnitz formerly accused Newton of introducing "occult qualities and miracles into philosophy."

I see no good reason why the views given in this volume should shock the religious feelings of any one. It is satisfactory, as showing how transient such impressions are, to remember that the greatest discovery ever made by man, namely, the law of the attraction of gravity, was also attacked by Leibnitz, "as subversive of natural, and inferentially of revealed, religion." A celebrated author and divine has written to me that "he has gradually learnt to see that it is just as noble a conception of the Deity to believe that He created a few original forms capable of self-development into other and needful forms, as to believe that He required a fresh act of creation to supply the voids caused by the action of His laws."

Why, it may be asked, until recently did nearly all the most eminent living naturalists and geologists disbelieve in the mutability of species. It cannot be asserted that organic beings in a state of nature are subject to no variation; it cannot be proved that the amount of variation in the course of long ages is a limited quantity; no clear distinction has been, or can be, drawn between species and well-marked varieties. It cannot be maintained that species when intercrossed are invariably sterile, and varieties invariably fertile; so that sterility is a special endowment and sign of creation. The belief that species were immutable productions was almost unavoidable as long as the history of the world was thought to be of short duration; and now that we have acquired some idea of the lapse of time, we are too apt to assume, without proof, that the geological record is so perfect that it would have afforded us plain evidence of the mutation of species, if they had undergone mutation.

But the chief cause of our natural unwillingness to admit that one species has given birth to other and distinct species, is that we are always slow in admitting great changes of which we do not see the steps. The difficulty is the same as that felt by so many geologists, when Lyell first insisted that long lines of inland cliffs had been formed, and great valleys excavated, by the agencies which we see still at work. The mind cannot possibly grasp the full meaning of the term of even a million years; it cannot add up and perceive the full effects of many slight variations, accumulated during an almost infinite number of generations.

Although I am fully convinced of the truth of the views given in this volume under the form of an abstract, I by no means expect to convince experienced naturalists whose minds are stocked with a multitude of facts all viewed, during a long course of years, from a point of view directly opposite to mine. It is so easy to hide our ignorance under such expressions as the "plan of creation," "unity of design," etc., and to think that we give an explanation when we only restate a fact. Any one whose disposition leads him to attach more weight to unexplained difficulties than to explanation of a certain number of facts will certainly reject the theory. A few naturalists, endowed with much flexibility of mind, and who have already begun to doubt the immutability of species, may be influenced by this volume; but I look with confidence to the future, to young and rising naturalists, who will be able to view both sides of the question with impartiality. Whoever is led to believe that species are mutable will do good service by conscientiously expressing his conviction; for thus only can the load of prejudice by which this subject is overwhelmed be removed.

Several eminent naturalists have of late published their belief that a multitude of reputed species in each genus are not real species; but that other species are real, that is, have been independently created. This seems to me a strange conclusion to arrive at. They admit that a multitude of forms, which till lately they themselves thought were special creations, and which are still thus looked at by the majority of naturalists, and which consequently have all the external characteristic features of true species, they admit that these have been produced by variation, but they refuse to extend the same view to other and slightly different forms. Nevertheless they do not pretend that they can define, or even conjecture, which are the created forms of life, and which are those produced by secondary laws. They admit variation as *vera causa* in one case, they arbitrarily reject it in another, and without assigning any distinction in the two cases. The day will come when this will be given as a curious illustration of the blindness of preconceived opinion. These authors seem no more startled at a miraculous act of creation than at an ordinary birth. But do they really believe that at innumerable periods in the earth's history certain elemental atoms have been commanded suddenly to flash into living tissues? Do they believe that at each supposed act of creation one individual or many were produced? Were all the infinitely numerous kinds of animals and plants created as egg or seed, or as full grown? And in the case of mammals, were they created bearing the false marks of nourishment from the mother's womb? Undoubtedly some of these same questions cannot be answered by those who believe in the appearance or creation of only a few forms of life, or of some one form alone. It has been maintained by several authors that it is as easy to believe in the creation of a million beings as of one; but Maupertuis' philosophical axiom "of least action" leads the mind more willingly to admit the smaller number; and certainly we ought not to believe that innumerable beings within each great class have been created with plain, but deceptive, marks of descent from a single parent.

As a record of a former state of things, I have retained in the foregoing paragraphs, and elsewhere, several sentences which imply that naturalists believe in the separate creation of each species; and I have been much censured for having thus expressed myself. But undoubtedly this was the general belief when the first edition of the present work appeared. I formerly spoke to very many naturalists on the subject of evolution, and never once met with any sympathetic agreement. It is probable that some did then believe in evolution, but they were either silent, or expressed themselves so ambiguously that it was not easy to understand their meaning. Now, things are wholly changed, and almost every naturalist admits the great principle of evolution. There are, however, some who still think that species have suddenly given birth, through quite unexplained means, to new and totally different forms; but, as I have attempted to show, weighty evidence can be opposed to the admission of great and abrupt modifications. Under a scientific point of view, and as leading to further investigation, but little advantage is gained by believing that new forms are suddenly developed in an inexplicable manner from old and widely different forms, over the old belief in the creation of species from the dust of the earth.

It may be asked how far I extend the doctrine of the modification of species. The question is difficult to answer, because the more distinct the forms are which we consider, by so much the arguments in favour of community of descent become fewer in number and less in force. But some arguments of the greatest weight extend very far. All the members of whole classes are connected together by a chain of affinities, and all can be classed on the same principle, in groups subordinate to groups. Fossil remains sometimes tend to fill up very wide intervals between existing orders. Organs in a rudimentary condition plainly show that an early progenitor had the organ in a fully developed condition; and this in some cases implies an enormous amount of modification in the descendants. Throughout whole classes various structures are formed on the same pattern, and at a very early age the embryos closely resemble each other. Therefore I cannot doubt that the theory of descent with modification embraces all the members of the same great class or kingdom. I believe that animals are descended from at most only four or five progenitors, and plants from an equal or lesser number.

Analogy would lead me one step farther, namely, to the belief that all animals and plants are descended from some one prototype. But analogy may be a deceitful guide. Nevertheless all living things have much in common, in their chemical composition, their cellular structure, their laws of growth, and their liability to injurious influences. We see this even in so trifling a fact as that the same poison often similarly affects plants and animals; or that the poison secreted by the gallfly produces monstrous growths on the wild rose or oak tree. With all organic beings, excepting perhaps some of the very lowest, sexual reproduction seems to be essentially similar. With all, as far as is at present known, the germinal vesicle is the same; so that all organisms start from a common origin. If we look even to the two main divisions—namely, to the animal and vegetable kingdoms—certain low forms are so far intermediate in character that naturalists have disputed to which kingdom they should be referred. As Professor Asa Gray has remarked, "the spores and other reproductive bodies of many of the lower algae may claim to have first a characteristically animal, and then an unequivocal vegetable, existence." Therefore, on the principle of natural selection with divergence of character, it does not seem incredible that, from such low and intermediate form, both animals and plants may have been developed; and, if we admit this, we must likewise admit that all the organic beings which have ever lived on this earth may be descended from some one primordial form. But this inference is chiefly grounded on analogy, and it is immaterial whether or not it be accepted. No doubt it is possible, as Mr. G. H. Lewes has urged, that at the first commencement of life many different forms are evolved; but if so, we may conclude that only a very few have left modified descendants. For, as I have recently remarked in regard to the members of each great kingdom, such as the Vertebrata, Articulata, etc., we have distinct evidence in their embryological, homologous, and rudimentary structures, that within each kingdom all the members are descended from a single progenitor.

When the views advanced by me in this volume, and by Mr. Wallace, or when analogous views on the origin of species are generally admitted, we can dimly foresee that there will be a considerable revolution in natural history. Systematists will be able to pursue their labours as at present; but they will not be incessantly haunted by the shadowy doubt whether this or that form be a true species. This, I feel sure and I speak after experience, will be no slight relief. The endless disputes whether or not some fifty species of British brambles are good species will cease. Systematists will have only to decide (not that this will be easy) whether any form be sufficiently constant and distinct from other forms, to be capable of definition; and if definable, whether the differences be sufficiently important to deserve a specific name. This latter point will become a far more essential consideration than it is at present; for differences, however slight, between any two forms, if not blended by intermediate gradations, are looked at by most naturalists as sufficient to raise both forms to the rank of species.

Hereafter we shall be compelled to acknowledge that the only distinction between species and well-marked varieties is, that the latter are known, or believed, to be connected at the present day by intermediate gradations whereas species were formerly thus connected. Hence, without rejecting the consideration of the present existence of intermediate gradations between any two forms, we shall be led to weigh more carefully and to value higher the actual amount of difference between them. It is quite possible that forms now generally acknowledged to be merely varieties may hereafter be thought worthy of specific names; and in this case scientific and common language will come into accordance. In short, we shall have to treat species in the same manner as those naturalists treat genera, who admit that genera are merely artificial combinations made for convenience. This may not be a cheering prospect; but we shall at least be freed from the vain search for the undiscovered and undiscoverable essence of the term species.

The other and more general departments of natural history will rise greatly in interest. The terms used by naturalists, of affinity, relationship, community of type, paternity, morphology, adaptive characters, rudimentary and aborted organs, etc., will cease to be metaphorical, and will have a plain signification. When we no longer look at an organic being as a savage looks at a ship, as something wholly beyond his comprehension; when we regard every production of nature as one which has had a long history; when we comtemplate every complex structure and instinct as the summing up of many contrivances, each useful to the possessor, in the same way as any great mechanical invention is the summing up of the labour, the experience, the reason, and even the blunders of numerous workmen; when we thus view each organic being, how far more interesting— I speak from experience—does the study of natural history become!

A grand and almost untrodden field of inquiry will be opened, on the causes and laws of variation, on correlation, on the effects of use and disuse, on the direct action of external conditions, and so forth. The study of domestic productions will rise immensely in value. A new variety raised by man will be a more important and interesting subject for study than one more species added to the infinitude of already recorded species. Our classifications will come to be, as far as they can be so made, genealogies; and will then truly give what may be called the plan of creation. The rules for classifying will no doubt become simpler when we have a definite object in view. We possess no pedigrees or amorial bearings; and we have to discover and trace the many diverging lines of descent in our natural genealogies, by characters of any kind which have long been inherited. Rudimentary organs will speak infallibly with respect to the nature of long-lost structures. Species and groups of species which are called aberrant, and which may fancifully be called living fossils, will aid us in forming a picture of the ancient forms of life. Embryology will often reveal to us the structure, in some degree obscured, of the prototypes of each great class.

When we can feel assured that all the individuals of the same species, and all the closely allied species of most genera, have, within a not very remote period descended from one parent, and have migrated from some one birth-place; and when we better know the many means of migration, then, by the light which geology now throws, and will continue to throw, on former changes of climate and of the level of the land, we shall surely be enabled to trace in an admirable manner the former migrations of the inhabitants of the whole world. Even at present, by comparing the differences between the inhabitants of the sea on the opposite sides of a continent, and the nature of the various inhabitants of that continent in relation to their apparent means of immigration, some light can be thrown on ancient geography.

The noble science of Geology loses glory from the extreme imperfection of the record. The crust of the earth with its imbedded remains must not be looked at as a well-filled museum, but as a poor collection made at hazard and at rare intervals. The accumulation of each great fossiliferous formation will be recognised as having depended on an unusual concurrence of favourable circumstances, and the blank intervals by a comparison of the preceding and succeeding organic forms. We must be cautious in attempting to correlate as strictly contemporaneous two formations which do not include many identical species, by the general succession of the forms of life. As species are produced and exterminated by slowly acting and still existing causes, and not by miraculous acts of creation; and as the most important of all cause of organic change is one which is almost independent of altered and perhaps suddenly altered physical conditions, namely, the mutual relation of organism to organism,—the improvement of one organism entailing the improvement or the extermination of others; it follows, that the amount of organic change in the fossils of consecutive formations probably serves as a fair measure of the relative, though not actual lapse of time. A number of species, however, keeping in a body might remain for a long period unchanged, whilst within the same period, several of these species by migrating into new countries and coming into competition with foreign associates, might become modified; so that we must not overrate the accuracy of organic change as a measure of time.

In the future I see open fields for far more important researches. Psychology will be securely based on the foundation already well laid by Mr. Herbert Spencer, that of the necessary acquirement of each mental power and capacity by gradation. Much light will be thrown on the origin of man and his history.

Authors of the highest eminence seem to be fully satisfied with the view that each species has been independently created. To my mind it accords better with what we know of the laws impressed on matter by the Creator, that the production and extinction of the past and present inhabitants of the world should have been due to secondary causes, like those determining the birth and death of the individual. When I view all beings not as special creations, but as the lineal descendants of some few beings which lived long before the first bed of the Cambrian system was deposited, they seem to me to become ennobled. Judging from the past, we may safely infer that not one living species will transmit its unaltered likeness to a distant futurity. And of the species now living very few will transmit progeny of any kind to a far distant futurity; for the manner in which all organic beings are grouped, shows that the greater number of species in each genus, and all the species in many genera, have left no descendants, but have become utterly extinct.

We can so far take a prophetic glance into futurity as to foretell that it will be the common and widely spread species, belonging to the larger and dominant groups within each class, which will ultimately prevail and procreate new and dominant species. As all the living forms of life are the lineal descendants of those which lived long before the Cambrian epoch, we may feel certain that the ordinary succession by generation has never once been broken, and that no cataclysm has desolated the whole world. Hence we may look with some confidence to a secure future of great length. And as natural selection works solely by and for the good of each being, all corporeal and mental endowments will tend to progress towards perfection.

It is interesting to contemplate a tangled bank, clothed with many plants of many kinds, with birds singing on the bushes, with various insects flitting about, and with worms crawling through the damp earth, and to reflect that these elaborately constructed forms, so different from each other, and dependent upon each other in so complex a manner, have all been produced by laws acting around us. These laws, taken in the largest sense, being Growth and Reproduction; Inheritance which is almost implied by reproduction; Variability from the indirect and direct action of the conditions of life, and from use and disuse: a Ratio of Increase so high as to lead to a Struggle for Life, and as a consequence to Natural Selection, entailing Divergence of Character and the Extension of less improved forms. Thus, from the war of nature, from famine and death, the most exalted object which we are capable of conceiving, namely, the production of the higher animals, directly follows. There is grandeur in this view of life, with its several powers, having been originally breathed by the Creator into a few forms or into one; and that, whilst this planet has gone cycling on according to the fixed law of gravity, from so simple a beginning endless forms most beautiful and most wonderful have been, and are being, evolved.

THE DESCENT OF MAN

CHAPTER XXI

General Summary and Conclusion

Main conclusion that man is descended from some lower form—Manner of development—Genealogy of man—Intellectual and moral faculties—Sexual selection—Concluding remarks.

A brief summary will be sufficient to recall to the reader's mind the more salient points in this work. Many of the views which have been advanced are highly speculative, and some no doubt will prove erroneous; but I have in every case given the reasons which have led me to one view rather than to another. It seemed worth while to try how far the principle of evolution would throw light on some of the more complex problems in the natural history of man. False facts are highly injurious to the progress of science, for they often endure long; but false views, if supported by some evidence, do little harm, for every one takes a salutary pleasure in proving their falseness; and, when this is done, one path toward error is closed and the road to truth is often at the same time opened.

The main conclusion here arrived at, and now held by many naturalists, who are well competent to form a sound judgment, is that man is descended from some less highly organized form. The grounds upon which this conclusion rests will never be shaken, for the close similarity between man and the lower animals in embryonic development, as well as in innumerable points of structure and constitution, both of high and of the most trifling importance—the rudiments which he retains, and the abnormal reversions to which he is occasionally liable—are facts which cannot be disputed. They have long been known, but, until recently, they told us nothing with respect to the origin of man. Now, when viewed by the light of our knowledge of the whole organic world, their meaning is unmistakable. The great principle of evolution stands up clear and firm when these groups of facts are considered in connection with others, such as the mutual affinities of the members of the same group, their geographical distribution in past and present times, and their geological succession. It is incredible that all these facts should speak falsely. He who is not content to look, like a savage, at the phenomena of nature as disconnected, cannot any longer believe that man is the work of a separate act of creation. He will be forced to admit that the close resemblance of the embryo of man to that, for instance, of a dog—the construction of his skull, limbs and whole frame on the same plan with that of other mammals, independently of the uses to which the parts may be put—the occasional reappearance of various structures, for instance of several muscles, which man does not normally possess, but which are common to the Quadrumana—and a crowd of analogous facts—all point in the plainest manner to the conclusion that man is the co-descendant with other mammals of a common progenitor.

We have seen that man incessantly presents individual differences in all parts of his body and in his mental faculties. These differences or variations seem to be induced by the same general causes, and to obey the same laws as with the lower animals. In both cases similar laws of inheritance prevail. Man tends to increase at a greater rate than his means of subsistence; consequently he is occasionally subjected to a severe struggle for existence, and natural selection will have affected whatever lies within its scope. A succession of strongly marked variations of a similar nature is by no means requisite; slight fluctuating differences in the individual suffice for the work of natural selection; not that we have any reason to suppose that in the same species all parts of the organization tend to vary to the same degree. We may feel assured that the inherited effects of the long-continued use or disuse of parts will have done much in the same direction with natural selection. Modifications formerly of importance, though no longer of any special use, are long-inherited. When one part is modified other parts change through the principle of correlation, of which we have instances in many curious cases of correlated monstrosities. Something may be attributed to the direct and definite action of the surrounding conditions of life, such as abundant food, heat or moisture; and, lastly, many characters of slight physiological importance, some indeed of considerable importance, have been gained through sexual selection.

No doubt man, as well as every other animal, presents structures, which seem to our limited knowledge, not to be now of any service to him, nor to have been so formerly, either for the general conditions of life, or in the relations of one sex to the other. Such structures cannot be accounted for by any form of selection, or by the inherited effects of the use and disuse of parts. We know, however, that many strange and strongly marked peculiarities of structure occasionally appear in our domesticated productions, and if their unknown causes were to act more uniformly, they would probably become common to all the individuals of the species. We may hope hereafter to understand something about the causes of such occasional modifications, especially through the study of monstrosities; hence, the labors of experimentalists, such as those of M. Camille Dareste, are full of promise for the future. In general we can only say that the cause of each slight variation and of each monstrosity lies much more in the constitution of the organism than in the nature of the surrounding conditions; though new and changed conditions certainly play an important part in exciting organic changes of many kinds.

Through the means just specified, aided perhaps by others as yet undiscovered, man has been raised to his present state. But since he attained to the rank of manhood, he has diverged into distinct races, or, as they may be more fitly called, sub-species. Some of these, such as the negro and European, are so distinct that, if specimens had been brought to a naturalist without any further information, they would undoubtedly have been considered by him as good and true species. Nevertheless, all the races agree in so many unimportant details of structure and in so many mental peculiarities that these can be accounted for only by inheritance from a common progenitor; and a progenitor thus characterized would probably deserve to rank as man.

It must not be supposed that the divergence of each race from the other races and of all from a common stock can be traced back to any one pair of progenitors. On the contrary, at every stage in the process of modification, all the individuals which were in any way better fitted for their conditions of life, though in different degrees, would have survived in greater numbers than the less well-fitted. The process would have been like that followed by man, when he does not intentionally select particular individuals, but breeds from all the superior individuals and neglects the inferior. He thus slowly but surely modifies his stock and unconsciously forms a new strain. So with respect to modifications acquired independently of selection, and due to variations arising from the nature of the organism and the action of the surrounding conditions, or from changed habits of life, no single pair will have been modified much

more than the other pairs inhabiting the same country, for all will have been continually blended through free intercrossing.

By considering the embryological structure of man—the homologies which he presents with the lower animals—the rudiments which he retains—and the reversions to which he is liable, we can partly recall in imagination the former condition of our early progenitors; and can approximately place them in their proper place in the zoological series. We thus learn that man is descended from a hairy, tailed quadruped, probably arboreal in its habits and an inhabitant of the Old World. This creature, if its whole structure had been examined by a naturalist, would have been classed among the Quadrumana, as surely as the still more ancient progenitor of the Old and New World monkeys. The Quadrumana and all the higher mammals are probably derived from an ancient marsupial animal and this through a long line of diversified forms, from some amphibian-like creature, and this again from some fish-like animal. In the dim obscurity of the past we can see that the early progenitor of all the Vertebrata must have been an aquatic animal, provided with branchiae with the two sexes united in the same individual, and with the most important organs of the body (such as the brain and heart) imperfectly or not at all developed. This animal seems to have been more like the larvae of the existing marine Ascidians than any other known form.

The high standard of our intellectual powers and moral disposition is the greatest difficulty which presents itself, after we have been driven to this conclusion on the origin of man. But every one who admits the principle of evolution must see that the mental powers of the higher animals, which are the same in kind with those of man, though so different in degree, are capable of advancement. Thus the interval between the mental powers of one of the higher apes and of a fish, or between those of an ant and scale-insect, is immense; yet their development does not offer any special difficulty; for with our domesticated animals the mental faculties are certainly variable, and the variations are inherited. No one doubts that they are of the utmost importance to animals in a state of nature. Therefore, the conditions are favorable for their development through natural selection. The same conclusion may be extended to man; the intellect must have been all-important to him, even at a very remote period, as enabling him to invent and use language, to make weapons, tools, traps, etc., whereby with the aid of his social habits he long ago became the most dominant of all living creatures.

A great stride in the development of the intellect will have followed, as soon as the half-art and half-instinct of language came into use; for the continued use of language will have reacted on the brain and produced an inherited effect; and this again will have reacted on the improvement of language. As Mr. Chauncey Wright has well remarked, the largeness of the brain in man relatively to his body, compared with the lower animals, may be attributed in chief part to the early use of some simple form of language—that wonderful engine which affixes signs to all sorts of objects and qualities, and excites trains of thought which would never arise from the mere impression of the senses, or if they did arise could not be followed out. The higher intellectual powers of man, such as those of ratiocination, abstraction, self-consciousness, etc., probably follow from the continued improvement and exercise of the other mental faculties.

The development of the moral qualities is a more interesting problem. The foundation lies in the social instincts, including under this term the family ties. These instincts are highly complex, and in the case of the lower animals give special tendencies toward certain definite actions; but the more important elements are love and the distinct emotion of sympathy. Animals endowed with the social instincts take pleasure in one another's company, warn one another of danger, defend and aid one another in many ways. These instincts do not extend to all the individuals of the species, but only to those of the same community. As they are highly beneficial to the species they have in all probability been acquired through natural selection.

A moral being is one who is capable of reflecting on his past actions and their motives—of approving of some and disapproving of others; and the fact that man is the one being who certainly deserves this designation is the greatest of all distinctions between him and the lower animals. But in the fourth chapter I have endeavored to show that the moral sense follows, firstly, from the enduring and everpresent nature of the social instincts; secondly, from man's appreciation of the approbation and disapprobation of his fellows; and, thirdly, from the high activity of his mental faculties, with past impressions extremely vivid; and in these latter respects he differs from the lower animals. . . .

The moral faculties are generally and justly esteemed as of higher value than the intellectual

powers. But we should bear in mind that the activity of the mind in vividly recalling past impressions is one of the fundamental though secondary bases of conscience. This affords the strongest argument for educating and stimulating in all possible ways the intellectual faculties of every human being. No doubt a man with a torpid mind, if his social affections and sympathies are well developed, will be led to good actions, and may have a fairly sensitive conscience. But whatever renders the imagination more vivid and strengthens the habit of recalling and comparing past impressions will make the conscience more sensitive, and may even somewhat compensate for weak social affections and sympathies.

The moral nature of man has reached its present standard partly through the advancement of his reasoning powers and consequently of a just public opinion, but especially from his sympathies having been rendered more tender and widely diffused through the effects of habit, example, instruction and reflection. It is not improbable that after long practice virtuous tendencies may be inherited. With the more civilized races the conviction of the existence of an all-seeing Deity has had a potent influence on the advance of morality. Ultimately man does not accept the praise or blame of his fellows as his sole guide, though few escape this influence, but his habitual convictions, controlled by reason, afford him the safest rule. His conscience then becomes the supreme judge and monitor. Nevertheless, the first foundation or origin of the moral sense lies in the social instincts, including sympathy; and these instincts no doubt were primarily gained, as in the case of the lower animals, through natural selection.

The belief in God has often been advanced as not only the greatest but the most complete of all the distinctions between man and the lower animals. It is, however, impossible, as we have seen, to maintain that this belief is innate or instinctive in man. On the other hand, a belief in all-pervading spiritual agencies seems to be universal; and apparently follows from a considerable advance in man's reason, and from a still greater advance in his faculties of imagination, curiosity and wonder. I am aware that the assumed instinctive belief in God has been used by many persons as an argument for His existence. But this is a rash argument, as we should thus be compelled to believe in the existence of many cruel and malignant spirits, only a little more powerful than man; for the belief in them is far more general than in a beneficient Deity. The idea of a universal and beneficient Creator does not seem to arise in the mind of man until he has been elevated by long-continued culture.

He who believes in the advancement of man from some low organized form will naturally ask, How does this bear on the belief in the immortality of the soul? The barbarous races of man, as Sir J. Lubbock has shown, possess no clear belief of this kind; but arguments derived from the primeval beliefs of savages are, as we have just seen, of little or no avail. Few persons feel any anxiety from the impossibility of determining at what precise period in the development of the individual, from the first trace of a minute germinal vesicle, man becomes an immortal being; and there is no greater cause for anxiety because the period cannot possibly be determined in the gradually ascending organic scale.

I am aware that the conclusions arrived at in this work will be denounced by some as highly irreligious; but he who denounces them is bound to show why it is more irreligious to explain the origin of man as a distinct species by descent from some lower form, through the laws of variation and natural selection, than to explain the birth of the individual through the laws of ordinary reproduction. The birth both of the species and of the individual are equally parts of that grand sequence of events, which our minds refuse to accept as the result of blind chance. The understanding revolts at such a conclusion, whether or not we are able to believe that every slight variation of structure, the union of each pair in marriage, the dissemination of each seed, and other such events have all been ordained for some special purpose. . . .

The main conclusion arrived at in this work, namely, that man is descended from some lowly organized form, will, I regret to think, be highly distasteful to many. But there can hardly be a doubt that we are descended from barbarians. The astonishment which I felt on first seeing a party of Fuegians on a wild and broken shore will never be forgotten by me, for the reflection at once rushed into my mind—such were our ancestors. These men were absolutely naked and bedaubed with paint, their long hair was tangled, their mouths frothed with excitement, and their expression was wild, startled and distrustful. They possessed hardly any arts, and like wild animals lived on what they could catch; they had no government, and were merciless to every one not of their own small tribe. He who has seen a savage in his native land will not feel much shame, if forced to acknowledge that the blood of some more humble creature flows in his veins. For my own part I would as soon be descended from that heroic little monkey who braved his dreaded enemy in order to save the life of his keeper, or from that old baboon, who, descending from the mountains, carried away in triumph his young comrade from a crowd of astonished dogs—as from a savage who delights to torture his enemies, offers up bloody sacrifices, practices infanticide without remorse, treats his wives like slaves, knows no decency, and is haunted by the grossest superstitions.

Man may be excused for feeling some pride at having risen, though not through his own exertions, to the very summit of the organic scale; and the fact of his having thus risen, instead of having been aboriginally placed there, may give him hope for a still higher destiny in the distant future. But we are not here concerned with hopes or fears, only with the truth as far as our reason permits us to discover it; and I have given the evidence to the best of my ability. We must, however, acknowledge, as it seems to me, that man, with all his noble qualities, with sympathy which feels for the most debased, with benevolence which extends not only to other men but to the humblest living creature, with his godlike intellect which has penetrated into the movements and constitution of the solar system—with all these exalted powers—man still bears in his bodily frame the indelible stamp of his lowly origin.

Herbert Spencer

Herbert Spencer (1820-1903) was the most celebrated of the "social Darwinists" of the late nineteenth century. For Spencer the entire universe was governed by the laws of evolution—not only living organisms, but also societies, governments and economies. He felt that society was evolving toward greater freedom for the individual and that the role of government was simply to maintain an atmosphere of free competition. Spencer identified the poor with the unfit in society; government should not coddle them. The weak and the unfit should engage in the struggle of life without government aid—this would assure "the survival of the fittest." Any attempt on the part of the government to better the lot of the poor would simply subvert the evolutionary process and make the future more difficult. In the selection below, Spencer applied these principles to sanitary legislation.

SOCIAL STATICS

SANITARY SUPERVISION

The current ideas respecting legislative interference in sanitary matters, do not seem to have taken the form of a definite theory. The Eastern Medical Association of Scotland does indeed hold "that it is the duty of the State to adopt measures for protecting the health as well as the property of its subjects;" and *The Times* lately asserted that "the Privy Council is chargeable with the health of the Empire;" but no considerable political party has adopted either of these dogmas by way of a distinct confession of faith.

That it comes within the proper sphere of government to repress nuisances is evident. He who contaminates the atmosphere breathed by his neighbour, is infringing his neighbour's rights. Men having equal claims to the free use of the elements, and having that exercise more or less limited by whatever makes the elements more or less unusable, are obviously trespassed against by any one who unnecessarily vitiates the elements, and renders them detrimental to health, or disagreeable to the senses; and in the discharge of its function as protector, a government is called upon to afford redress to those so trespassed against.

Beyond this, however, it cannot lawfully go. As already shown in several kindred cases, for a government to take from a citizen more property than is needful for the efficient defence of that citizen's rights, is to infringe his rights. And hence all taxation for sanitary superintendence coming, as it does, within this category, must be condemned.

The theory which Boards of Health and the like imply, is not only inconsistent with our definition of State-duty, but is open to strictures similar to those made in analogous cases. If, by saying "that it is the duty of the State to adopt measures for protecting the health of its subjects," it is meant (as it *is* meant by the majoriy of the medical profession) that the State should interpose between quacks and those who patronize them, or between the druggist and the artizan who wants a remedy for his cold—if it is meant that to guard people against empirical treatment, the State should forbid all unlicensed persons from prescribing; then the reply is, that to do so is directly to violate the moral law. Men's rights are infringed by these, as much as by all other, trade-interferences. The invalid is at liberty to buy medicine and advice from whomsoever he pleases; the unlicensed practitioner is at liberty to sell these to whosoever will buy. On no pretext can a barrier be set up between the two, without the law of equal freedom being broken; and least of all may the Government, whose office it is to uphold that law, become a transgressor of it.

Moreover this doctrine, that it is the duty of the State to protect the health of its subjects, cannot be established, for the same reason that its kindred doctrines cannot, namely, the impossibility of

From *Social Statics*, Abridged and Revised; together with *The Man Versus the State*, by Herbert Spencer. Copyright 1892 by D. Appleton and Company, New York.

saying how far the alleged duty shall be carried. Health depends on the fulfilment of numerous conditions—can be "protected" only by insuring that fulfilment. If, therefore, it is the duty of the State to protect the health of its subjects, it is its duty to see that all the conditions to health are fulfilled by them. The legislature must prescribe so many meals a day for each individual; fix the quantities and qualities of food for men, women and children; state the proportion of fluids, when to be taken, and of what kind; specify the amount of exercise, and define its character; describe the clothing to be employed; determine the hours of sleep; and to enforce these regulations it must employ officials to oversee every one's domestic arrangements. If, on the other hand, a universal supervision of private conduct is not meant, then there comes the question—Where, between this and no supervision at all, lies the boundary up to which supervision is a duty?

There is a manifest analogy between committing to Government-guardianship the physical health of the people, and committing to it their moral health. If the welfare of men's souls can be fitly dealt with by acts of parliament, why then the welfare of their bodies can be fitly dealt with likewise. The disinfecting society from vice may naturally be cited as a precedent for disinfecting it from pestilence. Purifying the haunts of men from noxious vapours may be held quite as legitimate as purifying their moral atmosphere. The fear that false doctrines may be instilled by unauthorized preachers, has its analogue in the fear that unauthorized practitioners may give deleterious medicines or advice. And the prosecutions once committed to prevent the one evil, countenance the penalties used to put down the other. Contrariwise, the arguments employed by the dissenter to show that the moral sanity of the people is not a matter for State-superintendence, are applicable, with a slight change of terms, to their physical sanity also.

Let no one think this analogy imaginary. The two notions are not only theoretically related; we have facts proving that they tend to embody themselves in similar institutions. There is an inclination on the part of the medical profession to get itself organized after the fashion of the clergy. Little do the public at large know how actively professional publications are agitating for State-appointed overseers of the public health. Take up the *Lancet,* and you will find articles written to show the necessity of making poor-law medical officers independent of Boards of Guardians, by appointing them for life, holding them responsible only to central authority, and giving them handsome salaries from the Consolidated Fund. The *Journal of Public Health* proposes that "every house on becoming vacant be examined by a competent person as to its being in a condition adapted for the safe dwelling in of the future tenants;" and to this end would raise by fees, chargeable on the landlords, "a revenue adequate to pay a sufficient staff of inspectors four or five hundred pounds a year each." A non-professional publication, echoing the appeal, says—"No reasonable men can doubt that if a proper system of ventilation were rendered imperative upon landlords, not only would the cholera and the epidemic diseases be checked, but the general standard of health would be raised." While the *Medical Times* shows its leanings by announcing, with marked approbation, that "the Ottoman Government has recently published a decree for the appointment of physicians to be paid by the State," who "are bound to treat gratuitously all—both rich and poor—who shall demand advice."

The most specious excuse for not extending to medical advice the principles of free trade, is the same as that given for not leaving education to be diffused under them; namely, that the judgment of the consumer is not a sufficient guarantee for the goodness of the commodity. The intolerance shown by orthodox surgeons and physicians towards unordained followers of their calling, is to be understood as arising from a desire to defend the public against quackery. Ignorant people, say they, cannot distinguish good treatment from bad, or skilful advisers from unskilful ones: hence it is needful that the choice should be made for them. And then, following in the track of priesthoods, for whose persecutions a similar defence has always been set up, they agitate for more stringent regulations against unlicensed practitioners, and descant upon the dangers to which men are exposed by an unrestricted system. Hear Mr. Wakley. Speaking of a recently-revived law relating to chemists and druggists, he says,—"It must have the effect of checking, to a vast extent, that frightful evil called counter-practice, exercised by unqualified persons, which has so long been a disgrace to the operation of the laws relating to medicine in this country, and which, doubtless, has been attended with a dreadful sacrifice of human life." (*Lancet,* Sept. 11, 1841.) And again, "There is not a chemist and druggist in the empire who would refuse to prescribe in his own shop in medical cases, or who would hesitate day by day to prescribe simple remedies for the ailments of infants and children." . . . "We had previously considered the evil to be of enormous magnitude, but it is quite clear that we had under-estimated the extent of the danger to which the public are exposed." (*Lancet,* Oct. 16, 1841.)

Any one may discern through these ludicrous exaggerations much more of the partizan than of the philanthropist. But let that pass. And without dwelling upon the fact that it is strange a "dreadful sacrifice of human life" should not have drawn the attention of the people themselves to this "frightful evil,"—without doing more than glance at the further fact, that nothing is said of those benefits conferred by "counter practice," which would at least form a considerable set off against this "evil of enormous magnitude;" let it be conceded that very many of the poorer class *are* injured by druggists' prescriptions and quack medicines. The allegation having been thus, for argument's sake, admitted in full, let us now consider whether it constitutes a sufficient plea for legal interference.

Inconvenience, suffering, and death, are the penalties attached by Nature to ignorance, as well as to incompetence—are also the means of remedying these. Partly by weeding out those of lowest development, and partly by subjecting those who remain to the never-ceasing discipline of experience, Nature secures the growth of a race who shall both understand the conditions of existence, and be able to act up to them. It is impossible in any degree to suspend this discipline by stepping in between ignorance and its consequences, without, to a corresponding degree, suspending the progress. If to be ignorant were as safe as to be wise, no one would become wise. And all measures which tend to put ignorance upon a par with wisdom, inevitably check the growth of wisdom. Acts of parliament to save silly people from the evils which putting faith in empirics may entail on them, do this, and are therefore bad. It is best to let the foolish man suffer the penalty of his foolishness. For the pain—he must bear it as well as he can: for the experience—he must treasure it up, and act more rationally in future. To others as well as to himself will his case be a warning. And by multiplication of such warnings, there cannot fail to be generated a caution corresponding to the danger to be shunned.

A sad population of imbeciles would our schemers fill the world with, could their plans last. A sorry kind of human constitution would they make for us—a constitution continually going wrong, and needing to be set right again—a constitution ever tending to self-destruction. Why the whole effort

of Nature is to get rid of such—to clear the world of them, and make room for better. Mark how the diseased are dealt with. Consumptive patients, with lungs incompetent to perform the duties of lungs, people with digestive organs that will not take up enough nutriment, people with defective hearts which break down under effort, people with any constitutional flaw preventing due fulfilment of the conditions of life, are continually dying out, and leaving behind those fit for the climate, food, and habits to which they are born. Even the less-imperfectly organized who, under ordinary circumstances, manage to live with comfort, are still the first to be carried off by adverse influences; and only such as are robust enough to resist these—that is, only such as are tolerably well adapted to both the usual and incidental necessities of existence, remain. And thus is the race kept free from vitiation. Of course this statement is in substance a truism; for no other arrangement of things is conceivable. But it is a truism to which most men pay little regard. And if they commonly overlook its application to body, still less do they note its bearing upon mind. Yet it is equally true here. Nature just as much insists on fitness between mental character and circumstances, as between physical character and circumstances; and radical defects are as much causes of death in the one case as in the other. He on whom his own stupidity, or vice, or idleness, entails loss of life, must, in the generalizations of philosophy, be classed with the victims of weak viscera or malformed limbs. In his case, as in the others, there exists a fatal non-adaptation; and it matters not in the abstract whether it be a moral, an intellectual, or a corporeal one. Beings thus imperfect are Nature's failures, and are recalled by her when found to be such. Along with the rest they are put upon trial. If they are sufficiently complete to live, they *do* live, and it is well they should live. If they are not sufficiently complete to live, they die, and it is best they should die. And however irregular the action of this law may appear—however it may seem that much chaff is left behind which should be winnowed out, and that much grain is taken away which should be left behind; yet due consideration must satisfy every one that the *average* effect is to purify society from those who are, *in some respect or other,* essentially faulty.

Of course, in so far as the severity of this process is mitigated by the spontaneous sympathy of men for one another, it is proper that it should be mitigated: albeit there is unquestionably harm done when sympathy is shown, without any regard to ultimate results. But the drawbacks hence arising are nothing like commensurate with the benefits otherwise conferred. Only when this sympathy prompts to a breach of equity—only when it originates an interference forbidden by the law of equal freedom—only when, by so doing, it suspends in some particular department of life the relationship between constitution and conditions, does it work pure evil. Then, however, it defeats its own end. It favours the multiplication of those worst fitted for existence, and, by consequence, hinders the multiplication of those best fitted for existence—leaving, as it does, less room for them. It tends to fill the world with those to whom life will bring most pain, and tends to keep out of it those to whom life will bring most pleasure. It inflicts positive misery, and prevents positive happiness.

Turning now to consider these impatiently-agitated schemes for improving our sanitary condition by act of parliament, the first criticism to be passed on them is that they are needless, inasmuch as there are already efficient influences at work gradually accomplishing every desideratum.

Seeing, as do the philanthropic of our day, like the congenitally blind to whom sight has just been given, they form very crude and very exaggerated notions of the evils to be dealt with. Some, anxious for the enlightenment of their fellows, collect statistics exhibiting a lamentable amount of ignorance; publish these; and the lovers of their kind are startled. Others dive into the dens where poverty hides itself, and shock the world with descriptions of what they see. Others, again, gather together information respecting crime, and make the benevolent look grave by their disclosures. Whereupon, in horror at these revelations, men keep thoughtlessly assuming that the evils have lately become greater, when in reality it is they who have become more observant of them. If few complaints have hitherto been heard about crime, and ignorance, and misery, it is not that in times past these were less widely spread, for the contrary is the fact; but it is that our forefathers thought little about them, and said little about them. Overlooking which circumstance, and forgetting that social evils have been undergoing a gradual amelioration, many entertain a needless alarm lest fearful consequences should ensue, if these evils are not immediately remedied, and a visionary hope that immediate remedy of them is possible.

. . . .

Even could State-agency compass for our towns the most perfect salubrity, it would be in the end better to remain as we are, rather than obtain such a benefit by such means. It is quite possible to give too much even for a great desideratum. However valuable good bodily health may be, it is dearly purchased when mental health goes in exchange. Whoso thinks that Government can supply sanitary advantages for nothing, or at the cost of more taxes only, is woefully mistaken. They must be paid for with character as well as with taxes.

Let it be again remembered that men cannot *make* force. All they can do is to avail themselves of force already existing, and employ it for working out this or that purpose. They cannot increase it; they cannot get from it more than its due effect; and as much as they expend of it for doing one thing, must they lack of it for doing other things. Thus it is now becoming a received doctrine, that what we call chemical affinity, heat, light, electricity, magnetism, and motion, are all manifestations of the same primordial force—that they are convertible into one another; and, as a corollary, that it is impossible to obtain in any one form of this force more than its equivalent in the previous form. Now this is equally true of the agencies acting in society. It is quite possible to divert the power at present working out one result, to the working out of some other result. But you cannot make more of it, and you cannot have it for nothing. Just as much better as this particular thing is done, so much worse must another thing be done.

Or, changing the illustration, and regarding society as an organism, we may say that it is impossible artificially to use up social vitality for the more active performance of one function, without diminishing the activity with which other functions are performed. So long as society is let alone, its various structures will go on developing in due subordination to one another. If some of them are very imperfect, and make no appreciable progress towards efficiency, it is because still more important organs are equally imperfect, and because the growth of these involves cessation of growth elsewhere. Be sure, also, that whenever there arises a special necessity for the better performance of any one function, or for the establishment of some new function, Nature will respond. Instance, in proof of this, the increase of particular manufacturing towns and sea-ports, or the formation of incorporated companies. Is there a rising demand for some commodity of general consumption? Immediately the organ secreting that commodity becomes more active, absorbs more people, begins to enlarge, and secretes in greater abundance. To interfere with this process by producing premature development in any particular direction, is inevitably to disturb the due balance of organization, by causing somewhere else a corresponding atrophy. At any given time the amount of a society's vital force is fixed. Dependent as is that vital force on the extent to which men have acquired fitness for a co-operative life—upon the efficiency with which they can combine as elements of the social organism, we may be quite certain that, while their characters remain constant, nothing can increase its total quantity. We may be also certain that this total quantity can produce only its equivalent of results; and that no legislators can get more from it, although by wasting it they may get less.

Already, in treating of Poor-Laws and National Education, we have examined in detail the reactions by which these attempts at a multiplication of results are defeated. In the case of sanitary administrations, a similar reaction may be traced; showing itself, among other ways, in the checking of social improvements which demand popular enterprise.

Should proof of this be asked, it may be found in the contrast between English energy and Continental helplessness. English engineers (Manby, Wilson, and Co.) established the first gas-works in Paris, after the failure of a French company; and many of the gas-works throughout Europe have been constructed by Englishmen. An English engineer (Miller) introduced steam navigation on the Rhone; another English engineer (Pritchard) succeeded in ascending the Danube by steam, after the French and Germans had failed. The first steamboats on he Loire were built by Englishmen (Fawcett and Preston); the great suspension bridge at Pesth has been built by an Englishman (Tierney Clark); and an Englishman (Vignolles) is now building a still greater suspension bridge over the Dnieper. Many Continental railways have had Englishmen as consulting engineers; and in spite of the celebrated Mining College at Freyburg, several of the mineral fields along the Rhine have been opened up by English capital employing English skill. Now why is this? Why were our coaches so superior to the diligences and eilwagen of our neighbours? Why did our railway-system develop so much faster? Why are our towns better drained, better paved, and better supplied with water? There was originally no greater mechanical aptitude, and no greater desire to progress, in us than in the connate nations of Northern Europe. If anything, we were comparatively deficient in these respects. Early improvements in the arts of life

were imported. The germs of our silk and woollen manufactures came from abroad. The first waterworks in London were erected by a Dutchman. How happens it, then, that we have now reversed the relationship? Manifestly the change is due to difference of discipline. Having been left in a greater degree than others to manage their own affairs, the English people have become self-helping, and have acquired great practical ability. While, conversely, that comparative helplessness of the paternally-governed nations of Europe, illustrated in the above facts, and commented upon by Laing, in his *Notes of a Traveller,* and by other observers, is a natural result of the State-superintendence policy—is the reaction attendant on the action of official mechanisms—is the atrophy corresponding to some artificial hypertrophy.

One apparent difficulty accompanying the doctrine now contended for remains to be noticed. If sanitary administration by the State be wrong, because it implies a deduction from the citizen's property greater than is needful for maintaining his rights, then is sanitary administration by municipal authorities wrong also for the same reason. Be it by general government or by local government, the levying of compulsory rates for drainage, and for paving and lighting, is inadmissible, as indirectly making legislative protection more costly than necessary, or, in other words, turning it into aggression (p. 123); and if so, it follows that neither the past, present, nor proposed methods of securing the health of towns are equitable.

This seems an awkward conclusion; nevertheless, as deducible from our general principle, we have no alternative but to accept it. How streets and courts are rightly to be kept in order remains to be considered. Respecting sewage there would be no difficulty. Houses might readily be drained on the same mercantile principle that they are now supplied with water. It is probably that in the hands of a private company, the resulting manure would not only pay the cost of collection, but would yield a considerable profit. But if not, the return on the invested capital would be made up by charges to those whose houses were drained: the alternative of having their connexions with the main sewer stopped, being as good a security for payment as the analogous ones possessed by water and gas companies. Paving and lighting would properly fall to the management of house-owners. Were there no public provision for such conveniences, house-owners would quickly find it their interest to furnish them. Some speculative building society having set the example of improvement in this direction, competition would do the rest. Dwellings without proper footways before them, and with no lamps to show the tenants to their doors, would stand empty, when better accommodation was offered. And good paving and lighting having thus become essential, landlords would combine for the more economical supply of them.

To the objection that the perversity of individual landlords and the desire of some to take unfair advantage of the rest, would render such an arrangement impracticable, the reply is that in new suburban streets, not yet taken to by the authorities, such an arrangement is, to a considerable extent, already carried out, and would be much better carried out but for the consciousness that it is merely temporary. Moreover, no adverse inference could be drawn, were it even shown that for the present such an arrangement *is* impracticable. So, also, was personal freedom once. So once was representative government, and is still with many nations. As repeatedly pointed out, the practicability of recognizing men's rights is proportionate to the degree in which men have become moral. That an organization dictated by the law of equal freedom cannot yet be fully realized, is no proof of its imperfection: is proof only of *our* imperfection. And as, by diminishing this, the process of adaptation has already fitted us for institutions which were once too good for us, so will it go on to fit us for others that may be too good for us now.

THE
TWENTIETH
CENTURY

The streets of our country are in turmoil
The Universities are filled with students rebelling and rioting,
Communists are seeking to destroy our country
Russia is threatening us with her might
And the Republic is in danger.
Yes—danger from within and without.
We need law and order.
Without law and order our nation can not survive.

Adolph Hitler 1932

Joseph Stalin

In the decade following the death of Lenin in 1924, Joseph Stalin (1879-1953) gradually emerged as the absolute dictator of Soviet Russia. Although a loyal Marxist-Leninist, Stalin firmly believed that Socialism should first be a success in one country before world-wide revolution was attempted. Although Lenin had successfully established Marxian Socialism in Russia, it was left to Stalin to make the system work. He followed Lenin's New Economic Policy until 1928, when he introduced the first Five Year Plan. The basic idea of this plan, declared completed in 1932, was to build up heavy industry in Russia and move the peasants onto collective farms. In January 1934, the 17th All-Union Communist Party Congress was held in Moscow and Joseph Stalin, as Secretary General of the Communist Party, gave a report on developments under the Five Year Plan. The following selection contains excerpts from that report. Note that Stalin mentions specifically the battles which had gone on within the party and the state to make Communism a success and his discussion of the Marxist concept of equality. He concludes by cautioning the members of the party not to become complacent because of what has been accomplished, but to continue to fight for the principles of Marx, Engels and Lenin. The second selection contains several articles from the Constitution of the Union of Soviet Socialist Republics, promulgated in 1936 and currently in force in Russia. The first twelve articles give legal sanction to some basic principles of Marxian Socialism, while Articles 118 through 133 state the rights and duties of a citizen. Compare these rights with those found in he "Declaration of the Rights of Man and Citizen" and "The Bill of Rights."

THE POLITICAL AND SOCIAL DOCTRINE OF COMMUNISM

III. THE PARTY

I come now to the question of the Party.

The present Congress is taking place under the flag of the complete victory of Leninism, under the flag of the liquidation of the remnants of anti-Leninist groups.

The anti-Leninist Trotskyist group has been defeated and scattered. Its organizers are now hanging around the backyards of the bourgeois parties abroad.

The anti-Leninist Right deviationist group has been defeated and scattered. Its organizers long ago renounced their views and are now trying very hard to expiate the sins they committed against the Party.

The national deviationist groups have been defeated and scattered. Their organizers long ago became finally merged with the interventionist émigrés, or else have recanted.

The majority of the adherents of these anti-revolutionary groups have been compelled to admit that the line of the Party was right and have capitulated before the Party.

At the Fifteenth Party Congress it was still necessary to prove that the Party line was right and to wage a struggle against certain anti-Leninist groups; and at the Sixteenth Party Congress the last adherents of these groups had to be dispatched. At this Congress, however, there is nothing to prove and, perhaps, no one to beat. Everyone now sees that the line of the Party has conquered.

The policy of industrializing the country has conquered. Its results are obvious to everyone. What argument can be advanced against this fact?

The policy of liquidating the kulaks and of mass collectivization has conquered. Its results also are obvious to everyone. What argument can be advanced against that fact?

The experience of our country has shown that it

From Joseph Stalin "Report of the Work of the Central Committee of the Communist Party of the Soviet Union" from *The Political and Social Doctrine of Communism*, International Conciliation Pamphlet No. 305, December 1934, the Carnegie Endowment for International Peace. Used by Permission of Johnson Reprint Corporation.

is quite possible to build socialism in a single country taken separately. What argument can be advanced against that fact?

Evidently, all these successes, and primarily the victory of the Five-Year Plan, have utterly demoralized and smashed to atoms all and sundry anti-Leninist groups.

It must be admitted that the Party today is as united as it never has been before.

I. Problems of Ideological-Political Leadership

Does this mean, however, that the fight is ended and that the further offensive of socialism is to be abandoned as something superfluous?

No, it does not mean that.

Does that mean that all is well in the Party, that there will be no more deviations and that we can now rest on our laurels?

No, it does not mean that.

The enemies of the Party, the opportunists of all shades, the national-deviationists of all types, have been defeated. But remnants of their ideologies still live in the minds of individual members of the Party, and not infrequently they find expression. The Party must not be regarded as something isolated from the people who surround it. It lives and works in its environment. It is not surprising that not infrequently unhealthy moods penetrate the Party from without. And the soil for such moods undoubtedly still exists in our country, if only for the reason that certain intermediary strata of the population still exist in town and country and represent the medium which fosters such moods.

The Seventeenth Conference of our Party declared that one of the fundamental political tasks in connection with the fulfilment of the Second Five-Year Plan is "to overcome the survivals of capitalism in economy and in the minds of men." This is an absolutely correct idea. But can we say that we have already overcome all the survivals of capitalism in economy? No, we cannot say that. Still less reason would there be for saying that we have overcome the survivals of capitalism in the minds of men. This cannot be said, not only because the development of the mind of man lags behind his economic position, but also because the capitalist environment exists, which tries to revive and support the survivals of capitalism in economy and in the minds of the people of the U.S.S.R., and against which we, Bolsheviks, must always keep our powder dry.

It goes without saying that these survivals cannot but create a favorable soil for the revival of the ideology of the defeated anti-Leninist groups in the minds of individual members of our Party. Add to this the not very high theoretical level of the majority of the members of our Party, the weak ideological work of the Party organs and the fact that our Party workers are overburdened with purely practical work, which deprives them of the opportunity of augmenting their theoretical knowledge, and you will understand whence comes the confusion on a number of problems of Leninism that exists in the minds of individual members of the Party, which not infrequently penetrates our press, and which helps to revive the survivals of the ideology of the defeated anti-Leninist groups.

That is why we cannot say that the fight is ended, and that there is no longer any need for the policy of the socialist offensive.

A number of problems of Leninism could be taken to demonstrate how tenacious the survivals of the ideology of the defeated anti-Leninist groups are in the minds of certain Party members.

Take for example the question of building classless socialist society. The Seventeenth Party Conference declared that we are marching towards classless socialist society. It goes without saying that classless society cannot come by itself. It has to be won and built by the efforts of all the toilers, by strengthening the organs of the dictatorship of the proletariat, by extending the class struggle, by abolishing classes, by liquidating the remnants of the capitalist classes in battles with the enemy, both internal and external.

The thing is clear, one would think.

And yet, who does not know that the promulgation of this clear and elementary thesis of Leninism has given rise to not a little confusion and unhealthy moods among a certain section of Party members? The thesis—advanced as a slogan—about our advancing towards classless society is interpreted by them as a spontaneous process. And they begin to reason in the following way: if it is classless society, then we can relax the class struggle, we can relax the dictatorship of the proletariat and generally abolish the State, which in any case has got to die out soon. And they drop into a state of moon-calf ecstasy in the expectation that soon there will be no classes and therefore no class struggle, and therefore no cares and worries, and therefore it is possible to lay down our arms and retire—to sleep and to wait for the advent of classless society.

There can be no doubt that this confusion of mind and these moods are as like as two peas to the well-known views of the Right deviationists who believe that the old must automatically grow into the new, and that one fine day we shall wake up and find ourselves in socialist society.

As you see, the remnants of the ideology of the defeated anti-Leninist groups can be revived, and have not lost their tenacity by a long way.

It goes without saying that if this confusion of mind and these non-Bolshevik moods overcame the majority of our Party, the Party would find itself demobilized and disarmed. . . .

Every Leninist knows, that is, if he is a real Leninist, that equality in the sphere of requirements and personal life is a piece of reactionary petty-bourgeois stupidity worthy of a primitive sect of ascetics, but not of socialist society organized on Marxian lines, because we cannot demand that all people should have the same requirements and tastes, that all people shall live their individual lives in the same way. And finally, are not differences in requirements and in personal life preserved among the workers? Does that mean that the workers are more remote from socialism than the members of an agricultural commune?

These people evidently think that socialism calls for equality, for leveling the requirements and the personal lives of the members of society. Needless to say, such an assumption has nothing in common with Marxism, with Leninism. By equality Marxism means, not equality in personal requirements and personal life, but the abolition of classes, i.e., a) the equal emancipation of all toilers from exploitation after the capitalists have been overthrown and expropriated, b) the equal abolition for all of private property in the means of production after they have been transformed into the property of the whole of society, c) the equal duty of all to work according to their ability and the equal right of all toilers to receive according to the amount of work they have done (socialist society), d) the equal duty of all to work according to their ability and the equal right of all toilers to receive according to their requirements (communist society). And Marxism starts out with the assumption that people's tastes and requirements are not, and cannot be, equal in quality or in quantity, either in the period of socialism or in the period of communism.

That is the Marxian conception of equality.

Marxism has not recognized, nor does it recognize, any other equality.

To draw from this the conclusion that socialism calls for equality, for the leveling of the requirements of the members of society, for the leveling of their tastes and of their personal lives, that according to Marxism all should wear the same clothes, and eat the same dishes and in the same quantity—means talking banalities and slandering Marxism.

It is time it was understood that Marxism is opposed to leveling. Even in *The Manifesto of the Communist Party* Marx and Engels scourged primitive utopian socialism and described it as reactionary because it preached "universal asceticism and social leveling in its crudest form." In his *Mr. Dühring Revolutionizes Science*, Engels devotes a whole chapter to the withering criticism of the "radical equalitarian socialism" proposed by Duhring to counteract Marxian socialism. And Engels wrote:

> . . . the real content of the proletarian demand for equality is the demand for the abolition of classes. Any demand for equality which goes beyond that of necessity passes into absurdity.

Lenin said the same thing:

> Engels was a thousand times right when he wrote: any demand for equality which goes beyond the demand for the abolition of classes is a stupid and absurd prejudice. Bourgeois professors tried to use the argument about equality in order to expose us by saying that we wanted to make all men equal. They tried to accuse the Socialists of an absurdity that they themselves invented. But owing to their ignorance they did not know that the Socialists—and precisely the founders of modern scientific socialism, Marx and Engels—said: equality is an empty phrase unless by equality is meant the abolition of classes. We want to abolish classes, and in that respect we are in favor of equality. But the claim that we want to make all men equal to each other is an empty phrase and a stupid invention of the intellectuals. (Lenin's speech, *On Deceiving the People with Slogans About Liberty and Equality.*)

Clear, one would think.

Bourgeois writers are fond of depicting Marxian socialism like the old tsarist barracks, where everything was subordinated to the "principle" of equality. Marxists cannot be responsible for the ignorance and stupidity of bourgeois writers.

There cannot be any doubt that the confusion in the minds of individual members of the Party concerning Marxian socialism and their infatuation with the equalitarian tendencies of agricultural communes, are as like as two peas to the petty-bourgeois views of our Leftist blockheads who at one time idealized the agricultural commune to such an extent that they even tried to implant the commune in the factories where skilled and unskilled workers, each working at his trade, had to put his wages into the common fund which was then shared out equally. We know what harm these infantile equalitarian exercises of our Leftist block-heads caused our industry.

As you see, the remnants of the ideology of the defeated anti-Party groups still display rather considerable tenacity.

It goes without saying that if these Leftist views were to triumph in the Party, the Party would cease to be Marxian, and the collective farm movement would finally be disorganized.

Or take for example the question of the slogan: "make every collective farmer well-to-do." This slogan not only affects collective farmers; it affects the workers to a far larger extent, because we want to make all the workers well-to-do, to enable them to lead a well-to-do and cultured existence.

One would think the point was clear. There would have been no use overthrowing capitalism in October, 1917, and building socialism for a number of years if we are not going to secure a life of plenty for our people. Socialism means, not poverty and privation, but the abolition of poverty and privation, the organization of a well-to-do and cultured life for all members of society.

And yet, this clear and essentially elementary slogan has caused perplexity, muddle, and confusion among a certain section of our Party members. Is not this slogan, they ask, a reversion to the old slogan, "enrich yourselves" that was rejected by the Party? If everyone becomes well-to-do, they continue to argue, and the poor cease to be with us, whom can we Bolsheviks rely upon in our work? How shall we be able to work without the poor?

This may sound funny, but the existence of such näive and anti-Leninist views among a section of the members of the Party is an undoubted fact, which we must take note of.

Apparently, these people do not understand that a wide gulf lies between the slogan "enrich yourselves" and the slogan "make the collective farmers well-to-do." In the first place only individual persons or groups can enrich themselves, whereas the slogan concerning a well-to-do existence affects, not individual persons or groups, but all collective farmers. Secondly, individual persons or groups enrich themselves for the purpose of subjecting other people, and of exploiting them, whereas the slogan concerning the well-to-do existence of all collective farmers—with the means of production in the collective farms socialized—excludes all possibility of the exploitation of some persons by others. Thirdly, the slogan, "enrich yourselves," was issued in the period of the initial stage of the New Economic Policy, when capitalism was partly restored, when the kulak was strong, when individual peasant farming predominated in the country, and collective farming was in a rudimentary state, whereas the slogan, "make every collective farmer well-to-do," was issued in the last stage of N.E.P., when the capitalist elements in industry had been destroyed, the kulaks in the countryside crushed, individual peasant farming forced into the background and the collective farms transformed into the predominant form of agriculture. I need not mention that the slogan, "make every collective farmer well-to-do," is not isolated, but is inseparably connected with he slogan, "make all collective farms Bolshevik farms."

Is it not clear that in essence the slogan, "enrich yourselves," was a call for the restoration of capitalism, whereas the slogan, "make every collective farmer well-to-do," is a call to finally crush the last remnants of capitalism by increasing the economic power of the collective farms and by transforming all collective farmers into well-to-do toilers?

Is it not clear that there is not, nor can there be, anything in common between these two slogans?

The argument that Bolshevik work and socialism are inconceivable without the existence of the poor is so stupid that one finds it embarrassing to talk about it. The Leninists rely upon the poor when there are capitalist elements and the poor who are exploited by the capitalists. But when the capitalist elements are crushed and the poor are emancipated from exploitation, the task of the Leninists is not to perpetuate and preserve poverty and the poor—the premises of whose existence have already been destroyed—but to abolish poverty and to raise the poor to a well-to-do standard of living. It would be absurd to think that socialism can be built on the basis of poverty and privation, on the basis of reducing personal requirements and the standard of living to the level of the poor who, moreover, refuse to remain poor any longer and are pushing their way upward to a well-to-do standard of living. Who wants this sort of socialism? This would not be socialism, but a caricature of socialism. Socialism can only be built up on the basis of a rapid growth of the productive forces of society, on the basis of an abundance of products and goods, on the basis of a well-to-do standard of living of the toilers and on he basis of the rapid growth of culture. For socialism, Marxian socialism, means, not the cutting down of personal requirements, but their universal expansion; not the restriction, or the abstention from satisfying these requirements, but the all-sided and full satisfaction of all the requirements of culturally-developed working people.

There cannot be any doubt that this confusion in the minds of certain members of the Party concerning poverty and prosperity is a reflection of the views of our Leftist blockheads, who idealize the poor as the eternal bulwark of Bolshevism under all conditions, and who regard the collective farms as the arena of fierce class struggle.

As you see, here too, on this question, the remnants of the ideology of the defeated anti-Party groups have not yet lost their tenacity.

It goes without saying that had such blockheaded views achieved victory in our Party, the collective farms would not have achieved the successes they achieved during the past two years, and they would have fallen to pieces in a very short time. . . .

After this, can it be said that all is well in the Party?

Clearly, it cannot.

Our tasks in the sphere of ideological and political work are:

1) To raise the theoretical level of the Party to its proper plane;

2) To intensify ideological work in all the links of the Party;

3) To carry on unceasing propaganda of Leninism in the ranks of the Party;

4) To train the Party organizations and the non-Party *active* which surrounds them in the spirit of Leninist internationalism;

5) Not to gloss over, but boldly to criticize the deviations of certain comrades from Marxism-Leninism;

6) Systematically to expose the ideology and remnants of the ideology of trends that are hostile to Leninism. . . .

I have now come to the end of my report, comrades.

What conclusions must be drawn from it?

Everybody now admits that our successes are great and extraordinary. In a relatively short period of time our country has been transferred to the rails of industrialization and collectivization. The First Five-Year Plan has been successfully carried out. This rouses a sense of pride and increases the confidence of our workers in their own strength. This is all very good, of course. But successes sometimes have their dark side. They sometimes give rise to certain dangers which, if allowed to develop, may wreck the whole cause. There is, for example, the danger that some of our comrades may have their heads turned by these successes. There have been cases like that, as you know. There is the danger that certain of our comrades, having become intoxicated with success, will get swelled-headed and begin to sooth themselves with boastful songs, such as: "We care for nobody," "We'll knock everybody into a cocked hat,"etc. This is by no means excluded, comrades. There is nothing more dangerous than moods of this kind, because they disarm the Party and demobilize its ranks. If such moods were to predominate in our Party we would be faced with the danger of all our successes being wrecked. Of course, the First Five-Year Plan has been successfully carried out. This is true. But this does not, and cannot, end the matter, comrades. Before us is the Second Five-Year Plan, which we must also carry out, and also successfully. You know that plans are carried out in the struggle against difficulties, in the process of overcoming difficulties. That means that there will be difficulties and there will be a struggle against them. Comrades Molotov and Kuibyshev will tell you about the Second Five-Year Plan. From their reports you will see what great difficulties we will have to overcome in order to carry out this great plan. That means that we must not lull the Party but rouse its vigilance, we must not lull it to sleep but keep it in a state of fighting preparedness, not disarm but arm it, not demobilize it but keep it in a state of mobilization for the purpose of fulfilling the Second Five-Year Plan.

Hence, the first conclusion: *we must not allow ourselves to be carried away by the successes achieved, and must not get swelled-headed.*

We achieved successes because we had the correct guiding line of the Party, and because we were able to organize the masses for the purpose of applying this line. Needless to say, without these conditions we would not have achieved the successes we have achieved, and of which we are justly proud. But it is a very rare thing for ruling parties to have a correct line and to be able to apply it. Look at the countries which surround us: are there many ruling parties there that have a correct line and are able to apply it? Strictly speaking, there are no longer any such parties in the world, because they are all living without prospects, are wallowing in the chaos of crises, and see no road to lead them out of the swamp. Our Party alone knows where to lead the cause, and it is leading it forward successfully. What is our Party's superiority due to? It is due to the fact that it is a Marxian Party, a Leninist Party. It is due to the fact that it is guided in its work by the tenets of Marx, Engels, and Lenin. There cannot be any doubt that as long as we remain true to these tenets, as long as we have this compass, we will achieve successes in our work.

It is said that in the West, in some countries, Marxism has already been destroyed. It is said that it was destroyed by the bourgeois-nationalist trend known as fascism. That is nonsense, of course. Only those who are ignorant of history can talk like that. Marxism is the scientific expression of the fundamental interests of the working class. More than eighty years have passed since Marxism stepped into the arena. During this time scores and hundreds of bourgeois governments have tried to destroy Marxism. And what happened? Bourgeois governments have come and gone, but Marxism still goes on. And it is impossible to destroy the working class.

More than that, Marxism has achieved complete victory on one-sixth of the globe and achieved victory in the very country in which Marxism was considered to have been utterly destroyed.

It is not an accident that the country in which Marxism achieved complete victory is now the only country in the world which knows no crisis and unemployment, whereas in all other countries, including the fascist countries, crisis and unemployment have been reigning for four years. No, comrades, it is not an accident.

Yes, comrades, our successes are due to the fact that we worked and fought under the banner of Marx, Engels, and Lenin.

Hence the second conclusion: *to remain loyal to the end to the great banner of Marx, Engels, and Lenin.*

The working class of the U.S.S.R. is strong, not only because it has a Leninist Party that has been tried in battles; it is strong, not only because it enjoys the support of millions of toiling peasants; it is strong also because it is supported and assisted by the world proletariat. The working class of the U.S.S.R. is part of the world proletariat, its vanguard; and our republic—is the offspring of the world proletariat. There can be no doubt that if it had not been supported by the working class in the capitalist countries it would not have been able to retain power, it would not have secured for itself the conditions for socialist construction and hence, it would not have achieved the successes that it did achieve. International ties between the working class of the U.S.S.R. and the workers of the capitalist countries, the fraternal alliance between the workers of the U.S.S.R. and the workers of all countries—this is one of the corner-stones of the strength and might of the Republic of Soviets. The workers in the West say that the working class of the U.S.S.R. is the shock brigade of the world proletariat. That is very good. It shows that the world proletariat is prepared to continue to render all the support it can to the working class of the U.S.S.R. But this imposes a very serious duty upon us. It means that we must prove worthy of the honorable title of the shock brigade of the proletarians of all countries. It imposes upon us the duty to work better, and to fight better, for the final victory of socialism in our country, for the victory of socialism in all countries.

Hence, the third conclusion: *to remain loyal to the end to the cause of proletarian internationalism, to the cause of the fraternal alliance of the proletarians of all countries.*

Such are the conclusions.

Long live the great and invincible banner of Marx, Engels, and Lenin!

CONSTITUTION OF THE UNION OF SOVIET SOCIALIST REPUBLICS

ARTICLE 1

The Union of Soviet Socialist Republics is a socialist state of workers and peasants.

ARTICLE 2

The political foundation of the U.S.S.R. is the Soviets of Working People's Deputies, which grew and became strong as a result of the overthrow of the power of the landlords and capitalists and the attainment of the dictatorship of the proletariat.

ARTICLE 3

All power in the U.S.S.R. is vested in the working people of town and country as represented by the Soviets of Working People's Deputies.

From *Constitution Fundamental Law of the Union of Soviet Socialist Republics* as amended by the Seventh Session of the Fifth Supreme Soviet of the U.S.S.R. Foreign Languages Publishing House, 1962, Moscow.

ARTICLE 4

The economic foundation of the U.S.S.R. is the socialist system of economy and the socialist ownership of the instruments and means of production, firmly established as a result of the abolition of the capitalist system of economy, private ownership of the instruments and means of production, and the exploitation of man by man.

ARTICLE 5

Socialist property in the U.S.S.R. exists either in the form of state property (belonging to the whole people) or in the form of co-operative and collective-farm property (the property of collective farms or co-operative societies).

ARTICLE 6

The land, its mineral wealth, waters, forests, the factories and mines, rail, water and air transport facilities, the banks, means of communication, large state-organised agricultural enterprises (state farms, machine and tractor stations, etc.), as well as municipal enterprises and the bulk of the dwelling-houses in the cities and industrial localities, are state property, that is, belong to the whole people.

ARTICLE 7

The enterprises of the collective farms and co-operative organisations, with their livestock, buildings, implements, and output, are the common, socialist property of the collective farms and co-operative organisations.

Every collective-farm household, in addition to its basic income from the collective farm, has for its own use a small plot of land attached to the house and, as its own property, a dwelling-house, livestock, poultry, and minor agricultural implements—in conformity with the Rules of the Agricultural Artel.

ARTICLE 8

The land occupied by the collective farms is made over to them for their free use for an unlimited time, that is, in perpetuity.

ARTICLE 9

In addition to the socialist system of economy, which is the predominant form of economy in the U.S.S.R., the law permits the small private undertakings of individual peasants and handicraftsmen based on their own labour and precluding the exploitation of the labour of others.

ARTICLE 10

The right of citizens to own, as their personal property, income and savings derived from work, to own a dwelling house and a supplementary husbandry, articles of household and articles of personal use and convenience, is protected by law, as is also the right of citizens to inherit personal property.

ARTICLE 11

The economic life of the U.S.S.R. is determined and guided by the state economic plan for the purpose of increasing the wealth of society as a whole, steadily raising the material and cultural standards of the working people and strengthening the independence of the U.S.S.R. and its capacity for defence.

ARTICLE 12

Work in the U.S.S.R. is a duty and a matter of honour for every able-bodied citizen, in accordance with the principle: "He who does not work, neither shall he eat".

The principle applied in the U.S.S.R. is that of socialism: "From each according to his ability, to each according to his work".

. . . .

ARTICLE 118

Citizens of the U.S.S.R. have the right to work, that is, the right to guaranteed employment and payment for their work in accordance with its quantity and quality.

The right to work is ensured by the socialist organisation of the national economy, the steady growth of the productive forces of Soviet society, the elimination of the possibility of economic crises, and the abolition of unemployment.

ARTICLE 119

Citizens of the U.S.S.R. have the right to rest and leisure.

The right to rest and leisure is ensured by the establishment of a seven-hour day for industrial, office, and professional workers, the reduction of the working day to six hours for arduous trades and to four hours in shops where conditions of work are particularly arduous; by the institution of annual vacations with full pay for industrial, office, and professional workers, and by the provision of a wide network of sanatoriums, holiday homes and clubs for the accommodation of the working people.

ARTICLE 120

Citizens of the U.S.S.R. have the right to maintenance in old age and also in case of sickness or disability.

This right is ensured by the extensive development of social insurance of industrial, office, and professional workers at state expense, free medical service for the working people, and the provision of a wide network of health resorts for the use of the working people.

ARTICLE 121

Citizens of the U.S.S.R. have the right to education.

This right is ensured by universal compulsory eight-year education; by extensive development of secondary polytechnical education, vocational-technical education, and secondary special and higher education based on close ties between the school, real life and production activities; by the utmost development of evening and extramural education; by free education in all schools; by a system of state grants; by instruction in schools in the native language, and by the organisation of free vocational, technical and agronomic training for the working people in the factories, state farms, and collective farms.

ARTICLE 122

Women in the U.S.S.R. are accorded all rights on an equal footing with men in all spheres of economic, government, cultural, political, and other social activity.

The possibility of exercising these rights is ensured by women being accorded the same rights as men to work, payment for work, rest and leisure, social insurance and education, and also by state protection of the interests of mother and child, state aid to mothers of large families and to unmarried mothers, maternity leave with full pay, and the provision of a wide network of maternity homes, nurseries and kindergartens.

ARTICLE 123

Equality of rights of citizens of the U.S.S.R., irrespective of their nationality or race, in all spheres of economic, government, cultural, political and other social activity, is an indefeasible law.

Any direct or indirect restriction of the rights of, or, conversely, the establishment of any direct or indirect privileges for, citizens on account of their race or nationality, as well as any advocacy of racial or national exclusiveness or hatred and contempt, are punishable by law.

ARTICLE 124

In order to ensure to citizens freedom of conscience, the church in the U.S.S.R. is separated from the state, and the school from the church. Freedom of religious worship and freedom of anti-religious propaganda is recognised for all citizens.

ARTICLE 125

In conformity with the interests of the working people, and in order to strengthen the socialist system, the citizens of the U.S.S.R. are guaranteed by law:

a) freedom of speech;

b) freedom of the press;

c) freedom of assembly, including the holding of mass meetings;

d) freedom of street processions and demonstrations.

These civil rights are ensured by placing at the disposal of the working people and their organisations printing presses, stocks of paper, public buildings, the streets, communications facilities and other material requisites for the exercise of these rights.

ARTICLE 126

In conformity with the interests of the working people, and in order to develop the organisational initiative and political activity of the masses of the people, citizens of the U.S.S.R. are guaranteed the right to unite in public organisations: trade unions, co-operative societies, youth organisations, sport and defence organisations, cultural, technical and scientific societies; and the most active and politically-conscious citizens in the ranks of the working class, working peasants and working intelligentsia voluntarily unite in the Communist Party of the Soviet Union, which is the vanguard of the working people in their struggle to build communist society and is the leading core of all organisations of the working people, both public and state.

ARTICLE 127

Citizens of the U.S.S.R. are guaranteed inviolability of the person. No person may be placed under arrest except by decision of a court or with the sanction of a procurator.

ARTICLE 128

The inviolability of the homes of citizens and privacy of correspondence are protected by law.

ARTICLE 129

The U.S.S.R. affords the right of asylum to foreign citizens persecuted for defending the interests of the working people, or for scientific activities, or for struggling for national liberation.

ARTICLE 130

It is the duty of every citizen of the U.S.S.R. to abide by the Constitution of the Union of Soviet Socialist Republics, to observe the laws to maintain labour discipline, honestly to perform public duties, and to respect the rules of socialist society.

ARTICLE 131

It is the duty of every citizen of the U.S.S.R. to safeguard and fortify public, socialist property as the sacred and inviolable foundation of the Soviet system, as the source of the wealth and might of the country, as the source of the prosperity and culture of all the working people.

Persons committing offences against public, socialist property are enemies of the people.

ARTICLE 132

Universal military service is law.

Military service in the Armed Forces of the U.S.S.R. is the honourable duty of citizens of the U.S.S.R.

ARTICLE 133

To defend the country is the sacred duty of every citizen of the U.S.S.R. Treason to the Motherland—violation of the oath of allegiance, desertion to the enemy, impairing the military power of the state, espionage—is punishable with all the severity of the law as the most heinous of crimes.

Benito Mussolini

Benito Mussolini (1883-1945) was the founder of the Italian Fascist party after World War I. In his early life Mussolini had been a Socialist and was the editor of a prominent Socialist newspaper *il Popolo d'Italia.* At the beginning of the first World War, he began to agitate for the entry of Italy into the war; for this he was expelled from the Socialist party. He served in World War I and after the war, because of the chaotic conditions in Italy, gathered together a group of ex-soldiers who formed the nucleus of the Fascist party. The party grew in size and finally achieved power in 1922, after the famous "March on Rome." For ten years there was no stated program for the party; the doctrines of Fascism emerged after a decade of evolution. This particular selection, the "Political and Social Doctrine of Fascism," was written by Mussolini in 1932 for the *Enciclopedia Italiana* and is the first major statement of the beliefs and doctrines of the party. Note in particular Mussolini's views on Marxian Socialism, democracy, religion, and the position of the individual in the Fascist state. Following this essay by Mussolini is a story which appeared in *The New York Times* in 1927, reporting Winston Churchill's visit to Italy and his opinion of Mussolini's government. Do you think that Churchill was merely being polite or did he really believe what he said? How does Churchill's feeling toward Communism affect his ideas?

THE POLITICAL AND SOCIAL DOCTRINE OF FASCISM

When, in the now distant March of 1919, I summoned a meeting at Milan through the columns of the *Popolo d'Italia* of the surviving members of the Interventionist Party who had themselves been in action, and who had followed me since the creation of Fascist Revolutionary Party (which took place in the January of 1915), I had no specific doctrinal attitude in my mind. I had a living experience of one doctrine only—that of Socialism, from 1903-4 to the winter of 1914—that is to say, about a decade: and from Socialism itself, even though I had taken part in the movement first as a member of the rank and file and then later as a leader, yet I had no experience of its doctrine in practice. My own doctrine, even in this period, had always been a doctrine of action. A unanimous, universally accepted theory of Socialism did not exist after 1905, when the revisionist movement began in Germany under the leadership of Bernstein, while under pressure of the tendencies of the time, a Left Revolutionary movement also appeared, which though never getting further than talk in Italy, in Russian Socialistic circles laid the foundations of Bolshevism. Reformation, Revolution, Centralization—already the echoes of these terms are spent—while in the great stream of Fascism are to be found ideas which began with Sorel, Peguy, with Lagerdelle in the "Mouvement Socialiste," and with the Italian trades-union movement which throughout the period 1904-14 was sounding a new note in Italian Socialist circles (already weakened by the betrayal of Giolitti) through Olivetti's *Pagine Libre,* Orano's *La Lupa,* and Enrico Leone's *Divenire Sociale.*

After the War, in 1919, Socialism was already dead as a doctrine: it existed only as a hatred. There remained to it only one possibility of action, especially in Italy, reprisals against those who had desired the War and who must now be made to "expiate" its results. The *Popolo d'Italia* was then given the sub-title of "The newspaper of ex-service men and producers," and the word producers was already the expression of a mental attitude. Fascism was not the nursling of a doctrine worked out beforehand with detailed elaboration; it was born of the need for action and it was itself from the beginning practical rather than theoretical; it was not merely another political party but, even in the first two years, in opposition to all political parties

From Benito Mussolini "The Political and Social Doctrines of Fascism" from *International Conciliation Pamphlet* No. 306 January, 1935, The Carnegie Endowment for International Peace. Used by permission of Johnson Reprint Corporation.

as such, and itself a living movement. The name which I then gave to the organization fixed its character. And yet, if one were to re-read, in the now dusty columns of that date, the report of the meeting in which the *Fasci Italiana di combattimento* were constituted, one would there find no ordered expression of doctrine, but a series of aphorisms, anticipations, and aspirations which, when refined by time from the original ore, were destined after some years to develop into an ordered series of doctrinal concepts, forming the Fascist political doctrine—different from all others either of the past or the present day.

"If the bourgeoisie," I said then, "think that they will find lightning-conductors in us, they are the more deceived; we must start work at once. . . . We want to accustom the working-class to real and effectual leadership, and also to convince them that it is no easy thing to direct an industry or a commercial enterprise successfully. . . . We shall combat every retrograde idea, technical or spiritual. . . . When the succession to the seat of government is open, we must not be unwilling to fight for it. We must make haste; when the present regime breaks down, we must be ready at once to take its place. It is we who have the right to the succession, because it was we who forced the country into the War, and led her to victory. The present method of political representation cannot suffice, we must have a representation direct from the individuals concerned. It may be objected against this program that it is a return to the conception of the corporation, but that is no matter. . . . Therefore, I desire that this assembly shall accept the revindication of national trades-unionism from the economic point of view. . . . "

Now is it not a singular thing that even on this first day in the Piazza San Sepolcro that word "corporation" arose, which later, in the course of the Revolution, came to express one of the creations of social legislation at the very foundation of the régime?

The years which preceded the march to Rome were years of great difficulty, during which the necessity for action did not permit of research or any complete elaboration of doctrine. The battle had to be fought in the towns and villages. There was much discussion, but—what was more important and more sacred—men died. They knew how to die. Doctrine, beautifully defined and carefully elucidated, with headlines and paragraphs, might be lacking; but there was to take its place something more decisive—Faith. Even so, anyone who can recall the events of the time through the aid of books, articles, votes of congresses, and speeches of great and minor importance—anyone who knows how to research and weigh evidence—will find that the fundamentals of doctrine were cast during the years of conflict. It was precisely in those years that Fascist thought armed itself, was refined, and began the great task of organization. The problem of the relation between the individual citizen and the State; the allied problems of authority and liberty; political and social problems as well as those specifically national—a solution was being sought for all these while at the same time the struggle against Liberalism, Democracy, Socialism, and the Masonic bodies was being carried on, contemporaneously with the "punitive expedition." But, since there was inevitably some lack of system, the adversaries of Fascism have disingenuously denied that it had any capacity to produce a doctrine of its own, though that doctrine was growing and taking shape under their very eyes, even though tumultuously; first, as happens to all ideas in their beginnings, in the aspect of a violent and dogmatic negation, and then in the aspect of positive construction which has found its realization in the laws and institutions of the régime as enacted successively in the years 1926, 1927, and 1928.

Fascism is now a completely individual thing, not only as a régime but as a doctrine. And this means that today Fascism, exercising its critical sense upon itself and upon others, has formed its own distinct and peculair point of view, to which it can refer and upon which, therefore, it can act in the face of all problems, practical or intellectual, which confront the world.

And above all, Fascism, the more it considers and observes the future and the development of humanity quite apart from political considerations of the moment, believes neither in the possibility nor the utility of perpetual peace. It thus repudiates the doctrine of Pacifism—born of a renunciation of the struggle and an act of cowardice in the face of sacrifice. War alone brings up to its highest tension all human energy and puts the stamp of nobility upon the peoples who have the courage to meet it. All other trials are substitutes, which never really put men into the position where they have to make the great decision—the alternative of life or death. Thus a doctrine which is founded upon this harmful postulate of peace is hostile to Fascism. And thus hostile to the spirit of Fascism, though accepted for what use they can be in dealing with particular political situations, are all the international leagues and societies which, as history will show, can be scattered to the winds when once strong national feeling is aroused by any motive—sentimental, ideal, or practical. This anti-pacifist spirit is carried by Fascism even into the life of the individual; the proud motto of the *Squadrista*, "Me ne frego," written on the bandage of the wound, is an act of philosophy not only stoic, the summary of a doctrine not only political—it is the education to combat, the acceptation of the risks which combat implies, and a new way of life for Italy. Thus the Fascist accepts life and loves it, knowing nothing of and despising suicide: he rather conceives of life as duty and struggle and conquest, life which should be high and full, lived for oneself, but above all for others—those who are at hand and those who are far distant, contemporaries, and those who will come after.

This "demographic" policy of the régime is the result of the above premise. Thus the Fascist loves in actual fact his neighbor, but this "neighbor" is not merely a vague and undefined concept, this love for one's neighbor puts no obstacle in the way of necessary educational severity, and still less to differentiation of status and to physical distance. Fascism repudiates any universal embrace, and in order to live worthily in the community of civilized peoples watches its contemporaries with vigilant eyes, takes good note of their state of mind and, in the changing trend of their interests, does not allow itself to be deceived by temporary and fallacious appearances.

Such a conception of life makes Fascism the complete opposite of that doctrine, the base of so-called scientific and Marxian Socialism, the materialist conception of history; according to which the history of human civilization can be explained simply through the conflict of interests among the various social groups and by the change and development in the means and instruments of production. That the changes in the economic field—new discoveries of raw materials, new methods of working them, and the inventions of science—have their importance no one can deny; but that these factors are sufficient to explain the history of humanity excluding all others is an absurd delusion. Fascism, now and always, believes in holiness and in heroism; that is to say, in actions influenced by no economic motive, direct or indirect. And if the economic conception of history be denied, according to which theory men are no more than puppets, carried to and fro by the waves of chance, while the real directing forces are quite out of their control, it follows that the existence of an unchangeable and unchanging

class-war is also denied—the natural progeny of the economic conception of history. And above all Fascism denies that class-war can be the preponderant force in the transformation of society. These two fundamental concepts of Socialism being thus refuted, nothing is left of it but the sentimental aspiration—as old as humanity itself—towards a social convention in which the sorrows and sufferings of the humblest shall be alleviated. But here again Fascism repudiates the conception of "economic" happiness, to be realized by Socialism and, as it were, at a given moment in economic evolution to assure to everyone the maximum of well-being. Fascism denies the materialist conception of happiness as a possibility, and abandons it to its inventors, the economists of the first half of the nineteenth century: that is to say, Fascism denies the validity of the equation, well-being-happiness, which would reduce men to the level of animals, caring for one thing only—to be fat and well-fed—and would thus degrade humanity to a purely physical existence.

After Socialism, Fascism combats the whole complex system of democratic ideology, and repudiates it, whether in its theoretical premises or in its practical application. Fascism denies that the majority, by the simple fact that it is a majority, can direct human society; it denies that numbers alone can govern by means of a periodical consultation, and it affirms the immutable, beneficial, and fruitful inequality of mankind, which can never be permanently leveled through the mere operation of a mechanical process such as universal suffrage. The democratic régime may be defined as from time to time giving the people the illusion of sovereignty, while the real effective sovereignty lies in the hands of other concealed and irresponsible forces. Democracy is a régime nominally without a king, but it is ruled by many kings—more absolute, tyrannical, and ruinous than one sole king, even though a tyrant. This explains why Fascism, having first in 1922 (for reasons of expediency) assumed an attitude tending towards republicanism, renounced this point of view before the march to Rome; being convinced that the question of political form is not today of prime importance, and after having studied the examples of monarchies and republics past and present reached the conclusion that monarchy or republicanism are not to be judged, as it were, by an absolute standard; but that they represent forms in which the evolution—political, historical, traditional, or psychological—of a particular country has expressed itself. Fascism supersedes the antithesis monarchy or republicanism, while democracy still tarries beneath the domination of this idea, forever pointing out the insufficiency of the first and forever the praising of the second as the perfect régime. Today, it can be seen that there are republics, innately reactionary and absolutist, and also monarchies which incorporate the most ardent social and political hopes of the future.

"Reason and science," says Renan (one of the inspired pre-Fascists) in his philosophical meditations, "are products of humanity, but to expect reason as a direct product of the people and a direct result of their action is to deceive oneself by a chimera. It is not necessary for the existence of reason that everybody should understand it. And in any case, if such a decimation of truth were necessary, it could not be achieved in a low-class democracy, which seems as though it must of its very nature extinguish any kind of noble training. The principle that society exists solely through the well-being and the personal liberty of all the individuals of which it is composed does not appear to be conformable to the plans of nature, in whose workings the race alone seems to be taken into consideration, and the individual sacrificed to it. It is greatly to be feared that the last stage of such a conception of democracy (though I must hasten to point out that the term 'democracy' may be interpreted in various ways) would end in a condition of society in which a degenerate herd would have no other preoccupation but the satisfaction of the lowest desires of common men." Thus Renan. Fascism denies, in democracy, the absurd conventional untruth of political equality dressed out in the garb of collective irresponsibility, and the myth of "happiness" and indefinite progress. But, if democracy may be conceived in diverse forms—that is to say, taking democracy to mean a state of society in which the populace are not reduced to impotence in the State—Fascism may write itself down as "an organized, centralized, and authoritative democracy."

Fascism has taken up an attitude of complete opposition to the doctrines of Liberalism, both in the political field and the field of economics. There should be no undue exaggeration (simply with the object of immediate success in controversy) of the importance of Liberalism in the last century, nor should what was but one among many theories which appeared in that period be put forward as a religion for humanity for all time, present and to come. Liberalism only flourished for half a century. It was born in 1830 in reaction against the Holy Alliance, which had been formed with the object of diverting the destinies of Europe back to the period before 1789, and the highest point of its success was the year 1848, when even Pius IX was a Liberal. Immediately after that date it began to decay, for if the year 1848 was a year of light and hope, the following year, 1849, was a year of darkness and tragedy. The Republic of Rome was dealt a mortal blow by a sister republic—that of France—and in the same year Marx launched the gospel of the Socialist religion, the famous Communist Manifesto. In 1851 Napoleon III carried out his far from Liberal *coup d'état* and reigned in France until 1870, when he was deposed by a popular movement as the consequence of a military defeat which must be counted as one of the most decisive in history. The victor was Bismarck, who knew nothing of the religion of liberty, or the prophets by which that faith was revealed. And it is symptomatic that such a highly civilized people as the Germans were completely ignorant of the religion of liberty during the whole of the nineteenth century. It was nothing but a parenthesis, represented by that body which has been called "The ridiculous Parliament of Frankfort," which lasted only for a short period. Germany attained her national unity quite outside the doctrines of Liberalism—a doctrine which seems entirely foreign to the German mind, a mind essentially monarchic—while Liberalism is the logical and, indeed, historical forerunner of anarchy. The stages in the achievement of German unity are the three wars of '64, '66, and '70, which were guided by such "Liberals" as Von Moltke and Bismarck. As for Italian unity, its debt to Liberalism is completely inferior in contrast to that which it owes to the work of Mazzini and Garibaldi, who were not Liberals. Had it not been for the intervention of the anti-Liberal Napoleon, we should not have gained Lombardy; and without the help of the again anti-Liberal Bismarck at Sadowa and Sedan it is very probable that we should never have gained the province of Venice in '66, or been able to enter Rome in '70. From 1870 to 1914 a period began during which even the very high priests of the religion themselves had to recognize the gathering twilight of their faith—defeated as it was by the decadence of literature and atavism in practice— that is to say, Nationalism, Futurism, Fascism. The era of Liberalism, after having accumulated an infinity of Gordian knots, tried to untie them in the slaughter of the World War—and never has any religion demanded of its votaries such a monstrous sacrifice. Perhaps the Liberal Gods were athirst for blood? But now, today, the Liberal faith must shut the doors of its deserted temples, deserted because the peoples of the world realize that its worship—agnostic in the field of economics and indifferent in the field of politics and morals—will lead, as it has already led, to certain ruin. In addition to this, let it be pointed out that all the political hopes of the present day are anti-Liberal, and it is therefore supremely ridiculous to try to classify this sole creed as outside the judgment of history, as though history were a hunting ground reserved for the professors of Liberalism alone—as though Liberalism were the final unalterable verdict of civilization.

But the Fascist negation of Socialism, Democracy, and Liberalism must not be taken to mean that Fascism desires to lead the world back to the state of affairs before 1789, the date which seems to be indicated as the opening years of the succeeding semi-Liberal century: we do not desire to turn back; Fascism has not chosen De Maistre for its high-priest. Absolute monarchy has been and can never return, any more than blind acceptance of ecclesiastical authority.

So, too, the privileges of the feudal system "have been," and the division of society into castes impenetrable from outside, and with no inter-communication among themselves: the Fascist conception of authority has nothing to do with such a polity. A party which entirely governs a nation is a fact entirely new to history, there are no possible references or parallels. Fascism uses in its construction whatever elements in the Liberal, Social, or Democratic doctrines still have a living value; it maintains what may be called the certainties which we owe to history, but it rejects all the rest—that is to say, the conception that there can be any doctrine of unquestioned efficacy for all times and all peoples. Given that the nineteenth century was the century of Socialism, of Liberalism, and of Democracy, it does not necessarily follow that the twentieth century must also be a century of Socialism, Liberalism, and Democracy: political doctrines pass, but humanity remains; and it may rather be expected that this will be a century of authority, a century of the Left, a century of Fascism. For if the nineteenth century was a century of individualism (Liberalism always signifying individualism) it may be expected that this will be the century of collectivism, and hence the century of the State. It is a perfectly logical deduction that a new doctrine can utilize all the still vital elements of previous doctrines.

No doctrine has ever been born completely new, completely defined and owing nothing to the past; no doctrine can boast a character of complete originality; it must always derive, if only historically, from the doctrines which have preceded it and develop into further doctrines which will follow. Thus the scientific Socialism of Marx is the heir of the Utopian Socialism of Fourier, of the Owens and of Saint-Simon; thus again the Liberalism of the eighteenth century is linked with all the advanced thought of the seventeenth century, and thus the doctrines of Democracy are the heirs of the Encyclopedists. Every doctrine tends to direct human activity towards a determined objective; but the action of men also reacts upon the doctrine, transforms it, adapts it to new needs, or supersedes it with something else. A doctrine then must be no more exercise in words, but a living act; and thus the value of Fascism lies in the fact that it is veined with pragmatism, but at the same time has a will to exist and a will to power, a firm front in face of the reality of "violence."

The foundation of Fascism is the conception of the State, its character, its duty, and its aim. Fascism conceives of the State as an absolute, in comparison with which all individuals or groups are relative, only to be conceived of in their relation to the State. The conception of the Liberal State is not that of a directing force, guiding the play and development, both material and spiritual, of a collective body, but merely a force limited to the function of recording results: on the other hand, the Fascist State is itself conscious, and has itself a will and a personality—thus it may be called the "ethic" State. In 1929, at the first five-yearly assembly of the Fascist régime, I said:

"For us Fascists, the State is not merely a guardian, preoccupied solely with the duty of assuring the personal safety of the citizens; nor is it an organization with purely material aims, such as to guarantee a certain level of well-being and peaceful conditions of life; for a mere council of administration would be sufficient to realize such objects. Nor is it a purely political creation, divorced from all contact with the complex material reality which makes up the life of the individual and the life of the people as a whole. The State, as conceived of and as created by Fascism, is a spiritual and moral fact in itself, since its political, juridical, and economic organization of the nation is a concrete thing: and such an organization must be in its origins and development a manifestation of the spirit. The State is the guarantor of security both internal and external, but it is also the custodian and transmitter of the spirit of the people, as it has grown up through the centuries in language, in customs, and in faith. And the State is not only a living reality of the present, it is also linked with the past and above all with the future, and thus transcending the brief limits of individual life, it represents the immanent spirit of the nation. The forms in which States express themselves may change, but the necessity for such forms is eternal. It is the State which educates its citizens in civic virtue, gives them a consciousness of their mission and welds them into unity; harmonizing their various interests through justice, and transmitting to future generations the mental conquests of science, of art, of law and the solidarity of humanity. It leads men from primitive tribal life to that highest expression of human power which is Empire: it links up through the centuries the names of those of its members who have died for its existence and in obedience to its laws, it holds up the memory of the leaders who have increased its territory and the geniuses who have illumined it with glory as an example to be followed by future generations. When the conception of the State declines, and disunifying and centrifugal tendencies prevail, whether of individuals or of particular groups, the nations where such phenomena appear are in their decline."

From 1929 until today, evolution, both political and economic, has everywhere gone to prove the validity of these doctrinal premises. Of such gigantic importance is the State. It is the force which alone can provide a solution to the dramatic contradictions of capitalism, and that state of affairs which we call the crisis can only be dealt with by the State, as between other States. Where is the shade of Jules Simon, who in the dawn of Liberalism proclaimed that, "The State must labor to make itself unnecessary, and prepare the way for its own dismissal"? Or of McCulloch, who, in the second half of the last century, affirmed that the State must guard against the danger of governing too much? What would the Englishman, Bentham, say today to the continual and inevitably-invoked intervention of the State in the sphere of economics, while according to his theories industry should ask no more of the State than to be left in peace? Or the German, Humboldt, according to whom the "lazy" State should be considered the best? It is true that the second wave of Liberal economists were less extreme than the first, and Adam Smith himself opened the door—if only very cautiously—which leads to State intervention in the economic field: but whoever says Liberalism implies individualism, and whoever says Fascism implies the State. Yet the Fascist State is unique, and an original creation. It is not reactionary, but revolutionary, in that it anticipates the solution of the universal political problems which elsewhere have to be settled in the political field by the rivalry of parties, the excessive power of the parliamentary régime and the irresponsibility of political assemblies; while it meets the problems of the economic field by a system of syndicalism which is continually increasing in importance, as much in the sphere of labor as of industry: and in the moral field enforces order, discipline, and obedience to that which is the determined moral code of the country. Fascism desires the State to be a strong and organic body, at the same time reposing upon broad and popular support. The Fascist State has drawn into itself even the economic activities of the nation, and, through the corporative social and educational institutions created by it, its influence reaches every aspect of the national life and includes, framed in their respective organizations, all the political, economic and spiritual forces of the nation. A State which reposes upon the support of millions of individuals who recognize its authority, are continually conscious of its power and are ready at once to serve it, is not the old tyrannical State of the medieval lord nor has it anything in common with the absolute governments either before or after 1789. The individual in the Fascist State is not annulled but rather multiplied, just in the same way that a soldier in a regiment is not diminished but rather increased by the number of his comrades. The Fascist State organizes the nation, but leaves a sufficient margin of liberty to the individual; the latter is deprived of all useless and possibly harmful freedom, but retains what is essential; the deciding power in this question cannot be the individual, but the State alone.

The Fascist State is not indifferent to the fact of religion in general, or to that particular and positive faith which is Italian Catholicism. The State professes no theology, but a morality, and in the Fascist State religion is considered as one of the deepest manifestations of the spirit of man, thus it is not only respected but defended and protected. The Fascist State has never tried to create its own God, as at one moment Robespierre and the wildest extremists of the Convention tried to do; nor does it vainly seek to obliterate religion from the hearts of men as does Bolshevism: Fascism respects the God of the ascetics, the saints and heroes, and equally, God as He is perceived and worshipped by simple people.

The Fascist State is an embodied will to power

and government: the Roman tradition is here an ideal of force in action. According to Fascism, government is not so much a thing to be expressed in territorial or military terms as in terms of morality and the spirit. It must be thought of as an empire—that is to say, a nation which directly or indirectly rules other nations, without the need for conquering a single square yard of territory. For Fascism, the growth of empire, that is to say the expansion of the nation, is an essential manifestation of vitality, and its opposite a sign of decadence. Peoples which are rising, or rising again after a period of decadence, are always imperialist; any renunciation is a sign of decay and of death. Fascism is the doctrine best adapted to represent the tendencies and the aspirations of a people, like the people of Italy, who are rising again after many centuries of abasement and foreign servitude. But empire demands discipline, the coordination of all forces and a deeply felt sense of duty and sacrifice: this fact explains many aspects of the practical working of the régime, the character of many forces in the State, and the necessarily severe measures which must be taken against those who would oppose this spontaneous and inevitable movement of Italy in the twentieth century, and would oppose it by recalling the outworn ideology of the nineteenth century—repudiated wheresoever there has been the courage to undertake great experiements of social and political has been the courage to undertake great experiments of social and political direction, and of order. If every age has its own characteristic doctrine, there are a thousand signs which point to Fascism as the characteristic doctrine of our time. For if a doctrine must be a living thing, this is proved by the fact that Fascism has created a living faith; and that this faith is very powerful in the minds of men, is demonstrated by those who suffered and died for it. demonstrated by those who have suffered and died for it.

Fascism has henceforth in the world the universality of all those doctrines which, in realizing themselves, have represented a stage in the history of the human spirit.

CHURCHILL EXTOLS FASCISMO FOR ITALY

"No political issue," he said, "can be judged apart from its atmosphere and environment. If I had been an Italian I am sure I would have been wholeheartedly from start to finish with Fascismo's triumphant struggle against the bestial appetite and passions of Leninism. But in England we have not yet had to face this danger in the same deadly form. We have our own way of doing things. But that we shall succeed in grapling with communism and choking the life out of it, of that I am absolutely sure." He also spoke of the international aspects of Fascismo, saying it rendered a service to the whole world in showing it how to deal with communism "It proved the necessary antidote to the communist poison," he added.

Referring to Premier Mussolini, Mr. Churchill said "I could not help being charmed, as so many other prople have been, by his gentle, simple bearing and his calm, detached poise, despite so many burdens and dangers. Anyone could see he thought of nothing but the lasting good, as he understood it, of the Italian people and that no lesser interest was of the slightest concern to him."

Adolph Hitler

Adolph Hitler (1889-1945), a native Austrian, founded the National Socialist German Workers Party, became the absolute dictator of Germany and, by 1940, ruler of practically all of Europe. Early in his life he developed a hatred for the Jews, Marxian Socialism, communism, and all races in the world not classified as Aryan. Shortly after World War I, Adolph Hitler joined with six others to form the Nazi Party and in February, 1920, Hitler published the twenty-five point program of the Nazi Party. Remember while reading these points that although the Fascist party did not develop its program until 1932, eleven years after it had been in power, the Nazi party had a program thirteen years *before* it achieved political power. In 1923 Adolph Hitler attempted to overthrow the government of the state of Bavaria, but was unsuccessful. He was arrested, tried and sentenced to a short term in prison, during which he completed most of his autobiography, *Mein Kampf* (My Battle). Remember that one of the fundamental points of National Socialism was the purity of the blood of all good Germans. In the second selection, a brief synopsis of a speech given by Hitler in 1931, note the promises Hitler made to the people of Germany if he and his party gained power. The third selection presents the famous Nuremberg Laws, promulgated in September, 1935, as first reported in *The New York Times.* Although additions and refinements were made at later dates, this is the original attempt of a nation to achieve racial purity through legislation.

TWENTY-FIVE POINTS OF THE NATIONAL SOCIALIST GERMAN WORKERS PARTY

The Programme of the Party of Hitler: The National Socialist German Workers' Party and Its General Conceptions, by Gottfried Feder

The National Socialist German Workers' Party at a great mass-meeting on February 25th, 1920, in the Hofbräuhaus-Festsaal in Munich announced their Programme to the world.

In section 2 of the Constitution of our Party this Programme is declared to be inalterable.

THE PROGRAMME

The Programme of the German Workers' Party is limited as to period. The leaders have no intention, once the aims announced in it have been achieved, of setting up fresh ones, merely in order to increase the discontent of the masses artificially, and so ensure the continued existence of our Party.

1. We demand the union of all Germans to form a Great Germany on the basis of the right of the self-determination enjoyed by nations.

2. We demand equality of rights for the German People in its dealings with other nations, and abolition of the Peace Treaties of Versailles and St. Germain.

3. We demand land and territory (colonies) for the nourishment of our people and for settling our superfluous population.

4. None but members of the nation may be citizens of the State. None but those of German blood, whatever their creed, may be members of the nation. No Jew, therefore, may be a member of the nation.

5. Anyone who is not a citizen of the State may live in Germany only as a guest and must be regarded as being subject to foreign laws.

6. The right of voting on the State's government and legislation is to be enjoyed by the citizen of the State alone. We demand therefore that all official appointments, of whatever kind, whether

From *National Socialism Basic Principles, Their Application by the Nazi Party's Foreign Organization, and the Use of Germans Abroad for Nazi Aims.* Prepared in the Special Unit of the Division of European Affairs by Raymond E. Murphy, Francis B. Stevens, Howard Trivers and Joseph M. Roland. United States Government Printing Office Washington: 1943.

in the Reich, in the country, or in the smaller localities, shall be granted to citizens of the State alone.

We oppose the corrupting custom of Parliament of filling posts merely with a view to party considerations, and without reference to character or capability.

7. We demand that the State shall make it its first duty to promote the industry and livelihood of citizens of the State. If it is not possible to nourish the entire population of the State, foreign nationals (non-citizens of the State) must be excluded from the Reich.

8. All non-German immigration must be prevented. We demand that all non-Germans, who entered Germany subsequent to August 2nd, 1914, shall be required forthwith to depart from the Reich.

9. All citizens of the State shall be equal as regards rights and duties.

10. It must be the first duty of each citizen of the State to work with his mind or with his body. The activities of the individual may not clash with the interests of the whole, but must proceed within the frame of the community and be for the general good.

We demand therefore:

11. Abolition of incomes unearned by work.

ABOLITION OF THE THRALDOM OF INTEREST

12. In view of the enormous sacrifice of life and property demanded of a nation by every war, personal enrichment due to a war must be regarded as a crime against the nation. We demand therefore ruthless confiscation of all war gains.

13. We demand nationalisation of all businesses which have been up to the present formed into companies (Trusts).

14. We demand that the profits from wholesale trade shall be shared out.

15. We demand extensive development of provision for old age.

16. We demand creation and maintenance of a healthy middle class, immediate communalisation of wholesale business premises, and their lease at a cheap rate to small traders, and that extreme consideration shall be shown to all small purveyors to the State, district authorities and smaller localities.

17. We demand land-reform suitable to our national requirements, passing of a law for confiscation without compensation of land for communal purposes; abolition of interest on land loans, and prevention of all speculation in land.[1]

We demand ruthless prosecution of those whose activities are injurious to the common interest. Sordid criminals against the nation, usurers, profiteers, etc. must be punished with death, whatever their creed or race.

19. We demand that the Roman Law, which serves the materialistic world order, shall be replaced by a legal system for all Germany.

20. With the aim of opening to every capable and industrious German the possibility of higher education and of thus obtaining advancement, the State must consider a thorough re-construction of our national system of education. The curriculum of all educational establishments must be brought into line with the requirements of practical life. Comprehension of the State idea (State sociology) must be the school objective, beginning with the first dawn of intelligence in the pupil. We demand development of the gifted children of poor parents, whatever their class or occupation, at the expense of the State.

21. The State must see to raising the standard of health in the nation by protecting mothers and infants, prohibiting child labour, increasing bodily efficiency by obligatory gymnastics and sports laid down by law, and by extensive support of clubs engaged in the bodily development of the young.

22. We demand abolition of a paid army and formation of a national army.

23. We demand legal warfare against conscious political lying and its dissemination in the Press. In order to facilitate creation of a German national Press we demand:

(a) that all editors of newspapers and their assistants, employing the German language, must be members of the nation;

(b) that special permission from the State shall be necessary before non-German newspapers may appear. These are not necessarily printed in the German language;

(c) that non-Germans shall be prohibited by law from participation financially in or influencing German newspapers, and that the penalty for

---

1. On April 13th, 1928, Adolf Hitler made the following declaration:

It is necessary to reply to the false interpretation on the part of our opponents of Point 17 of the Programme of the N.S.D.A.P.

Since the N.S.D.A.P. admits the principle of private property, it is obvious that the expression "confiscation without compensation" merely refers to possible legal powers to confiscate, if necessary, land illegally acquired, or not administered in accordance with national welfare. It is directed in accordance with national welfare. It is directed in the first instance against the Jewish companies which speculate in land.

MUNICH, *April 13th 1928.*

(signed) ADOLF HITLER.

contravention of the law shall be suppression of any such newspaper, and immediate deportation of the non-German concerned in it.

It must be forbidden to publish papers which do not conduce to the national welfare. We demand legal prosecution of all tendencies in art and literature of a kind likely to disintegrate our life as a nation, and the suppression of institutions which militate against the requirements above-mentioned.

24. We demand liberty for all religious denominations in the State, so far as they are not a danger to it and do not militate against the moral feelings of the German race.

The Party, as such, stands for positive Christianity, but does not bind itself in the matter of creed to any particular confession. It combats the Jewish-materialist spirit within us and without us,

and is convinced that our nation can only achieve permanent health from within on the principle:

THE COMMON INTEREST BEFORE SELF

25. That all the fore-going may be realised we demand the creation of strong central power of the State. Unquestioned authority of the politically centralised Parliament over the entire Reich and its organisations; and formation of Chambers for classes and occupations for the purpose of carrying out the general laws promulgated by the Reich in the various States of the confederation.

The leaders of the Party swear to go straight forward—if necessary to sacrifice their lives—in securing fulfilment of the foregoing Points.

MUNICH, *February 24th, 1920.*

A SPEECH BY ADOLPH HITLER

What will be done if our party gets power? The world must not expect fireworks from me, the contrary is the case. True, Germany, which is on its sick bed today, will need an entirely different treatment from that prescribed by the Versailles quack doctors since 1919.

As will be remembered Germany's reputation as a commercial nation of the first order before the war was based on Germany's progressive conservatism and her solid honesty was almost a proverbial trademark. One of my chief aims is to restore the world wide credit of German commerce, industry and finance.

It must not be believed that Germany and I stand for anything but the old forgotten virtues of our forefathers, the frugality, inner discipline and honesty which are the cornerstones of any state

and commonwealth. . . . Of course things in Germany must be reshaped entirely. You must realize the masses who are going to sweep our delegates into control are thoroughly disgusted and disappointed with all events since Germany signed the Versaille Treaty. Those millions behind me today are not expecting me to preserve the present system. Quite the contrary is the case. They are yearning for a new state, new ideals and heroic conceptions instead of the banal platitudes our parliamentarianism has bestowed on them these last years. Those masses want to feel some one single-head is responsible and not the ubiquitous anonymity of the state bourgeoise party system.

From *The New York Times*, Tuesday, December 8, 1931. © 1931 by The New York Times Company. Reprinted by permission.

NUREMBERG LAWS

National Socialist Germany definitely flung down the gauntlet before the feet of Western liberal opinion tonight when the Reichstag, assembled for a special session here (Nuremberg) in connection with the "Party Day of Freedom," decreed a series of laws that put Jews beyond the legal and social pale of the German nation and in token of this act proclaimed the Swastika banner to be the sole flag of the German Reich. . . .

The new laws provide: (1) German citizenship with full political rights depend on the special

grant of a Reich citizenship Charter, to be given only to those of German or racially related blood who have proved by their attitude that they are willing and fit loyally to serve the German people and the Reich.

This deprives Jews of German citizenship, it leaves them to the status of "state members," and Germans found undeserving of the Reich citizen-

From *The New York Times*, Monday, September 16, 1935. © 1935 by The New York Times Company. Reprinted by permission.

ship may likewise be reduced to this status, which, among other disadvantages entails loss of the vote. (2) Marriages between Jews and citizens of German or racially related blood as well as extra marital sexual relations between them, are forbidden and will be punished by penal servitude or imprisonment. Jews must not engage feminine domestic help of German or racially related blood under 45 years old. Jews likewise are forbidden to show the German national flag, but may under protection of the state show the Jewish colors of white and blue. Violations of the last two provisions are punishable by imprisonment up to one year or a fine or both. (3) The Reich or national flag is the Swastika flag, which is also the flag of commerce to be flown by German merchant ships. . . .

These laws, which General Goering himself called momentous, were introduced with speeches by Hitler and General Goering and adopted unanimously and with many cheers by the Reichstag, which by like unanimity and cheers rendered itself voiceless at the beginning of the session.

At the request of Dr. Wilhelm Frick, Minister of the Interior, the Reichstag abolished its own rules of procedure and placed itself "under the principle of leadership," to be exercised by General Goering. This motion is as important as any of the laws passed, for it formally abolished the Reichstag as a deliberative body and reduced it to a mere division of the National Socialist Party. That, Dr. Frick explained, brought the Reichstag in step with the new epoch.

Friedrich Nietzsche

Friedrich Nietzsche (1844-1900) is perhaps the most misunderstood thinker of modern times. Yet he saw the direction of western civiliation more clearly than most men. The place to begin with Nietzsche is his attitude toward Christianity. He considered Christianity to be a religion for the weak; Christianity denied life rather than affirming life. Christian morality was a morality for slaves. Meekness, humility and the other Christian virtues were devices used by the weak to disarm and destroy the strong, to bring the strong down to the level of the weak. Christianity, then, was responsible for the decadent condition of western civilization. Yet, ironically, western man had killed God. Nietzsche expressed his unqualified atheism with his famous dictum—"God is dead." These aspects of his thought are illustrated in the first part of the reading below. The second portion consists of two extracts from his *Thus Spake Zarathustra*. Zarathustra tells man what he must do now that there can be no faith in the supernatural. Since God is dead, there can be no cosmic meaning to life. There are no longer any absolutes. Therefore, man must overcome himself—he must raise himself above human nature if he is to find meaning in life. Nietzsche meant that man must rise above what his culture has made him. The man who does so Zarathustra calls the "overman." (Overman is a better translation of the German word Übermensch than the term Superman as used in the text by the translator). The overman has the will to live. He will rise above traditional values, and thus will rescue his decadent civilization. Finally, some myths about Nietzsche should be laid to rest. First, he did not go insane because of his atheism, but rather because of a syphilitic condition contracted in his youth. Furthermore, he was neither racist nor anti-Semitic, despite the perversion of his thought by some theorists of National Socialism. He deplored nationalism and militarism. He did not urge a super race; his overman was a spiritual giant. When properly understood, it is clear that Nietzsche was the prophet of twentieth-century nihilism, of totalitarianism and the less appealing aspects of modern mass society. Prophets, however, do not make their prophesies come true. They only prophesy.

THE WILL TO POWER

152.

The physiology of Nihilistic religions. —All in all, the *Nilhilistic* religions are *systematised histories of sickness* described in religious and moral terminology.

In pagan cultures it is around the interpretation of the great annual cycles that the religious cult turns; in Christianity it is around a cycle of *paralytic phenomena.*

153.

This *Nihilistic* religion gathers together all the *decadent elements* and things of like order which it can find in antiquity, viz.:—

(*a*) The *weak* and the *botched* (the refuse of the ancient world, and that of which it rid itself with most violence).

(*b*) Those who are *morally obsessed* and *anti-pagan.*

(*c*) Those who are *weary of politics* and indifferent (the *blasé* Romans), the *denationalised,* who know not what they are.

(*d*) Those who are tired of themselves—who are happy to be party to a subterranean conspiracy.

From Friedrich Nietzsche, *The Will to Power,* Volume I translated by Anthony M. Ludovici, Vol. 14 of *The Complete Works of Friedrich Nietzsche,* General editor, Oscar Levy [1909-1911] New York: Russell & Russell, 1964, Used by permission.

154.

Buddha versus *Christ.*—Among the Nihilistic religions, Christianity and *Buddhism* may always be sharply distinguished. *Buddhism* is the expression of a *fine evening,* perfectly sweet and mild—it is a sort of gratitude towards all that lies hidden, including that which it entirely lacks, viz., bitterness, disillusionment, and resentment. Finally it possesses lofty intellectual love; it has got over all the subtlety of philosophical contradictions, and is even resting after it, though it is precisely from that source that it derives its intellectual glory and its glow as of a sunset (it originated in the higher classes).

Christianity is a degenerative movement, consisting of all kinds of decaying and excremental elements: it is *not* the expression of the downfall of a race, it is, from the root, an agglomeration of all the morbid elements which are mutually attractive and which gravitate to one another. . . . It is therefore *not* a national religion, *not* determined by race: it appeals to the disinherited everywhere; it consists of a foundation of resentment against all that is successful and dominant: it is in need of a symbol which represents the damnation of everything successful and dominant. It is opposed to every form of *intellectual* movement, to all philosophy: it takes up the cudgels for idiots, and utters a curse upon all intellect. Resentment against those who are gifted, learned, intellecutally independent: in all these it suspects the element of success and domination.

. . . .

185.

The *"Christian Ideal"* put on the stage with Jewish astuteness—these are the fundmental *psychological forces* of its "nature":—

Revolt against the ruling spiritual powers;

The attempt to make those virtues which facilitate the *happiness of the lowly,* a standard of all values—in fact, to call *God* that which is no more than the self-preservative instinct of that class of man possessed of least vitality;

Obedience and absolute *abstention* from war and resistance, justified by this ideal;

The love of one another as a result of the love of God.

The trick: The *denial* of all *natural mobilia,* and their transference to the spiritual world beyond . . . the exploitation of *virtue* and its *veneration* for wholly interested motives, gradual *denial* of virtue in everything that is not Christian.

. . . .

248.

Christian moral quackery.—Pity and contempt succeed each other at short intervals, and at the sight of them I feel as indignant as if I were in the presence of the most despicable crime. Here error is made a duty—a virtue, misapprehension has become a knack, the destructive instinct is systematised under the name of "redemption"; here every operation becomes a wound, an amputation of those very organs whose energy would be the prerequisite to a return of health. And in the best of cases no cure is effected; all that is done is to exchange one set of evil symptoms for another set. . . . And this pernicious nonsense, this systematised profanation and castration of life, passes for holy and sacred; to be in its service, to be an instrument of this art of healing—that is to say, to be a priest, is to be rendered distinguished, reverent, holy, and sacred. God alone could have been the Author of this supreme art of healing; redemption is only possible as a revelation, as an act of grace, as an unearned gift, made by the Creator Himself.

Proposition I.: Spiritual healthiness is regarded as morbid, and creates suspicion. . . .

Proposition II.: The prerequisites of a strong, exuberant life—strong desires and passions—are reckoned as objections against strong and exuberant life.

Proposition III.: Everything which threatens danger to man, and which can overcome and ruin him, is evil, must be rejected—and should be torn root and branch from his soul.

Proposition IV.: Man converted into a weak creature, inoffensive to himself and others, crushed by humility and modesty, and conscious of his weakness,—in fact, the "sinner,"—this is the desirable type, and one which one can *produce* by means of a little spiritual surgery. . . .

THE JOYFUL WISDOM

125.

The Madman.—Have you ever heard of the madman who on a bright morning lighted a lantern and ran to the market-place calling out unceasingly: "I seek God! I seek God!"—As there were many people standing about who did not believe in God, he caused a great deal of amusement. Why! is he lost? said one. Has he strayed away like a child? said another. Or does he keep himself hidden? Is he afraid of us? Has he taken a sea-voyage? Has he emigrated?—the people cried out laughingly, all in a hubbub. The insane man jumped into their midst and transfixed them with his glances. "Where is God gone?" he called out. "I mean to tell you! *We have killed him,*—you and I! We are all his murderers! But how have we done it? How were we able to drink up the sea? Who gave us the sponge to wipe away the whole horizon? What did we do when we loosened this earth from its sun? Whither does it now move? Whither do we move? Away from all suns? Do we not dash on unceasingly? Backwards, sideways, forwards, in all directions? Is there still an above and below? Do we not stray, as through infinite nothingness? Does not empty space breathe upon us? Has it ot become colder? Does not night come on continually, darker and darker? Shall we not have to light lanterns in the morning? Do we not hear the noise of the grave-diggers who are burying God? Do we not smell the divine putrefaction?—for even Gods putrefy! God is dead! God remains dead! And we have killed him! How shall we console ourselves, the most murderous of all murderers? The holiest and the mightiest that the world has hitherto possessed, has bled to death under our knife,—who will wipe the blood from us? With what water could we cleanse ourselves? What lustrums, what sacred games shall we have to devise? Is not the magnitude of this deed too great for us? Shall we not ourselves have to become Gods, merely to seem worthy of it? There never was a greater event,—and on account of it, all who are born after us belong to a higher history than any history hitherto!"—Here the madman was silent and looked again at his hearers; they also were silent and looked at him in surprise. At last he threw his lantern on the ground, so that it broke in pieces and was extinguished. "I come too early," he then said, "I am not yet at the right time. This prodigious event is still on its way, and is travelling,—it has not yet reached men's ears. Lightning and thunder need time, the light of the stars needs time, deeds need time, even after they are done, to be seen and heard. This deed is as yet further from them than the furthest star,—*and yet they have done it!*"—It is further stated that the madman made his way into different churches on the same day, and there intoned his *Requiem aeternam deo.* When led out and called to account, he always gave the reply: "What are these churches now, if they are not the tombs and monuments of God?"—

From Friedrich Nietzsche, *The Joyful Wisdom,* translated by Thomas Common, Volume 10 of *The Complete Works of Friedrich Nietzsche,* General Editor, Oscar Levy [1909-1911] New York: Russell & Russell, 1964. Used by permission.

THUS SPAKE ZARATHUSTRA

ZARATHUSTRA'S PROLOGUE

I.

When Zarathustra was thirty years old, he left his home and the lake of his home, and went into the mountains. There he enjoyed his spirit and his solitude, and for ten years did not weary of it. But at last his heart changed,—and rising one morning with the rosy dawn, he went before the sun, and spake thus unto it:

Thou great star! What would be thy happiness if thou hadst not those for whom thou shinest!

For ten years hast thou climbed hither unto my cave: thou wouldst have wearied of thy light and of the journey, had it not been for me, mine eagle, and my serpent.

But we awaited thee every morning, took from thee thine overflow, and blessed thee for it.

Lo! I am weary of my wisdom, like the bee that

From Friedrich Nietzsche, *Thus Spake Zarathustra,* translated by Thomas Common, Vol. 11 of *the Complete Works of Friedrich Nietzsche,* General editor, Oscar Levy [1909-1911] New York: Russell & Russell, 1964. Used by permission.

hath gathered too much honey; I need hands outstretched to take it.

I would fain bestow and distribute, until the wise have once more become joyous in their folly, and the poor happy in their riches.

Therefore must I descend into the deep: as thou doest in the evening, when thou goest behind the sea, and givest light also to the nether-world, thou exuberant star!

Like thee must I *go down*, as men say, to whom I shall descend.

Bless me, then, thou tranquil eye, that canst behold even the greatest happiness without envy!

Bless the cup that is about to overflow, that the water may flow golden out of it, and carry everywhere the reflection of thy bliss!

Lo! This cup is again going to empty itself, and Zarathustra is again going to be a man.

Thus began Zarathustra's down-going.

2.

Zarathustra went down the mountain alone, no one meeting him. When he entered the forest, however, there suddenly stood before him an old man, who had left his holy cot to seek roots. And thus spake the old man to Zarathustra:

"No stranger to me is this wanderer: many years ago passed he by. Zarathustra he was called; but he hath altered.

Then thou carriedst thine ashes into the mountains: wilt thou now carry thy fire into the valleys? Fearest thou not the incendiary's doom?

Yea, I recognise Zarathustra. Pure is his eye, and no loathing lurketh about his mouth. Goeth he not along like a dancer?

Altered is Zarathustra; a child hath Zarathustra become; an awakened one is Zarathustra: what wilt thou do in the land of the sleepers?

As in the sea hast thou lived in solitude, and it hath borne thee up. Alas, wilt thou now go ashore? Alas, wilt thou again drag thy body thyself?"

Zarathustra answered: "I love mankind."

"Why," said the saint, "did I go into the forest and the desert? Was it not because I loved men far too well?

Now I love God: men, I do not love. Man is a thing too imperfect for me. Love to man would be fatal to me."

Zarathustra answered: "What spake I of love! I am bringing gifts unto men."

"Give them nothing," said the saint. "Take rather part of their load, and carry it along with them—that will be most agreeable unto them: if only it be agreeable unto thee!

If, however, thou wilt give unto them, give them no more than an alms, and let them also beg for it!"

"No," replied Zarathustra, "I give no alms. I am not poor enough for that."

The saint laughed at Zarathustra, and spake thus: "Then see to it that they accept thy treasures! They are distrustful of anchorites, and do not believe that we come with gifts.

The fall of our footsteps ringeth too hollow through their streets. And just as at night, when they are in bed and hear a man abroad long before sunrise, so they ask themselves concerning us: Where goeth the thief?

Go not to men, but stay in the forest! Go rather to the animals! Why not be like me—a bear amongst bears, a bird amongst birds?"

"And what doeth the saint in the forest?" asked Zarathustra.

The saint answered: "I make hymns and sing them; and in making hymns I laugh and weep and mumble: thus do I praise God.

With singing, weeping, laughing, and mumbling do I praise the God who is my God. But what dost thou bring us as a gift?"

When Zarathustra had heard these words, he bowed to the saint and said: "What should I have to give thee! Let me rather hurry hence lest I take aught away from thee!"—And thus they parted from one another, the old man and Zarathustra, laughing like schoolboys.

When Zarathustra was alone, however, he said to his heart: "Could it be possible! This old saint in the forest hath not yet heard of it, that *God is dead!*"

3.

When Zarathustra arrived at the nearest town which adjoineth the forest, he found many people assembled in the market-place; for it had been announced that a rope-dancer would give a performance. And Zarathustra spake thus unto the people:

I teach you the Superman. Man is something that is to be surpassed. What have ye done to surpass man?

All beings hitherto have created something beyond themselves: and ye want to be the ebb of that great tide, and would rather go back to the beast than surpass man?

What is the ape to man? A laughing-stock, a thing of shame. And just the same shall man be to the Superman: a laughing-stock, a thing of shame.

Ye have made your way from the worm to man, and much within you is still worm. Once were ye apes, and even yet man is more of an ape than any of the apes.

Even the wisest among you is only a disharmony and hybrid of plant and phantom. But do I bid you become phantoms or plants?

Lo, I teach you the Superman!

The Superman is the meaning of the earth. Let your will say: The Superman *shall be* the meaning of the earth!

I conjure you, my brethren, *remain true to the earth,* and believe not those who speak unto you of superearthly hopes! Poisoners are they, whether they know it or not.

Despisers of life are they, decaying ones and poisoned ones themselves, of whom the earth is weary: so away with them!

Once blasphemy against God was the greatest blasphemy; but God died, and therewith also those blasphemers. To blaspheme the earth is now the dreadfulest sin, and to rate the heart of the unknowable higher than the meaning of the earth!

Once the soul looked contemptuously on the body, and then that contempt was the supreme thing:—the soul wished the body meagre, ghastly, and famished. Thus it thought to escape from the body and the earth.

Oh, that soul was itself meagre, ghastly, and famished; and cruelty was the delight of that soul!

But ye, also, my brethren, tell me: What doth your body say about your soul? Is your soul not poverty and pollution and wretched self-complacency?

Verily, a polluted stream is man. One must be a sea, to receive a polluted stream without becoming impure.

Lo, I teach you the Superman: he is that sea; in him can your great contempt be submerged.

What is the greatest thing ye can experience? It is the hour of great contempt. The hour in which even your happiness becometh loathsome unto you, and so also your reason and virtue.

The hour when ye say: "What good is my happiness! It is poverty and pollution and wretched self-complacency. But my happiness should justify existence itself!"

The hour when ye say: "What good is my reason! Doth it long for knowledge as the lion for his food? It is poverty and pollution and wretched self-complacency!"

The hour when ye say: "What good is my virtue! As yet it hath not made me passionate. How weary I am of my good and my bad! It is all poverty and pollution and wretched self-complacency!"

The hour when ye say: "What good is my justice! I do not see that I am fervour and fuel. The just, however, are fervour and fuel!"

The hour when we say: "What good is my pity! Is not pity the cross on which he is nailed who loveth man? But my pity is not a crucifixion."

Have ye ever spoken thus? Have ye ever cried thus? Ah! would that I had heard you crying thus!

It is not your sin—it is your self-satisfaction that crieth unto heaven; your very sparingness in sin crieth unto heaven!

Where is the lightning to lick you with its tongue? Where is the frenzy with which ye should be inoculated?

Lo, I teach you the Superman: he is that lightning, he is that frenzy!—

When Zarathustra had thus spoken, one of the people called out: "We have now heard enough of the rope-dancer; it is time now for us to see him!" And all the people laughed at Zarathustra. But the rope-dancer, who thought the words applied to him, began his performance.

4.

Zarathustra, however, looked at the people and wondered. Then he spake thus:

Man is a rope stretched between the animal and the Superman—a rope over an abyss.

A dangerous crossing, a dangerous wayfaring, a dangerous looking-back, a dangerous trembling and halting.

What is great in man is that he is a bridge and not a goal: what is lovable in man is that he is an *over-going* and a *down-going.*

I love those that know not how to live except as down-goers, for they are the over-goers.

I love the great despisers, because they are the great adorers, and arrows of longing for the other shore.

I love those who do not first seek a reason beyond the stars for going down and being sacrifices, but sacrifice themselves to the earth, that the earth of the Superman may hereafter arrive.

I love him who liveth in order to know, and seeketh to know in order that the Superman may hereafter live. Thus seeketh he his own down-going.

I love him who laboureth and inventeth, that he

may build the house for the Superman, and prepare for him earth, animal, and plant: for thus seeketh he his own down-going.

I love him who loveth his virtue: for virtue is the will to down-going, and an arrow of longing.

I love him who reserveth no share of spirit for himself, but wanteth to be wholly the spirit of his virtue: thus walketh he as spirit over the bridge.

I love him who maketh his virtue his inclination and destiny: thus, for the sake of his virtue, he is willing to live on, or live no more.

I love him who desireth not too many virtues. One virtue is more of a virtue than two, because it is more of a knot for one's destiny to cling to.

I love him whose soul is lavish, who wanteth no thanks and doth not give back: for he always bestoweth, and desireth not to keep for himself.

I love him who is ashamed when the dice fall in his favour, and who then asketh: "Am I a dishonest player?"—for he is willing to succumb.

I love him who scattereth golden words in advance of his deeds, and always doeth more than he promiseth: for he seeketh his own down-going.

I love him who justifieth the future ones, and redeemeth the past ones: for he is willing to succumb through the present ones.

I love him who chasteneth his God, because he loveth his God: for he must succumb through the wrath of his God.

I love him whose soul is deep even in the wounding, and may succumb through a small matter: thus goeth he willingly over the bridge.

I love him whose soul is so overfull that he forgetteth himself, and all things are in him: thus all things become his down-going.

I love him who is of a free spirit and a free heart: thus is his head only the bowels of his heart; his heart, however, causeth his down-going.

I love all who are like heavy drops falling one by one out of the dark cloud that lowereth over man: they herald the coming of the lightning, and succumb as heralds.

Lo, I am a herald of the lightning, and a heavy drop out of the cloud: the lightning, however, is the *Superman.*—

5.

When Zarathustra had spoken these words, he again looked at the people, and was silent. "There they stand," said he to his heart; "there they laugh: they understood me not; I am not the mouth for these ears.

Must one first batter their ears, that they may learn to hear with their eyes? Must one clatter like kettledrums and penitential preachers? Or do they only believe the stammerer?

They have something whereof they are proud. What do they call it, that which maketh them proud? Culture, they call it; it distinguisheth them from the goatherds.

They dislike, therefore, to hear of 'contempt' of themselves. So I will appeal to their pride.

I will speak unto them of the most contemptible thing: that, however, is *the last man!*"

And thus spake Zarathustra unto the people:

It is time for man to fix his goal. It is time for man to plant the germ of his highest hope.

Still is his soil rich enough for it. But that soil will one day be poor and exhausted, and no lofty tree will any longer be able to grow thereon.

Alas! there cometh the time when man will no longer launch the arrow of his longing beyond man—and the string of his bow will have unlearned to whizz!

I tell you: one must still have chaos in one, to give birth to a dancing star. I tell you: ye have still chaos in you.

Alas! There cometh the time when man will no longer give birth to any star. Alas! There cometh the time of the most despicable man, who can no longer despise himself.

Lo! I show you *the last man.*

"What is love? What is creation? What is longing? What is a star?"—so asketh the last man and blinketh.

The earth hath then become small, and on it there hoppeth the last man who maketh everything small. His species is ineradicable like that of the ground-flea; the last man liveth longest.

"We have discovered happiness"—say the last men, and blink thereby.

They have left the regions where it is hard to live; for they need warmth. One still loveth one's neighbour and rubbeth against him; for one needeth warmth.

Turning ill and being distrustful, they consider sinful: they walk warily. He is a fool who still stumbleth over stones or men!

A little poison now and then: that maketh pleasant dreams. And much poison at last for a pleasant death.

One still worketh, for work is a pastime. But one is careful lest the pastime should hurt one.

One no longer becometh poor or rich; both are too burdensome. Who still wanteth to rule? Who still wanteth to obey? Both are too burdensome.

No shepherd, and one herd! Every one wanteth

the same; every one is equal: he who hath other sentiments goeth voluntarily into the mad-house.

"Formerly all the world was insane,"—say the subtlest of them, and blink thereby.

They are clever and know all that hath happened: so there is no end to their raillery. People still fall out, but are soon reconciled—otherwise it spoileth their stomachs.

They have their little pleasures for the day, and their little pleasures for the night: but they have a regard for health.

"We have discovered happiness,"—say the last men, and blink thereby.—

And here ended the first discourse of Zarathustra, which is also called "The Prologue": for at this point the shouting and mirth of the multitude interrupted him. "Give us this last man, O Zarathustra,"—they called—"make us into these last men! Then will we make thee a present of the Superman!" And all the people exulted and smacked their lips. Zarathustra, however, turned sad, and said to his heart:

"They understand me not: I am not the mouth for these ears.

Too long, perhaps, have I lived in the mountains; too much have I hearkened unto the brooks and trees: now do I speak unto them as unto the goatherds.

Calm is my soul, and clear, like the mountains in the morning. But they think me cold, and a mocker with terrible jests.

And now do they look at me and laugh: and while they laugh they hate me too. There is ice in their laughter."

6.

Then, however, something happened which made every mouth mute and every eye fixed. In the meantime, of course, the rope-dancer had commenced his performance: he had come out at a little door and was going along the rope which was stretched between two towers, so that it hung above the market-place and the people. When he was just midway across, the little door opened once more, and a gaudily-dressed fellow like a buffoon sprang out, and went rapidly after the first one. "Go on, halt-foot," cried his frightful voice, "go on, lazy-bones, interloper, sallow-face!—lest I tickle thee with my heel! What dost thou here between the towers? In the tower is the place for thee, thou shouldst be locked up; to one better than thyself thou blockest the way!"—And with every word he came nearer and nearer the first one.

When, however, he was but a step behind, there happened the frightful thing which made every mouth mute and every eye fixed:—he uttered a yell like a devil, and jumped over the other who was in his way. The latter, however, when he thus saw his rival triumph, lost at the same time his head and his footing on the rope; he threw his pole away, and shot downwards faster than it, like an eddy of arms and legs, into the depth. The market-place and the people were like the sea when the storm cometh on: they all flew apart and in disorder, especially where the body was about to fall.

Zarathustra, however, remained standing, and just beside him fell the body, badly injured and disfigured, but not yet dead. After a while consciousness returned to the shattered man, and he saw Zarathustra kneeling beside him. "What art thou doing there?" said he at last, "I knew long ago that the devil would trip me up. Now he draggeth me to hell: wilt thou prevent him?"

"On mine honour, my friend," answered Zarathustra, "there is nothing of all that whereof thou speakest: there is no devil and no hell. Thy soul will be dead even sooner than thy body: fear, therefore, nothing any more!"

The man looked up distrustfully. "If thou speakest the truth," said he, "I lose nothing when I lose my life. I am not much more than an animal which hath been taught to dance by blows and scanty fare."

"Not at all," said Zarathustra, "thou hast made danger thy calling; therein there is nothing contemptible. Now thou perishest by thy calling: therefore will I bury thee with mine own hands."

When Zarathustra had said this the dying one did not reply further; but he moved his hand as if he sought the hand of Zarathustra in gratitude.

7.

Meanwhile the evening came on, and the market-place veiled itself in gloom. Then the people dispersed, for even curiosity and terror become fatigued. Zarathustra, however, still sat beside the dead man on the ground, absorbed in thought: so he forgot the time. But at last it became night, and a cold wind blew upon the lonely one. Then arose Zarathustra and said to his heart:

Verily, a fine catch of fish hath Zarathustra made to-day! It is not a man he hath caught, but a corpse.

Sombre is human life, and as yet without meaning: a buffoon may be fateful to it.

I want to teach men the sense of their existence,

which is the Superman, the lightning out of the dark cloud—man.

But still am I far from them, and my sense speaketh not unto their sense. To men I am still something between a fool and a corpse.

Gloomy is the night, gloomy are the ways of Zarathustra. Come, thou cold and stiff companion! I carry thee to the place where I shall bury thee with mine own hands.

LXXIII.—THE HIGHER MAN

1.

When I came unto men for the first time, then did I commit the anchorite folly, the great folly: I appeared on the market-place.

And when I spake unto all, I spake unto none. In the evening, however, rope-dancers were my companions, and corpses; and I myself almost a corpse.

With the new morning, however, there came unto me a new truth: then did I learn to say: "Of what account to me are market-place and populace and populace-noise and long populace-ears!"

Ye higher men, learn *this* from me: On the market-place no one believeth in higher men. But if ye will speak there, very well! The populace, however, blinketh: "We are all equal."

"Ye higher men,"—so blinketh the populace—"there are no higher men, we are all equal; man is man, before God—we are all equal!"

Before God!—Now, however, this God hath died. Before the populace, however, we will not be equal. Ye higher men, away from the market-place!

2.

Before God!—Now however this God hath died! Ye higher men, this God was your greatest danger.

Only since he lay in the grave have ye again arisen. Now only cometh the great noontide, now only doth the higher man become—master!

Have ye understood this word, O my brethren? Ye are frightened: do your hearts turn giddy? Doth the abyss here yawn for you? Doth the hell-hound here yelp at you?

Well! Take heart! ye higher men! Now only travaileth the mountain of the human future. God hath died: now do *we* desire—the Superman to live.

3.

The most careful ask to-day: "How is man to be maintained?" Zarathustra however asketh, as the first and only one: "How is man to be *surpassed?*"

The Superman, I have at heart; *that* is the first and only thing to me—and *not* man: not the neighbour, not the poorest, not the sorriest, not the best.—

O my brethren, what I can love in man is that he is an over-going and a down-going. And also in you there is much that maketh me love and hope.

In that ye have despised, ye higher men, that maketh me hope. For the great despisers are the great reverers.

In that ye have despaired, there is much to honour. For ye have not learned to submit yourselves, ye have not learned petty policy.

For to-day have the petty people become master: they all preach submission and humility and policy and diligence and consideration and the long *et cetera* of petty virtues.

Whatever is of the effeminate type, whatever originateth from the ervile type, and especially the populace-mishmash:—*that* wisheth now to be master of all human destiny—o disgust! Disgust! Disgust!

That asketh and asketh and never tireth: "How is man to maintain himself best, longest, most pleasantly;" Thereby—are they the masters of to-day.

These masters of to-day—surpass them, O my brethren—these petty people: *they* are the Superman's greatest danger!

Surpass, ye higher men, the petty virtues, the petty policy, the sand-grain considerateness, the ant-hill trumpery, the pitiable comfortableness, the "happiness of the greatest number"—!

And rather despair than submit yourselves. And verily, I love you, because ye know not to-day how to live, ye higher men! For thus do *ye* live—best!

4.

Have ye courage, O my brethren? Are ye stout-hearted? *Not* the courage before witnesses, but anchorite and eagle courage, which not even a God any longer beholdeth?

Cold souls, mules, the blind and the drunken, I do not call stout-hearted. He hath heart who knoweth fear, but *vanquisheth* it; who seeth the abyss, but with *pride*.

He who seeth the abyss, but with eagle's eyes,—he who with eagle's talons *graspeth* the abyss: he hath courage.— —

5.

"Man is evil"—so said to me for consolation, all the wisest ones. Ah, if only it be still true to-day! For the evil is man's best force.

"Man must become better and eviler"—so do *I* teach. The evilest is necessary for the Superman's best.

It may have been well for the preacher of the petty people to suffer and be burdened by men's sin. I, however, rejoice in great sin as my great *consolation.—*

Such things, however, are not said for long ears. Every word, also, is not suited for every mouth. These are fine, far-away things: at them sheep's claws shall not grasp!

6.

Ye higher men, think ye that I am here to put right what ye have put wrong?

Or that I wished henceforth to make snugger couches for you sufferers? Or show you restless, miswandering, misclimbing ones, new and easier footpaths?

Nay! Nay! Three times Nay! Always more, always better ones of your types shall succumb,—for ye shall always have it worse and harder. Thus only—

—Thus only groweth man aloft to the height where the lightning striketh and shattereth him: high enough for the lightning!

Towards the few, the long, the remote go forth my soul and my seeking: of what account to me are your many little, short miseries:

Ye do not yet suffer enough for me! For ye suffer from yourselves, ye have not yet suffered *from man.* Ye would lie if ye spake otherwise! None of you suffereth from what *I* have suffered.— —

7.

It is not enough for me that the lightning no longer doeth harm. I do not wish to conduct it away: it shall learn—to work for *me.—*

My wisdom hath accumulated long like a cloud, it becometh stiller and darker. So doeth all wisdom which shall one day bear *lightnings.—*

Unto these men of to-day will I not be *light,* nor be called light. *Then*—will I blind: lightning of my wisdom! put out their eyes!

8.

Do not will anything beyond your power: there is a bad falseness in those who will beyond their power.

Especially when they will great things! For they awaken distrust in great things, these subtle false-coiners and stage-players:—

—Until at last they are false towards themselves, squint-eyed, whited cankers, glossed over with strong words, parade virtues and brilliant false deeds.

Take good care there, ye higher men! For nothing is more precious to me, and rarer, than honesty.

Is this to-day not that of the populace? The populace however knoweth not what is great and what is small, what is straight and what is honest: it is innocently crooked, it ever lieth.

9.

Have a good distrust to-day, ye higher men, ye enheartened ones! Ye open-hearted ones! And keep your reasons secret! For this to-day is that of the populace.

What the populace once learned to believe without reasons, who could—refute it to them by means of reasons?

And on the market-place one convinceth with gestures. But reasons make the populace distrustful.

And when truth hath once triumphed there, then ask yourselves with good distrust: "What strong error hath fought for it?"

Be on your guard also against the learned! They hate you, because they are unproductive! They have cold, withered eyes before which every bird is umplumed.

Such persons vaunt about not lying: but inability to lie is still far from being love to truth. Be on your guard!

Freedom from fever is still far from being knowledge! Refrigerated spirits I do not believe in. He who cannot lie, doth not know what truth is.

10.

If ye would go up high, then use your own legs! Do not get yourselves *carried* aloft; do not seat yourselves on other people's backs and heads!

Thou hast mounted, however, on horseback? Thou now ridest briskly up to thy goal? Well, my friend! But thy lame foot is also with thee on horseback!

When thou reachest thy goal, when thou alightest from thy horse: precisely on thy *height*, thou higher man,—then wilt thou stumble!

11.

Ye creating ones, ye higher men! One is only pregnant with one's own child.

Do not let yourselves be imposed upon or put upon! Who then is *your* neighbour? Even if ye act "for your neighbour"—ye still do not create for him!

Unlearn, I pray you, this "for," ye creating ones: your very virtue wisheth you to have naught to do with "for" and "on account of" and "because." Against these false little words shall ye stop your ears.

"For one's neighbour," is the virtue only of the petty people: there it is said "like and like," and "hand washeth hand":—they have neither the right nor the power for *your* self-seeking!

In your self-seeking, ye creating ones, there is the foresight and foreseeing of the pregnant! What no one's eye hath yet seen, namely, the fruit—this, sheltereth and saveth and nourisheth your entire love.

Where your entire love is, namely, with your child, there is also your entire virtue! Your work, your will is *your* "neighbour": let no false values impose upon you!

12.

Ye creating ones, ye higher men! Whoever hath to give birth is sick; whoever hath given birth, however, is unclean.

Ask women: one giveth birth, not because it giveth pleasure. The pain maketh hens and poets cackle.

Ye creating ones, in you there is much uncleanness. That is because ye have had to be mothers.

A new child: oh, how much new filth hath also come into the world! Go apart! He who hath given birth shall wash his soul!

13.

Be not virtuous beyond your powers! And seek nothing from yourselves opposed to probability!

Walk in the footsteps in which your fathers' virtue hath already walked! How would ye rise high, if your fathers' will should not rise with you?

He, however, who would be a firstling, let him take care lest he also become a lastling! And where the vices of your fathers are, there should ye not set up as saints!

He whose fathers were inclined for women, and for strong wine and flesh of wildboar swine; what would it be if he demanded chastity of himself?

A folly would it be! Much, verily, doth it seem to me for such a one, if he should be the husband of one or of two or of three women.

And if he founded monasteries, and inscribed over their portals: "The way to holiness,"—I should still say: What good is it! it is a new folly!

He hath founded for himself a penance-house and refuge-house: much good may it do! But I do not believe in it.

In solitude there groweth what any one bringeth into it—also the brute in one's nature. Thus is solitude inadvisable unto many.

Hath there ever been anything filthier on earth than the saints of the wilderness? *Around them* was not only the devil loose—but also the swine.

14.

Shy, ashamed, awkward, like the tiger whose spring hath failed—thus, ye higher men, have I often seen you slink aside. A *cast* which ye made had failed.

But what doth it matter, ye dice-players! Ye had not learned to play and mock, as one must play and mock! Do we not ever sit at a great table of mocking and playing?

And if great things have been a failure with you, have ye yourselves therefore—been a failure? And if ye yourselves have been a failure, hath man therefore—been a failure? If man, however, hath been a failure: well then! never mind!

15.

The higher its type, always the seldomer doth a thing succeed. Ye higher men here, have ye not all—been failures?

Be of good cheer; what doth it matter? How much is still possible! Learn to laugh at yourselves, as ye ought to laugh!

What wonder even that ye have failed and only half-succeeded, ye half-shattered ones! Doth not—man's *future* strive and struggle in you?

Man's furthest, profoundest, star-highest issues, his prodigious powers—do not all these foam through one another in your vessel?

What wonder that many a vessel shattereth! Learn to laugh at yourselves, as ye ought to laugh! Ye higher men, Oh, how much is still possible!

And verily, how much hath already succeeded! How rich is this earth in small, good, perfect things, in well-constituted things!

Set around you small, good, perfect things, ye higher men. Their golden maturity healeth the heart. The perfect teacheth one to hope.

16.

What hath hitherto been the greatest sin here on earth? Was it not the word of him who said: "Woe unto them that laugh now!"

Did he himself find no cause for laughter on the earth? Then he sought badly. A child even findeth cause for it.

He—did not love sufficiently: otherwise would he also have loved us, the laughing ones! But he hated and hooted us; wailing and teeth-gnashing did he promise us.

Must one then curse immediately, when one doth not love? That—seemeth to me bad taste. Thus did he, however, this absolute one. He sprang from the populace.

And he himself just did not love sufficiently; otherwise would he have raged less because people did not love him. All great love doth not *seek* love:—it seeketh more.

Go out of the way of all such absolute ones! They are a poor sickly type, a populace-type: they look at this life with ill-will, they have an evil eye for this earth.

Go out of the way of all such absolute ones! They have heavy feet and sultry hearts:—they do not know how to dance. How could the earth be light to such ones!

17.

Tortuously do all good things come nigh to their goal. Like cats they curve their backs, they purr inwardly with their approaching happiness,—all good things laugh.

His step betrayeth whether a person already walketh on *his own* path: just see me walk! He, however, who cometh nigh to his goal, danceth.

And verily, a statue have I not become, not yet do I stand there stiff, stupid and stony, like a pillar; I love fast racing.

And though there be on earth fens and dense afflictions, he who hath light feet runneth even across the mud, and danceth, as upon well-swept ice.

Lift up your hearts, my brethren, high, higher! And do not forget your legs! Lift up also your legs, ye good dancers, and better still, if ye stand upon your heads!

18.

This crown of the laugher, this rose-garland crown: I myself have put on this crown, I myself have consecrated my laughter. No one else have I found to-day potent enough for this.

Zarathustra the dancer, Zarathustra the light one, who beckoneth with his pinions, one ready for flight, beckoning unto all birds, ready and prepared, a blissfully light-spirited one:—

Zarathustra the soothsayer, Zarathustra the sooth-laugher, no impatient one, no absolute one, one who loveth leaps and side-leaps; I myself have put on this crown!

19.

Lift up your hearts, my brethren, high, higher! And do not forget your legs! Lift up also your legs, ye good dancers, and better still if ye stand upon your heads!

There are also heavy animals in a state of happiness, there are club-footed ones from the beginning. Curiously do they exert themselves, like an elephant which endeavoureth to stand upon its head.

Better, however, to be foolish with happiness than foolish with misfortune, better to dance awkwardly than walk lamely. So learn, I pray you, my wisdom, ye higher men: even the worst thing hath two good reverse sides,—

—Even the worst thing hath good dancing-legs: so learn, I pray you, ye higher men, to put yourselves on your proper legs!

So unlearn, I pray you, the sorrow-sighing, and all the populace-sadness! Oh, how sad the buffoons of the populace seem to me to-day! This to-day, however, is that of the populace.

20.

Do like unto the wind when it rusheth forth from its mountain-caves: unto its own piping will it dance; the seas tremble and leap under its footsteps.

That which giveth wings to asses, that which milketh the lionesses:—praised be that good, unruly spirit, which cometh like a hurricane unto all the present and unto all the populace,—

—Which is hostile to thistle-heads and puzzle-heads, and to all withered leaves and weeds:—praised be this wild, good, free spirit of the storm, which danceth upon fens and afflictions, as upon meadows!

Which hateth the consumptive populace-dogs, and the ill-constituted, sullen brood:—praised be this spirit of all free spirits, the laughing storm, which bloweth dust into the eyes of all the melanopic and melancholic!

Ye higher men, the worst thing in you is that ye

have none of you learned to dance as ye ought to dance—to dance beyond yourselves! What doth it matter that ye have failed!

How many things are still possible! So *learn* to laugh beyond yourselves! Lift up your hearts, ye good dancers, high! higher! And do not forget the good laughter!

This crown of the laugher, this rose-garland crown: to you my brethren do I cast this crown! Laughing have I consecrated; ye higher men, *learn,* I pray you—to laugh!

Jean-Paul Sartre

Jean-Paul Sartre (1905-   ) is a leading figure in twentieth-century existentialism. Active in the French resistance from 1941 to 1945, Sartre first published his *Being and Nothingness* in Paris in 1943, in the midst of the Nazi occupation. An atheist, Sartre saw man as an essentially lonely being, with no guide for his decisions except his own will. In the short selection below, Sartre defines freedom and responsibility.

BEING AND NOTHINGNESS

III. FREEDOM AND RESPONSIBILITY

Although the considerations which are about to follow are of interest primarily to the ethicist, it may nevertheless be worthwhile after these descriptions and arguments to return to the freedom of the for-itself and to try to understand what the fact of this freedom represents for human destiny.

The essential consequence of our earlier remarks is that man being condemned to be free carries the weight of the whole world on his shoulders; he is responsible for the world and for himself as a way of being. We are taking the word "responsibility" in its ordinary sense as "consciousness (of) being the incontestable author of an event or of an object." In this sense the responsibility of the for-itself is overwhelming since he is the one by whom it happens that *there is* a world; since he is also the one who makes himself be, then whatever may be the situation in which he finds himself, the for-itself must wholly assume this situation with its peculiar coefficient of adversity, even though it be insupportable. He must assume the situation with the proud consciousness of being the author of it, for the very worst disadvantages or the worst threats which can endanger my person have meaning only in and through my project; and it is on the ground of the engagement which I am that they appear. It is therefore senseless to think of com-

plaining since nothing foreign has decided what we feel, what we live, or what we are.

Furthermore this absolute responsibility is not resignation; it is simply the logical requirement of the consequences of our freedom. What happens to me happens through me, and I can neither affect myself with it nor revolt against it nor resign myself to it. Moreover everything which happens to me is *mine.* By this we must understand first of all that I am always equal to what happens to me *qua* man, for what happens to a man through other men and through himself can be only human. The most terrible situations of war, the worst tortures do not create a non-human state of things; there is no non-human situation. It is only through fear, flight, and recourse to magical types of conduct that I shall decide on the non-human, but this decision is human, and I shall carry the entire responsibility for it. But in addition, the situation is *mine* because it is the image of my free choice of myself, and everything which it presents to me is *mine* in that this represents me and symbolizes me. Is it not I who decide the coefficient of adversity in things and even their unpredictability by deciding myself?

Thus there are no *accidents* in a life; a community event which suddenly bursts forth and involves me in it does not come from the outside. If I am mobilized in a war, this war is *my* war; it is in my image and I deserve it. I deserve it first because I could always get out of it by suicide or by desertion; these ultimate possibles are those which must always be present for us when there is a question of envisaging a situation. For lack of getting out of it, I have *chosen* it. This can be due to inertia, to cowardice in the face of public opinion, or because I prefer certain other values to the value of the refusal to join in the war (the good opinion of my relatives, the honor of my family, *etc.*). Anyway you look at it, it is a matter of a choice. This choice will be repeated later on again and again without a break until the end of the war. Therefore we must agree with the statement by J. Romains, "In war there are no innocent victims." If therefore I have preferred war to death or to dishonor, everything takes place as if I bore the entire responsibility for this war. Of course others have declared it, and one might be tempted perhaps to consider me as a simple accomplice. But this notion of complicity has only a juridical sense, and it does not hold here. For it depended on me that for me and by me this war should not exist, and I have decided that it does exist. There was no compulsion here, for the compulsion could have got no hold on a freedom. I did not have any excuse; for as we have said repeatedly in this book, the peculiar character of human-reality is that it is without excuse. Therefore it remains for me only to lay claim to this war.

But in addition the war is *mine* because by the sole fact that it arises in a situation which I cause to be and that I can discover it there only by engaging myself for or against it, I can no longer distinguish at present the choice which I make of myself from the choice which I make of the war. To live this war is to choose myself. There can be no question of considering it as "four years of vacation" or as a "reprieve," as a "recess," the essential part of my responsibilities being elsewhere in my married, family, or professional life. In this war which I have chosen I choose myself from day to day, and I make it mine by making myself. If it is going to be four empty years, then it is I who bear the responsibility for this.

Finally, as we pointed out earlier, each person is an absolute choice of self from the standpoint of a world of knowledges and of techniques which this choice both assumes and illumines; each person is an absolute upsurge at an absolute date and is perfectly unthinkable at another date. It is therefore a waste of time to ask what I should have been if this war had not broken out, for I have chosen myself as one of the possible meanings of the epoch which imperceptibly led to war. I am not distinct from this same epoch; I could not be transported to another epoch without contradiction. Thus *I am* this war which restricts and limits and makes comprehensible the period which preceded it. In this sense we may define more precisely the responsibility of the for-itself if to the earlier quoted statement, "There are no innocent victims," we add the words, "We have the war we deserve." Thus, totally free, undistinguishable from the period for which I have chosen to be the meaning, as profoundly responsible for the war as if I had myself declared it, unable to live without integrating it in *my* situation, engaging myself in it wholly and stamping it with my seal, I must be without remorse or regrets as I am without excuse; for from the instant of my upsurge into being, I carry the weight of the world by myself alone without anything or any person being able to lighten it.

Yet this responsibility is of a very particular type. Someone will say, "I did not ask to be born." This is a naive way of throwing greater emphasis on our facticity. I am responsible for everything, in fact, except for my very responsibility, for I am not the foundation of my being. Therefore everything takes place as if I were compelled to be responsible. I am *abandoned* in the world, not in the sense that I might remain abandoned and passive in a hostile universe like a board floating on the water, but rather in the sense that I find myself suddenly alone and without help, engaged in a world for which I bear the whole responsibility without being able, whatever I do, to tear myself away from this responsibility for an instant. For I am responsible for my very desire of fleeing responsibilities. To make myself passive in the world, to refuse to act upon things and upon Others is still to choose myself, and suicide is one mode among others of being-in-the-world. Yet I find an absolute responsibility for the fact that my facticity (here the fact of my birth) is directly inapprehensible and even inconceivable, for this fact of my birth never appears as a brute fact but always across a projective reconstruction of my for-itself. I am ashamed of being born or I am astonished at it or I rejoice over it, or in attempting to get rid of my life I affirm that I live and I assume this life as bad. Thus in a certain sense I *choose* being born. This choice itself is integrally affected with facticity since I am not able not to choose, but this facticity in turn will appear only in so far as I surpass it toward my ends. Thus facticity is everywhere but inapprehensible; I never encounter anything except my responsibility. That is why I can not ask, "*Why* was I born?" or curse the day of my birth or declare that I did not ask to be born, for these various attitudes toward my birth—*i.e.,* toward the *fact* that I realize a presence in the world—are absolutely nothing else but ways of assuming this birth in full responsibility and of making it *mine.* Here again I encounter only myself and my projects so that finally my abandonment—*i.e.,* my facticity—consists simply in the fact that I am condemned to be wholly responsible for myself. I am the being which *is* in such a way that in its being its being is in question. And this "is" of my being *is as* present and inapprehensible.

Under these conditions since every event in the world can be revealed to me only as an *opportunity* (an opportunity made use of, lacked, neglected, *etc.*), or better yet since everything which happens to us can be considered as a *chance* (*i.e.,* can appear to us only as a way of realizing this being which is in question in our being) and since others as transcendences-transcended are themselves only *opportunities* and *chances,* the responsibility of the for-itself extends to the entire world as a peopled-world. It is precisely thus that the for-itself apprehends itself in anguish; that is, as a being which is neither the foundation of its own being nor of the Other's being nor of the in-itselfs which form the world, but a being which is compelled to decide the meaning of being—within it and everywhere outside of it. The one who realizes in anguish his condition as *being* thrown into a responsibility which extends to his very abandonment has no longer either remorse or regret or excuse; he is no longer anything but a freedom which perfectly reveals itself and whose being resides in this very revelation. But as we pointed out at the beginning of this work, most of the time we flee anguish in bad faith.

Carl Becker

Carl Becker (1873-1945) was a distinguished historian and professor of history at several American universities. His intellect, his wit, his philosophical bent of mind and his ability to make the past pertinent to the present are evident in his many articles and books, including the following essay in which he questioned the permanence of liberalism. *Liberalism—a Way Station* was written in 1932, in the midst of the Great Depression.

LIBERALISM—A WAY STATION

One day, talking with a Cornell student from Brooklyn about the difficulty of getting jobs in this time of depression, I asked him, with ironical intent, what he thought of liberty. He replied: "I've never been through it; I don't drive a car." There may have been less irony in my question than in his answer. The answer, at all events, suggested that liberty is perhaps no more than a small station on the main traveled road of human history—a place which humanity passes rapidly through.

I am referring to that liberty which for the last century and a half has commonly been associated with democratic government. "It is evident," wrote DeTocqueville in 1835, "that a great democratic revolution is going on among us." From the vantage of 1932, we can see that this democratic revolution was the outstanding political event of the nineteenth century. During all that time the public issues which chiefly engaged statesmen were these. What is the best form of government? What are the proper functions of government? What are the rights properly reserved to the individual? How can the powers of government and the rights of the individual be definitely guaranteed in constitutional form? Between 1789 and 1871, the chief occupation of statesmen and publicists, one might almost say, was the manufacture of constitutions, the construction of locked-vaults and strong-rooms for safeguarding the rights of the individual. The emancipation of the individual from class or corporate or governmental restraint—this was the democratic revolution noted by DeTocqueville. To be a Conservative was to be, with whatever reservations, against such emancipation. To be a Liberal was to be, with whatever reservations, in favor of it.

Liberalism was the doctrine that rationalized this emancipation of the individual. In its most naive form it comes to us from the eighteenth century. In that optimistic age the middle-class man, conscious of his virtues and desiring to rise in a world in which he was repressed by royal tyranny and class privilege, naturally believed in liberty; and while the Revolution had as yet occurred only in men's minds, it seemed to him that liberty was achieved as soon as it was adequately defined: liberty—that is to say, "the right of every one to do whatever does not injure others." Meanwhile, slow-footed time brought its heavy baggage of experience. The great Revolution came, bequeathing to the nineteenth century its furious fanaticisms and hatreds, its partial achievements, its hopes deferred, its fears and disillusionments. Often checked, the Revolution was never quite suppressed; and the liberal creed lived on, toned down by the impact of many defeats, and reduced to classic form by John Stuart Mill in his famous book *On Liberty*.

In restating the liberal creed, the hard-headed if forward-looking utilitarians of the Victorian age adapted it realistically to the needs of the business men and bankers who rode to power on the swelling tide of the industrial revolution. Liberty was still defined as the "right to do whatever does not injure others." But of the things one could do that did not injure others, not the least important, since it benefited every one concerned, was to engage in any legitimate business and make a private profit by buying in the cheapest and selling in the dearest market available. Free competition— this also, as well as political and intellectual freedom, was one of the natural rights proclaimed by the great Revolution, or at least one of the privileges so clearly demonstrated by Bentham to be useful to society. At a much clearer date Cecil Rhodes announced that "philanthropy is all very well, but philanthropy plus five per cent is a good deal better." The impregnable strength of nineteenth century liberalism was chiefly in this, that it recognized the high value of philanthropy plus five per cent: it united liberty and competition in the holy bonds of wedlock, made liberty useful by setting it up in business, and sanctified competition by annointing it with the incense of human freedom.

With this battery of principles, the middle and lower classes gradually edged their way, through many an unguarded opening, into the "political country" hitherto held chiefly by the aristocrats. If in the end the gates were opened to the common man by those within rather than forced by those without, it was not that the upper classes wanted democarcy, but that upper-class statesmen could do with more votes. Yet with whatever concessions in theory or compromises in practice the democratic revolution may have been accomplished, all was still done in the name of liberty; and never was the prestige of liberalism so high as in that age of brass and iron when those shoddy substitutes for the ideal (the Third Republic, the German Empire, the Austro-Hungarian *Compromise*, a household suffrage thrown as a sop to tenants on entailed estates) were complacently exhibited as examples of "democracy triumphant."

This Indian Summer of liberal content was nevertheless no more than a brief season. The moment of victory was in truth the beginning of defeat, since with all the famous "liberties" formally conferred on the individual the great role of nineteenth century liberalism was ended. When all statesmen loved the common man, sufficiently so at least to solicit his vote, and even the priests, as Georges Sorel said, "claim to be the best of democrats . . . and if a little persuasion is exerted . . . will have illuminations on the anniversary of August 10, 1792," where *then* was the enemy? The enemy appeared soon enough, but most disconcertingly: on two fronts, panoplied partly in conservative partly in liberal armor, and bearing banners strangely resembling both those which liberalism had carried to victory and those others which it had trampled in the dust.

The prophets of democracy had supposed that when political Liberty appeared economic Equality would come trailing affectionately along. *Laissez-faire,* free competition—what a wealth of subtle dialectic was employed to exhibit the social utility of these cleanly-kept but unfurnished concepts! The prophets of democracy could not force that the industrial revolution, superimposed on a régime of free competition, would give to the possessors of machines and the instruments of production powers and privileges which would have reduced dead and gone kings and nobles, could they have imagined them, to envious admiration. Before the end of the nineteenth century it was clear to the discerning that liberal democracy had belied the hopes of its prophets. Liberty, that liberty which was to have enlightened and emancipated the world, had ironically given birth to a brood of mean-faced tyrants, and so far from walking hand in hand with equality was to be found consorting chiefly, and secretly, with puffed and bedizzened privilege.

The first to feel the new oppressions were the industrial workers. Sooner or later, therefore, in every country they organized political parties committed to the defence of their class interests. These new parties had all much the same practical program—to obtain for the masses a larger share of the social income. They had all much the same social philosophy: some brand of Marxian socialism, which proclaimed the coming social revolution and the end of the competitive system. Not *laissez-faire* but socialization, not a competitive but a regulated economy, not individual liberty for private profit but restraint of the individual for the welfare of all—such was the new gospel of socialism that arose to contend with the old gospel of liberalism.

Confronted with the rising power of socialism, the possessing classes closed their ranks. Landed aristocrats, recently dispossessed by the political revolution, united with the aristocracy of bonded bourgeois wealth created by the industrial revolution, to defend the régime of liberal democracy. They were now all good conservatives since they wished to conserve the existing régime, all good liberals since the régime they wished to conserve was the one liberals had so long heralded and fought for. With the issue thus reshaped, with conservative-liberals to the right of them and revolutionary socialists to the left of them, the old Liberal parties, not well knowing whether to be guided by their humanitarian impulses or by their individualist principles, could only stand irresolute, while their once loyal followers deserted to one camp or the other. This process of dissolution was well under way in continental countries before the war. In England it is more recently that the great Liberal party of Gladstone has dropped to third place. For some years now its chief function as J.M. Keynes so aptly puts it, has been "to serve the State by supplying the Conservative party with

leaders and the Laborites with ideas;" and we need not be surprised that it has at present so few of either, having in the last twenty years surrendered so many of both.

Of all the leaders thus lost to he Liberal party, the most notable is undoubtedly Ramsay MacDonald, whose career throws a brilliant light on the predicament from which all old-fashioned liberals now strive with indifferent success to extricate themselves. Aristocratic in his avocations and in his demeanor, he lives by preference the life of a gentleman and a scholar; inheriting the Scots' canny caution and thoroughly rooted in British tradition, he understands the high virtue of compromise and has always set his face against violence, not always with pleasant consequences to himself; nevertheless, being eminently humane, he has consistently preached social reform in behalf of the poor; being eminently reasonable and reasonably ambitious, he has called himself a socialist but has risen to power as a leader of the Labor party; and yet through all the vicissitudes of an exciting career he has managed to preserve the liberal point of view, watching his step both ways, often uncertain whether to be counselled by his conscience which bids him budge with the masses, or by the fiend who bids him budge-not with the classes: the upshot of which is that he has been three times prime minister, and today, deprived of a party, stands in splendid isolation, discreetly holding a faded socialist flag and courageously leading a conservative House of Commons. All this is but an abstract and brief chronicle of Liberalism in our time.

Before the war this game could be played without fatalities. The liberals had so expertly socialized their program, the socialists had so expediently denatured their revolutionary doctrine, that there was not bewteen them (for example, between the liberalism of Lloyd George and the socialism of Ramsay MacDonald) the difference of the twentieth part of one poor scruple. But the harsh implications of anti-liberal doctrine, now fast becoming real issues, have revealed to liberals and socialists alike the puerility of their playboy disputes. The Marxian, communist, anti-liberal revolution has actually occurred in Russia. The fascist, anti-liberal revolution has occurred in Italy. We have only to remove our heads from the sand to see, on the arena of western civilization, old fundamental issues clearly defined, old fundamental conflicts realistically staged: on the one side, a ruthlessly regulated economy as it appears in Soviet Russia or in Fascist Italy; on the other, a free competitive economy (made workable by whatever patchwork of socialistic devices) as it appears in Great Britain and the United States.

As the implications of these contrasted systems become more apparent, the predicament in which all liberals find themselves (and in the liberal camp all tepid, skimmed-milk socialists are now huddled for shelter) becomes more acute, becomes even, if we wish to do anything about it, really pathetic. Our predicament arises from the fact that, having been long enamored of both liberty and equality, we are now ever more insistently urged (by the gods that be, those wooden-faced *croupiers* at life's gaming table) to choose between them and the truth is we cannot with a clear conscience or a light heart choose either without the other. So we stand irresolute, pulled one way by our humane sympathies, another by our traditional ideals. As we are humane, we look with compassion on the "looped and windowed raggedness" of the poor, invoke on their behalf the sacred principle of equality, and perhaps secretly admire, at the safe distance of three thousand miles, the high Russian endeavor to realize it in practice. Yet we shudder at the thought of blood, and assure the bolsheviks that the Great Society cannot be created by cutting off heads of suppressing freedom of speech (for which, in the distant past, so much blood was ruthlessly shed!) Although humane lovers of the masses, we are, on the other hand, highly differentiated individuals who prize our liberties, including the liberty of not belonging to the masses whom we love; and having been long unaccustomed to authority arbitrarily exercised, we hate Mussolini for the professors he has silenced, and write letters to the *Nation* protesting, in the name of liberty, against his brusk tyrannies. Yet we find it impossible not to denounce, in our own country where we are still free to denounce them, those oppression that have emerged under the aegis of the very liberty we invoke. Choose? Oh me, that word choose! We cannot choose liberty without denouncing the drastic methods now being taken to obtain equality, or choose equality so obtained without betraying liberty.

Choose as we will or can; the event is less likely to be decided by our choices than by the dumb pressure of common men and machines. The intellectual liberty we so highly prize is of little moment to the average man, since he rarely uses it, while the liberties he can make use of are just now of diminishing value to him. Of the many liberties which, in our free democratic society, the average man now enjoys (if that is the word), I will mention the one which concerns him most. He is free to take any job that offers, if any offers; if none offers, free to look for one that will pay a bare living wage, or less: if none is found, free to stand in line begging a crust from charity, or from the government that makes him a free man. What the average man wants, more than he wants this kind of liberty, is security; and when the pressure of adverse circumstances becomes adequate he will support those who can and will give it to him. The average man likes of course to do what he pleases, but he is averse to being made responsible for what it is that he pleases to do. Instinctively suspicious of eccentricity, he is nowise irked by conformity. The equality of mediocrity gives him all the liberty he cares for really, since he is not measurably different from the great majority of people, and does not wish to be. Give him security, and within security the liberty to do and to think what most people do and think—give him bread and motor cars—and he will never know, or soon forget, that liberty has departed.

And the machines, unfortunately for us perhaps, appear to be on the side of the average man. Having invented the machines, we must make the best of them. Master them we will, no doubt. Master them we do. But a prime condition of our mastering them is that we should adapt our conduct to their necessities. To make the best use of the machines we must meet them more than halfway, since they care nothing for us while we care greatly for them. It is the machines that make life complicated, at the same time that they impose on it a high tempo; and what the machines demand of the individual living in a closely intermeshed society running at top speed is not eccentricity, however cultivated and engaging, but conformity. The idle curiosity, the mental vagabondage of the brooding, reflective mind, the machines will indeed accept, but at high discount rates only; they put a premium on the immediately realizable virtues—on promptness, regularity, precision, effortless adaptability to the accelerated movement and rhythm of modern life.

Liberty is one of those magic words that have, on the world's state, their entrances and their exits, playing meanwhile their brief parts. One wonders whether the role of liberty, in its modern mask, is nearly played out. Is liberalism as we have understood it for a hundred years past no more than rationalization, an intellectual by-product of democracy? Is democracy itself but a passing phase, a loose and extravagant method of government, practicable only in relatively simple agricultural societies suddenly dowered with unaccustomed wealth by the industrial revolution? If so, then is equality not, as we have fondly supposed, the blood brother and indispensable accomplice of liberty? Will equalitarianism, in its turn, prove to be a new rationalization, an intellectual by-product of complex, economically interdependent industrial societies working inevitably, and no doubt impersonally, towards stability and equilibrium? These are questions which, in this time of disturbance and failing confidence, the reflecting mind cannot put lightly aside.

Dietrich Bonhoeffer

Dietrich Bonhoeffer (1906-1945) was a German Protestant clergyman. A fierce critic of National Socialism, he became a leader of the church's resistance to Hitler. He was the director of a secret theological school from 1935 until it was closed by the Gestapo in 1940. Arrested in 1943, Bonhoeffer remained a prisoner until 1945 when he was hanged. The following selection, taken from his *Letters and Papers from Prison* demonstrates his unyielding faith both in God and in the future.

LETTERS AND PAPERS FROM PRISON

AFTER TEN YEARS

Ten years is a long stretch in a man's life. Time is the most precious gift in our possession, for it is the most irrevocable. This is what makes it so disturbing to look back upon time we have lost. Time lost is time when we have not lived a full human life, time unenriched by experience, creative endeavour, enjoyment and suffering. Time lost is time we have not filled, time left empty. The past ten years have not been like that. Our losses have been immeasurable, but we have not lost time. True, knowledge and experience, which are realized only in retrospect, are mere abstractions compared with the reality, compared with the life we have actually lived. But just as the capacity to forget is a gift of grace, so memory, the recalling of the lessons we have learnt, is an essential element in responsible living. In the following pages I hope to put on record some of the lessons we have learnt and the experiences we have shared during the past ten years. These are not just individual experiences; they are not arranged in an orderly way, there is no attempt to discuss them or to theorize about them. All I have done is to jot down as they come some of the discoveries made by a circle of like-minded friends, discoveries about the business of human life. The only connexion between them is that of concrete experience. There is nothing new or startling about them, for they have been known long before. But to us has been granted the privilege of learning them anew by first-hand experience. I cannot write a single word about these things without a deep sense of gratitude for the fellowship of spirit and community of life we have been allowed to enjoy and preserve throughout these years.

No Ground Beneath Our Feet

Surely there has never been a generation in the course of human history with so little ground under its feet as our own. Every conceivable alternative seems equally intolerable. We try to escape from the present by looking entirely to the past or the future for our inspiration, and yet, without indulging in fanciful dreams, we are able to wait for the success of our cause in quietness and confidence. It may be, however, that the responsible, thinking people of earlier generations who stood at a turning-point of history felt just as we do, for the very reason that something new was being born which was not discernible in the alternatives of the present.

Who Stands His Ground?

The great masquerade of evil has wrought havoc with all our ethical preconceptions. This appearance of evil in the guise of light, beneficence and historical necessity is utterly bewildering to anyone nurtured in our traditional ethical systems. But for the Christian who frames his life on the Bible it simply confirms the radical evilness of evil.

The failure of rationalism is evident. With the best of intentions, but with a naive lack of realism, the rationalist imagines that a small dose of reason will be enough to put the world right. In his short-sightedness he wants to do justice to all sides, but in the melee of conflicting forces he gets trampled upon without having achieved the slightest effect. Disappointed by the irrationality of the world, he realizes at last his futility, retires from the fray, and weakly surrenders to the winning side.

Worse still is the total collapse of moral fanaticism. The fanatic imagines that his moral purity will prove a match for the power of evil, but like a bull he goes for the red rag instead of the man who carries it, grows weary and succumbs. He becomes entangled with non-essentials and falls into the trap set by the superior ingenuity of his adversary.

Then there is the man with a conscience. He fights single-handed against overwhelming odds in situations which demand a decision. But there are so many conflicts going on, all of which demand some vital choice—with no advice or support save that of his own conscience—that he is torn to pieces. Evil approaches him in so many specious and deceptive guises that his conscience becomes nervous and vacillating. In the end he contents himself with a salved instead of a clear conscience, and starts lying to his conscience as a means of avoiding despair. If a man relies exclusively on his conscience he fails to see how a bad conscience is sometimes more wholesome and strong than a deluded one.

When men are confronted by a bewildering variety of alternatives, the path of *duty* seems to offer a sure way out. They grasp at the imperative as the one certainty. The responsibility for the imperative rests upon its author, not upon its executor. But when men are confined to the limits of duty, they never risk a daring deed on their own responsibility, which is the only way to score a bull's eye against evil and defeat it. The man of duty will in the end be forced to give the devil his due.

What then of the man of *freedom?* He is the man who aspires to stand his ground in the world, who values the necessary deed more highly than a clear conscience or the duties of his calling, who is ready to sacrifice a barren principle for a fruitful compromise or a barren mediocrity for a fruitful radicalism. What then of him? He must beware lest his freedom should become his own undoing. For in choosing the lesser of two evils he may fail to see that the greater evil he seeks to avoid may prove the lesser. Here we have the raw material of tragedy.

Some seek refuge from the rough-and-tumble of public life in the sanctuary of their own private virtue. Such men, however, are compelled to seal their lips and shut their eyes to the njustice around them. Only at the cost of self-deception can they keep themselves pure from the defilements incurred by responsible action. For all that they achieve, that which they leave undone will still torment their peace of mind. They will either go to pieces in face of this disquiet, or develop into the most hypocritical of all Pharisees.

Who stands his ground? Only the man whose ultimate criterion is not in his reason, his principles, his conscience, his freedom or his virtue, but who is ready to sacrifice all these things when he is called to obedient and responsible action in faith and exclusive allegiance to God. The responsible man seeks to make his whole life a response to the question and call of God.

Civil Courage?

What lies behind the complaint about the dearth of civil courage? The last ten years have produced a rich harvest of bravery and self-sacrifice, but hardly any civil courage, even among ourselves. To attribute this to personal cowardice would be an all too facile psychology. Its background must be sought elsewhere. In the course of a long history we Germans have had to learn the necessity and the power of obedience. The subordination of all individual desires and opinions to the call of duty has given meaning and nobility to life. We have looked upwards, not in servile fear, but in free trust, seeing our duty as a call, and the call as a vocation. This readiness to follow a command from above rather than our own private opinion of what was best was a sign of a legitimate self-distrust. Who can deny that in obedience, duty and calling we Germans have again and again excelled in bravery and self-sacrifice? But the German has preserved his freedom—what nation has talked so passionately of freedom as we have, from Luther to the idealists?—by seeking deliverance from his own will through service to the community. Calling and freedom were two sides of the same thing. The trouble was, he did not understand his world. He forgot that submissiveness and self-sacrifice could be exploited for evil ends. Once that happened, once the exercise of the calling itself became questionable, all the ideals of the German would begin to totter. Inevitably he was convicted of a fundamental failure: he could not see that in certain circumstances free and responsible action might have to take precedence over duty and calling. As a compensation he developed in one direction an irresponsible unscrupulousness, and in another an agonising scrupulosity which invariably frustrated action. Civil courage, however, can only grow out of the free responsibility of free men. Only now are we Germans beginning to discover the meaning of free responsibility. It depends upon a God who demands bold action as the free response of faith, and who promises forgiveness and consolation to the man who becomes a sinner in the process.

Of Success

Though success can never justify an evil deed or the use of questionable means, it is not an ethically neutral thing. All the same it remains true that historical success creates the only basis of the continuance of life, and it is still a moot point whether it is ethically more responsible to behave like Don Quixote and enter the lists against a new age, or to admit one's defeat, accept the new age and agree to serve it. In the last resort success makes history, and the Disposer of history is always bringing good out of evil over the heads of the history-makers. To ignore the ethical significance of success is to betray a superficial acquaintance with history and a defective sense of responsibility. So it is all to the good that we have been forced for once to grapple seriously with this problem of ethics of success. All the time goodness is successful we can afford the luxury of regarding success as having no ethical significance. But the problem arises when success is achieved by evil means. It is no good then behaving as an arm-chair critic and disputing the issue, for that is to refuse to face the facts. Nor is opportunism any help, for that is to capitulate before success. We must be determined not to be outraged critics or mere opportunists. We must take our full share of responsibility for the moulding of history, whether it be a victors or vanquished. It is only by refusing to allow any event to deprive us of our responsibility for history, because we know that is a responsibility laid upon us by God, that we shall achieve a relation to the events of history far more fruitful than criticism or opportunism. To talk about going down fighting like heroes in face of certain defeat is not really heroic at all, but a failure to face up to the future. The ultimate question the man of responsibility asks is not, How can I extricate myself heroically from the affair? but, How is the coming generation to live? It is only in this way that fruitful solutions can arise, even if for the time being they are humiliating. In short, it is easier by

far to act on abstract principle than from concrete responsibility. The rising generation will always instinctively discern which of the two we are acting upon. For it is their future which is at stake.

Of Folly

Folly is a more dangerous enemy to the good than malice. You can protest against malice, you can unmask it or prevent it by force. Malice always contains the seeds of its own destruction, for it always makes men uncomfortable, if nothing worse. There is no defence against folly. Neither protests nor force are of any avail against it, and it is never amenable to reason. If facts contradict personal prejudices, there is no need to believe them, and if they are undeniable, they can simply be pushed aside as exceptions. Thus the fool, as compared with the scoundrel, is invariably self-complacent. And he can easily become dangerous, for it does not take much to make him aggressive. Hence folly requires much more cautious handling than malice. We shall never again try to reason with the fool, for it is both useless and dangerous.

To deal adequately with folly it is essential to recognize it for what it is. This much is certain, it is a moral rather than an intellectual defect. There are men of great intellect who are fools, and men of low intellect who are anything but fols, a discovery we make to our surprise as a result of particular circumstances. The impression we derive is that folly is acquired rather than congenital; it is acquired in certain circumstances where men make fools of themselves or allow others to make fools of them. We observe further that folly is less common in the unsociable or the solitary than in individuals or groups who are inclined or condemned to sociability. From this it would appear that folly is a sociological problem rather than one of psychology. It is a special form of the operation of historical circumstances upon men, a psychological by-product of definite external factors. On closer inspection it would seem that any violent revolution, whether political or religious, produces an outburst of folly in a large part of mankind. Indeed, it would seem to be almost a law of psychology and sociology. The power of one needs the folly of the other. It is not that certain aptitudes of men, intellectual aptitudes for instance, become stunted or destroyed. Rather, the upsurge of power is so terrific that it deprives men of an independent judgment, and they give up trying—more or less unconsciously—to assess the new state of affairs for themselves. The fool can often be stubborn, but this must not mislead us into thinking he is independent. One feels, somehow, especially in conversation with him, that it is impossible to talk to the man himself, to talk to him personally. Instead, one is confronted with a series of slogans, watch-words, and the like, which have acquired power over him. He is under a curse, he is blinded, his very humanity is being prostituted and exploited. Once he has surrendered his will and become a mere tool, there are no lengths of evil to which the fool will not go, yet all the time he is unable to see that it is evil. Here lies the danger of a diabolical exploitation of humanity, which can do irreparable damage to the human character.

But it is just at this point that we realize that the fool cannot be saved by education. What he needs is redemption. There is nothing else for it. Until then it is no earthly good trying to convince him by rational argument. In this state of affairs we can well understand why it is no use trying to find out what "the people" really think, and why this quesion is also so superfluous for the man who thinks and acts responsibly. As the Bible says, "the fear of the Lord is the beginning of wisdom." In other words, the only cure for folly is spiritual redemption, for that alone can enable a man to live as a responsible person in the sight of God.

But there is a grain of consolation in these reflections on human folly. There is no reason for us to think that the majority of men are fools under all circumstances. What matters in the long run is whether our rulers hope to gain more from the folly of men, or from their independence of judgement and their shrewdness of mind.

Contempt For Humanity?

There is a very real danger of our drifting into an attitude of contempt for humanity. We know full well that it would be very wrong, and that it would lead to a sterile relationship with our fellow men. Perhaps the following considerations will save us from this temptation. The trouble about it is that it lands us into the worst mistake of our enemies. The man who despises others can never hope to do anything with them. The faults we despise in others are always, to some extent at least, our own too. How often have we expected from others more than we are prepared to do ourselves! Why have we until now held such lofty views about human nature? Why have we not recognized its frailty and liability to temptation? We must form our estimate of men less from their achievements and failures, and more from their suffering. The only profitable relationship to others—and especially to our weaker brethren—is one of love, that is the will to hold fellowship with them. Even God did not despise humanity, but became Man for man's sake.

Immanent Righteousness

It is one of the most astounding discoveries, but one of the most incontrovertible, that evil—often in a surprisingly short time—proves its own folly and defeats its own object. That is not to say that every evil deed is at once followed automatically by retribution. But it does mean that the deliberate transgression of the divine law on the plea of self-preservation has the opposite effect of self-destruction. This is something we have learnt from our own experience, and it can be interpreted in various ways. But one certain conclusion we can draw from it seems to be that social life is governed by certain laws more powerful than any other factors which may claim to be determinative. Hence it is not only unjust, but positively unwise to ignore these laws. Perhaps that is why Aristotle and St. Thomas Aquinas made prudence one of the cardinal virtues. Prudence and folly are not ethical *adiaphora*, as some Neo-protestant and *Gesinnungs*-ethics have tried to make out. The prudent man sees not only the possibilities of every concrete situation, but also the limits to human behaviour which are set by the eternal laws of social life. The prudent man acts virtuously and the virtuous man prudently.

It is true that all great historical action is constantly disregarding these laws. But it makes all the difference in the world whether it does so on principle, as though it contained a justification of its own, or whether it is still realized that to break these laws is sin, even if it be unavoidable, and that it can only be justified if the law is at once reinstated and respected. It is not necessarily hypocrisy when the declared aim of political action is the restoration of the law and not just blatant self-preservation. The world *is* simply ordered in such a way that a profound respect for the absolute laws and human rights is also the best means of self-preservation. While these laws may on occasion be broken in case of necessity, to proclaim that necessity as a principle and to take the law into our own hands is bound to bring retribution sooner or later. The immanent righteousness of history only rewards and punishes the deeds of men, the eternal righteousness of God tries and judges their hearts.

A Few Articles Of Faith On The Sovereignty Of God In History

I believe that God both can and will bring good out of evil. For that purpose he needs men who make the best use of everything. I believe God will give us all the power we need to resist in all time of distress. But he never gives it in advance, lest we should rely upon ourselves and not on him alone. A faith as strong as this should allay all our fears for the future. I believe that even our errors and mistakes are turned to good account. It is no harder for God to cope with them than with what we imagine to be our good deeds. I believe God is not just timeless fate, but that he waits upon and answers sincere prayer and responsible action.

Confidence

There is hardly one of us who has not known what it is to be betrayed. We used to find the figure of Judas an enigma, but now we know him only too well. The air we breathe is so infested with mistrust that it almost chokes us. But where we have managed to pierce through this layer of mistrust we have discovered a confidence scarce dreamed of hitherto. Where we do trust we have learnt to entrust our very lives to the hands of others. In face of all the many constructions to which our actions and our lives have been inevitably exposed we have learnt to trust without reserve. We know that hardly anything can be more reprehensible than the sowing and encouragement of mistrust, and that our duty is rather to do everything in our power to strengthen and foster confidence among men. Trust will always be one of the greatest, rarest and happiest blessings of social life, though it can only emerge on the dark background of a necessary mistrust. We have learnt never to trust a scoundrel an inch, but to give ourselves to the trustworthy without reserve.

The Sense Of Quality

Unless we have the courage to fight for a revival of a wholesome reserve between man and man, all human values will be submerged in anarchy. The impudent comtempt for such reserve is as much the mark of the rabble as interior uncertainty, as haggling and cringing for the favour of the insolent, as lowering oneself to the level of the rabble is the way to becoming no better than the rabble oneself. Where self-respect is abandoned, where the feeling for human quality and the power of reserve decay, chaos is at the door. Where impudence is tolerated for the sake of material comfort, self-respect is abandoned, the flood-gates are opened, and chaos bursts the dams we were pledged to defend. That is a crime against humanity. In other ages it may have been the duty of Christians to champion the equality of all men. Our duty to-day, however, is passionately to defend the sense of reserve between man and man. We shall be accused of acting for our own interests, of being anti-social. Such cheap jibes must be placidly accepted. They are the invariable protests of the rabble against decency and order. To be pliant and uncertain is to fail to realize what is at stake, and no doubt it goes a good way to justify those jibes. We are witnessing the levelling down of all ranks of society, but at the same time we are watching the birth of a new sense of nobility, which is binding together a circle of men from all the previous classes of society. Nobility springs from and thrives on self-sacrifice and courage and an unfailing sense of duty to oneself and society. It expects due deference to itself, but shows an equally natural deference to others, whether they be of higher or of lower degree. From start to finish it demands a recovery of a lost sense of quality and of a social order based upon quality. Quality is the bitterest enemy of concent in all its forms. Socially it implies the cessation of all place-hunting, of the cult of the "star." It requires an open eye both upwards and downwards, especially in the choice of one's closest friends. Culturally it means a return from the newspaper and the radio to the book, from feverish activity to unhurried leisure, from dissipation to recollection, from sensationalism to reflection, from virtuosity to art, from snobbery to modesty, from extravagance to moderation. Quantities are competitive, qualities complementary.

Sympathy

We must never forget that most men only learn wisdom by personal experience. This explains, first, why so few people are capable of taking precautions in advance—they always think they will be able somehow or other to circumvent the danger. Secondly, it explains their insensibility to the sufferings of others. Sympathy grows in proportion to the fear of approaching disaster. There is a good deal of excuse on ethical grounds for this attitude. Nobody wants to meet fate head-on: inward calling and strength for action are only acquired in face of actual danger. Nobody is responsible for all the suffering and injustice in the world, and nobody wants to set himself up as the judge of the universe. Psychologically, our lack of imagination, sensitivity and mental agility is balanced by a steady composure, an unruffled power of concentration and an immense capacity for suffering. But from a Christian point of view, none of these mitigating circumstances can atone for the absence of the most important factor, that is a real breadth of sympathy. Christ avoided suffering until his hour had come, but when it did come he seized it with both hands as a free man and mastered it. Christ, as the Scriptures tell us, bore all our human sufferings in his own body as if they were his own—a tremendous thought—and submitted to them freely. Of course, we are not Christs, we do not have to redeem the world by any action or suffering of our own. There is no need for us to lay upon ourselves such an intolerable burden. We are not lords, but instruments in the hand of the Lord of history. Our capacity to sympathize with others in their sufferings is strictly limited. We are not Christs, but if we want to be Christians we must show something of Christ's breadth of sympathy by acting responsibly, by grasping our "hour," by facing danger like free men, by displaying a real sympathy which springs not from fear, but from the liberating and redeeming love of Christ for all who suffer. To look on without lifting a helping hand is most un-Christian. The Christian does not have to wait until he suffers himself; the sufferings of his brethren for whom Christ died are enough to awaken his active sympathy.

Of Suffering

It is infinitely easier to suffer in obedience to a human command than to accept suffering as free, responsible men. It is infinitely easier to suffer with others than to suffer alone. It is infinitely easier to suffer as public heroes than to suffer apart and in ignominy. It is infinitely easier to suffer physical death than to endure spiritual suffering. Christ suffered as a free man alone, apart and in ignominy, in body and in spirit, and since that day many Christians have suffered with him.

Present and Future

We always used to think it was one of the elementary rights of man that he should be able to plan his life in advance, both private life and professional. That is a thing of the past. The pressure of events is forcing us to give up "being anxious for the morrow." But it makes all the difference in the world whether we accept this willingly and in faith (which is what the Sermon on the Mount means) or under compulsion. For most people not to plan for the future means to live irresponsibly and frivolously, to live just for the moment, while some few continue to dream of better times to come. But we cannot take either of these courses. We are still left with only the narrow way, a way often hardly to be found, of living every day as if it were our last, yet in faith and responsibility living as though a splendid future still lay before us. "Houses and fields and vineyards shall yet again be brought in this land," cries Jeremiah just as the Holy City is about to be destroyed, a striking contrast to his previous prophecies of woe. It is a divine sign and pledge of better things to come, just when all seems blackest. Thinking and acting for the sake of the coming generation, but taking each day as it comes without fear and anxiety—that is the spirit in which we are being forced to live in practice. It is not easy to be brave and hold out, but it is imperative.

Optimism

It is more prudent to be a pessimist. It is an insurance against disappointment, and no one can say "I told you so," which is how the prudent condemns the optimist. The essence of optimism is that it takes no account of the present, but it is a source of inspiration, of vitality and hope where others have resigned; it enables a man to hold his head high, to claim the future for himself and not to abandon it to his enemy. Of course there is a foolish, shifty kind of optimism which is rightly condemned. But the optimism which is will for the future should never be despised, even if it is proved wrong a hundred times. It is the health and vitality which a sick man should never impugn. Some men regard it as frivolous, and some Christians think it is irreligious to hope and prepare oneself for better things to come in his life. They believe in chaos, disorder and catastrophe. That, they think, is the meaning of present events, and in sheer resignation or pious escapism they surrender all responsibility for the preservation of life and for the generations yet unborn. To-morrow may be the day of judgement. If it is, we shall gladly give up working for a better future, but not before.

Insecurity And Death

During recent years we have come to know death at close quarters. We are sometimes startled at the placidity with which we hear of the death of one of our contemporaries. We cannot hate death as we used to, for we have discovered some good in it after all, and have almose come to terms with it. Fundamentally we feel that we really belong to death already, and that every new day is a miracle. It would hardly be true to say that we welcome death—although we all know that *accidie* which should be avoided like the plague—we are too curious for that, or to put it more seriously, we still hope to see some sense in the broken fragments of our life. Nor do we try and romanticize death, for life is too precious for that. Still less are we inclined to see in danger the meaning of life—we are not desperate enough for that, and we know too much about the joys life has to offer. And we know too much about life's anxieties also, and all the havoc wrought by prolonged insecurity. We still love life, but I do not think that death can take us by surprise now. After all we have been through during the war we hardly dare admit our hope that we shall not die a sudden and unexpect-

ed death for some trivial accident, but rather in dedication to some noble cause. It is not the external circumstances, but the spirit in which we face it, that makes death what it can be, a death freely and voluntarily accepted.

Are We Still Serviceable?

We have been the silent witnesses of evil deeds. Many storms have gone over our heads. We have learnt the art of deception and of equivocal speech. Experience has made us suspicious of others, and prevented us from being open and frank. Bitter conflicts have made us weary and even cynical. Are we still serviceable? It is not the genius that we shall need, not the cynic, not the misanthropist, not the adroit tactician, but honest, straightforward men. Will our spiritual reserves prove adequate and our candour with ourselves remorseless enough to enable us to find our way back again to simplicity and straightforwardness?

Vatican Council II

Vatican Council II (1962-1965), the twenty-first Ecumenical Council of the Catholic Church, was convoked by Pope John XXIII to bring the Church into closer contact with the outside world and make it more responsive to the needs of men of the 20th Century. As Pope John told one visitor, "We intend to let in a little fresh air." The Council sought to renew the Catholic Church to bring about a greater emphasis on the dignity of man and to work toward the unity of mankind. Its deliberations resulted in the publication of sixteen documents, two of the most important being *The Pastoral Constitution on the Church in the Modern World* and *Declaration on Religious Freedom*. The first selection is the first chapter of the *Church in the Modern World* which contains the essence of the Council's thinking on the dignity of the human person, a concept which had been ignored in many societies of the 20th Century. Note in this reading the discussion of human conscience and also the section stating the desire of the Church to enter into dialogue with all, even with unbelievers. The second selection, taken from the *Declaration on Religious Freedom,* stresses the right of a human being to practice his religious beliefs without coercion or prohibition from either church or state. Although the church was slow in acknowledging the validity of the principle of religious freedom, Pope Paul VI, who had succeeded Pope John in 1963, called it one of the major texts of the Council.

THE PASTORAL CONSTITUTION ON THE CHURCH IN THE MODERN WORLD

PART I

The Church and Man's Calling

11. The People of God believes that it is led by the Lord's Spirit, Who fills the earth. Motivated by this faith, it labors to decipher authentic signs of God's presence and purpose in the happenings, needs and desires in which this People has a part along with other men of our age. For faith throws a new light on everything, manifests God's design for man's total vocation, and thus directs the mind to solutions which are fully human.

This council, first of all, wishes to assess in this light those values which are most highly prized today and to relate them to their divine source. Insofar as they stem from endowments conferred by God on man, these values are exceedingly good. Yet they are often wrenched from their rightful function by the taint in man's heart, and hence stand in need of purification.

What does the Church think of man? What needs to be recommended for the upbuilding of contemporary society? What is the ultimate significance of human activity throughout the world? People are waiting for an answer to these questions. From the answers it will be increasingly clear that the People of God and the human race in whose midst it lives render service to each other. Thus the mission of the Church will show its religious, and by that very fact, its supremely human character.

CHAPTER I

The Dignity of the Human Person

12. According to the almost unanimous opinion of believers and unbelievers alike, all things on earth should be related to man as their center and crown.

But what is man? About himself he has expressed, and continues to express, many divergent and even contradictory opinions. In these he often exalts himself as the absolute measure of all things or debases himself to the point of despair. The result is doubt and anxiety. The Church certainly understands these problems. Endowed with light from God, she can offer solutions to them, so that man's true situation can be portrayed and his defects explained, while at the same time his dignity and destiny are justly acknowledged.

For Sacred Scripture teaches that man was created "to the image of God," is capable of knowing and loving his Creator, and was appointed by Him as master of all earthly creatures that he might subdue them and use them to God's glory. "What is man that you should care for him? You have made him little less than the angels, and crowned him with glory and honor. You have given him rule over the works of your hands, putting all things under his feet" (Ps. 8:5-7).

But God did not create man as a solitary, for from the beginning "male and female he created them" (Gen. 1:27). Their companionship produces the primary form of interpersonal communion. For by his innermost nature man is a social being, and unless he relates himself to others he can neither live nor develop his potential.

Therefore, as we read elsewhere in Holy Scripture God saw "all that he had made, and it was very good" (Gen. 1:31).

13. Although he was made by God in a state of holiness, from the very onset of his history man abused his liberty, at the urging of the Evil One. Man set himself against God and sought to attain his goal apart from God. Although they knew God, they did not glorify him as God, but their senseless minds were darkened and they served the creature rather than the Creator. What divine revelation makes known to us agrees with experience. Examining his heart, man finds that he has inclinations toward evil too, and is engulfed by manifold ills which cannot come from his good Creator. Often refusing to acknowledge God as his beginning, man has disrupted also his proper relationship to his own ultimate goal as well as his whole relationship toward himself and others and all created things.

Therefore man is split within himself. As a result, all of human life, whether individual or collective, shows itself to be a dramatic struggle between good and evil, between light and darkness. Indeed, man finds that by himself he is incapable of battling the assaults of evil successfully, so that everyone feels as though he is bound by chains. But the Lord Himself came to free and strengthen man, renewing him inwardly and casting out that "prince of this world" (John 12:31) who held him in the bondage of sin. For sin has diminished man, blocking his path to fulfillment.

From *The Sixteen Documents of Vatican II and the Instruction on the Liturgy.* Printed by the Daughters of St. Paul, Boston, Mass. Translation reprinted with permission of the National Catholic News Service, Washington D.C..

The call to grandeur and the depths of misery, both of which are a part of human experience, find their ultimate and simultaneous explanation in the light of this revelation.

14. Though made of body and soul, man is one. Through his bodily composition he gathers to himself the elements of the material world; thus they reach their crown through him, and through him raise their voice in free praise of the Creator. For this reason man is not allowed to despise his bodily life; rather he is obliged to regard his body as good and honorable since God has created it and will raise it up on the last day. Nevertheless, wounded by sin, man experiences rebellious stirrings in his body. But the very dignity of man postulates that man glorify God in his body and forbid it to serve the evil inclinations of his heart.

Now, man is not wrong when he regards himself as superior to bodily concerns, and as more than a speck of nature or a nameless constituent of the city of man. For by his interior qualities he outstrips the whole sum of mere things. He plunges into the depths of reality whenever he enters into his own heart; God, Who probes the heart, awaits him there; there he discerns his proper destiny beneath the eyes of God. Thus, when he recognizes in himself a spiritual and immortal soul, he is not being mocked by a fantasy born only of physical or social influences, but is rather laying hold of the proper truth of the matter.

15. Man judges rightly that by his intellect he surpasses the material universe, for he shares in the light of the divine mind. By relentlessly employing his talents through the ages he has indeed made progress in the practical sciences and in technology and the liberal arts. In our times he has won superlative victories, especially in his probing of the material world and in subjecting it to himself. Still he has always searched for more penetrating truths, and finds them. For his intelligence is not confined to observable data alone, but can with genuine certitude attain to reality itself as knowable, though in consequence of sin that certitude is partly obscured and weakened.

The intellectual nature of the human person is perfected by wisdom and needs to be, for wisdom gently attracts the mind of man to a quest and a love for what is true and good. Steeped in wisdom, man passes through visible realities to those which are unseen.

Our era needs such wisdom more than bygone ages if the discoveries made by man are to be further humanized. For the future of the world stands in peril unless wiser men are forthcoming. It should also be pointed out that many nations, poorer in economic goods, are quite rich in wisdom and can offer noteworthy advantages to others.

It is, finally, through the gift of the Holy Spirit that man comes by faith to the contemplation and appreciation of the divine plan.

16. In the depths of his conscience, man detects a law which he does not impose upon himself, but which holds him to obedience. Always summoning him to love good and avoid evil, the voice of conscience when necessary speaks to his heart: do this, shun that. For man has in his heart a law written by God; to obey it is the very dignity of man; according to it he will be judged. Conscience is the most secret core and sanctuary of a man. There he is alone with God, Whose voice echoes in his depths. In a wonderful manner conscience reveals that law which is fulfilled by love of God and neighbor. In fidelity to conscience, Christians are joined with the rest of men in the search for truth, and for the genuine solution to the numerous problems which arise in the life of individuals from social relationships. Hence the more right conscience holds sway, the more persons and groups turn aside from blind choice and strive to be guided by the objective norms of morality. Conscience frequently errs from invincible ignorance without losing its dignity. The same cannot be said for a man who cares but little for truth and goodness, or for a conscience which by degrees grows practically sightless as a result of habitual sin.

17. Only in freedom can man direct himself toward goodness. Our contemporaries make much of this freedom and pursue it eagerly; and rightly to be sure. Often however they foster it perversely as a license for doing whatever pleases them, even if it is evil. For its part, authentic freedom is an exceptional sign of the divine image within man. For God has willed that man remain "under the control of his own decisions," so that he can seek his Creator spontaneously, and come freely to utter and blissful perfection through loyalty to Him. Hence man's dignity demands that he act according to a knowing and free choice that is personally motivated and prompted from within, not under blind internal impulse nor by mere external pressure. Man achieves such dignity when, emancipating himself from all captivity to passion, he pursues his goal in a spontaneous choice of what is good, and procures for himself through effective and skilful action, apt helps to that end. Since man's freedom has been damaged by sin, only by the aid of God's grace can he bring such a

relationship with God into full flower. Before the judgment seat of God with man must render an account of his own life, whether he has done good or evil.

18. It is in the face of death that the riddle of human existence grows most acute. Not only is man tormented by pain and by the advancing deterioration of his body, but even more so by a dread of perpetual extinction. He rightly follows the intuition of his heart when he abhors and repudiates the utter ruin and total disappearance of his own person. He rebels against death because he bears in himself an eternal seed which cannot be reduced to sheer matter. All the endeavors of technology, though useful in the extreme, cannot calm his anxiety; for prolongation of biological life is unable to satisfy that desire for higher life which is inescapably lodged in his breast.

Although the mystery of death utterly beggars the imagination, the Church has been taught by divine revelation and firmly teaches that man has been created by God for a blissful purpose beyond the reach of earthly misery. In addition, that bodily death from which man would have been immune had he not sinned will be vanquished, according to the Christian faith, when man who was ruined by his own doing is restored to wholeness by an almighty and merciful Saviour. For God has called man and still calls him so that with his entire being he might be joined to Him in an endless sharing of a divine life beyond all corruption. Christ won this victory when He rose to life, for by His death He freed man from death. Hence to every thoughtful man a solidly established faith provides the answer to his anxiety about what the future holds for him. At the same time faith gives him the power to be united in Christ with his loved ones who have already been snatched away by death; faith arouses the hope that they have found true life with God.

19. The root reason for human dignity lies in man's call to communion with God. From the very circumstance of his origin man is already invited to converse with God. For man would not exist were he not created by God's love and constantly preserved by it; and he cannot live fully according to truth unless he freely acknowledges that love and devotes himself to His Creator. Still, many of our contemporaries have never recognized this intimate and vital link with God, or have explicitly rejected it. Thus atheism must be accounted among the most serious problems of this age, and is deserving of closer examination.

The word atheism is applied to phenomena which are quite distinct from one another. For while God is expressly denied by some, others believe that man can assert absolutely nothing about Him. Still others use such a method to scrutinize the question of God as to make it seem devoid of meaning. Many, unduly transgressing the limits of the positive sciences, contend that everything can be explained by this kind of scientific reasoning alone, or by contrast, they altogether disallow that there is any absolute truth. Some laud man so extravagantly that their faith in God lapses into a kind of anemia, though they seem more inclined to affirm man than to deny God. Again some form for themselves such a fallacious idea of God that when they repudiate this figment they are by no means rejecting the God of the Gospel. Some never get to the point of raising questions about God, since they seem to experience no religious stirrings nor do they see why they should trouble themselves about religion. Moreover, atheism results not rarely from a violent protest against the evil in this world, or from the absolute character with which certain human values are unduly invested, and which thereby already accords them the stature of God. Modern civilization itself often complicates the approach to God not for any essential reason but because it is so heavily engrossed in earthly affairs.

Undeniably, those who willfully shut out God from their hearts and try to dodge religious questions are not following the dictates of their consciences, and hence are not free of blame; yet believers themselves frequently bear some responsibility for this situation. For, taken as a whole, atheism is not a spontaneous development but stems from a variety of causes, including a critical reaction against religious beliefs, and in some places against the Christian religion in particular. Hence believers can have more than a little to do with the birth of atheism. To the extent that they neglect their own training in the faith, or teach erroneous doctrine, or are deficient in their religious, moral or social life, they must be said to conceal rather than reveal the authentic face of God and religion.

20. Modern atheism often takes on a systematic expression which, in addition to other causes, stretches the desire for human independence to such a point that it poses difficulties against any kind of dependence on God. Those who profess atheism of this sort maintain that it gives man freedom to be an end unto himself, the sole artisan and creator of his own history. They claim that this freedom cannot be reconciled with the affir-

mation of a Lord Who is author and purpose of all things, or at least that this freedom makes such an affirmation altogether superfluous. Favoring this doctrine can be the sense of power which modern technical progress generates in man.

Not to be overlooked among the forms of modern atheism is that which anticipates the liberation of man especially through his economic and social emanicpation. This form argues that by its nature religion thwarts this liberation by arousing man's hope for a deceptive future life, thereby diverting him from the constructing of the earthly city. Consequently when the proponents of this doctrine gain governmental power they vigorously fight against religion, and promote atheism by using, especially in the education of youth, those means of pressure which public power has at its disposal.

21. In her loyal devotion to God and men, the Church has already repudiated and cannot cease repudiating, sorrowfully but as firmly as possible, those poisonous doctrines and actions which contradict reason and the common experience of humanity, and dethrone man from his native excellence.

Still, she strives to detect in the atheistic mind the hidden causes for the denial of God; conscious of how weighty are the questions which atheism raises, and motivated by love for all men, she believes these questions ought to be examined seriously and more profoundly.

The Church holds that the recognition of God is in no way hostile to man's dignity, since this dignity is rooted and perfected in God. For man was made an intelligent and free member of society by God Who created him; but even more important, he is called as a son to commune with God and share in His happiness. She further teaches that a hope related to the end of time does not diminish the importance of intervening duties but rather undergirds the acquittal of them with fresh incentives. By contrast, when a divine substructure and the hope of life eternal are wanting, man's dignity is most grievously lacerated, as current events often attest; riddles of life and death, of guilt and of grief go unsolved with the frequent result that men succumb to despair.

Meanwhile every man remains to himself an unsolved puzzle, however obscurely he may perceive it. For on certain occasions no one can entirely escape the kind of self-questioning mentioned earlier, especially when life's major events take place. To this questioning only God fully and most certainly provides an answer as He summons man to higher knowledge and humbler probing.

The remedy which must be applied to atheism, however, is to be sought in a proper presentation of the Church's teaching as well as in the integral life of the Church and her members. For it is the function of the Church, led by the Holy Spirit Who renews and purifies her ceaselessly, to make God the Father and His Incarnate Son present and in a sense visible. This result is achieved chiefly by he witness of a living and mature faith, namely, one trained to see difficulties clearly and to master them. Many martyrs have given luminous witness to this faith and continue to do so. This faith needs to prove its fruitfulness by penetrating the believer's entire life, including its worldly dimensions, and by activating him toward justice and love, especially regarding the needy. What does the most reveal God's presence, however, is the brotherly charity of the faithful who are united in spirit as they work together for the faith of the Gospel and who prove themselves a sign of unity.

While rejecting atheism, root and branch, the Church sincerely professes that all men, believers and unbelievers alike, ought to work for the rightful betterment of this world in which all alike live; such an ideal cannot be realized, however, apart from sincere and prudent dialogue. Hence the Church protests against the distinction which some state authorities make between believers and unbelievers, with prejudice to the fundamental rights of the human person. The Church calls for the active liberty of believers to build up in this world God's temple too. She courteously invites atheists to examine the Gospel of Christ with an open mind.

Above all the Church knows that her message is in harmony with the most secret desires of the human heart when she champions the dignity of the human vocation, restoring hope to those who have already despaired of anything higher than their present lot. Far from diminishing man, her message brings to his development light, life and freedom. Apart from this message nothing will avail to fill up the heart of man: "Thou hast made us for Thyself," O Lord, "and our hearts are restless till they rest in Thee."

22. The truth is that only in the mystery of the incarnate Word does the mystery of man take on light. For Adam, the first man, was a figure of Him Who was to come, namely Christ the Lord. Christ, the final Adam, by the revelation of the mystery of the Father and His love, fully reveals man to man himself and makes his supreme calling clear. It is not surprising, then, that in Him all the aforemen-

tioned truths find their root and attain their crown.

He Who is "the image of the invisible God" (Col. 1:15), is Himself the perfect man. To the sons of Adam He restores the divine likeness which had been disfigured from the first sin onward. Since human nature as He assumed it was not annulled, by that very fact it has been raised up to a divine dignity in our respect too. For by His incarnation the Son of God has united Himself in some fashion with every man. He worked with human hands, He thought with a human mind, acted by human choice and loved with a human heart. Born of the Virgin Mary, He has truly been made one of us, like us in all things except sin.

As an innocent lamb He merited for us life by the free shedding of His own blood. In Him God reconciled us to Himself and among ourselves; from bondage to the devil and sin He delivered us, so that each one of us can say with the Apostle: The Son of God "loved me and gave Himself up for me" (Gal. 2:20). By suffering for us He not only provided us with an example for our imitation, He blazed a trail, and if we follow it, life and death are made holy and take on a new meaning.

The Christian man, conformed to the likeness of that Son Who is the firstborn of many brothers, received "the first fruits of the Spirit" (Rom. 8:23) by which he becomes capable of discharging the new law of love. Through this Spirit, who is "the pledge of our inheritance" (Eph. 1:14), the whole man is renewed from within, even to the achievement of "the redemption of the body" (Rom. 8:23): "If the Spirit of him who raised Jesus from the death dwells in you, then he who raised Jesus Christ from the dead will also bring to life your mortal bodies because of his Spirit who dwells in you" (Rom. 8:11). Pressing upon the Christian to be sure, are the need and the duty to battle against evil through manifold tribulations and even to suffer death. But, linked with the paschal mystery and patterned on the dying Christ, he will hasten forward to resurrection in the strength which comes from hope.

All this holds true not only for Christians, but for all men of good will in whose hearts grace works in an unseen way. For, since Christ died for all men, and since the ultimate vocation of man is in fact one, and divine, we ought to believe that the Holy Spirit in a manner known only to God offers to every man the possibility of being associated with this paschal mystery.

Such is the mystery of man, and it is a great one, as seen by believers in the light of Christian revelation. Through Christ and in Christ, the riddles of sorrow and death grow meaningful. Apart from His Gospel, they overwhelm us. Christ has risen, destroying death by His death; He has lavished life upon us so that, as sons in the Son, we can cry out in the Spirit: Abba, Father!

DECLARATION ON RELIGIOUS FREEDOM

1. A sense of the dignity of the human person has been impressing itself more and more deeply on the consciousness of contemporary man, and the demand is increasingly made that men should act on their own judgment, enjoying and making use of a responsible freedom, not driven by coercion but motivated by a sense of duty. The demand is likewise made that constitutional limits should be set to the powers of government, in order that there may be no encroachment on the rightful freedom of the person and of associations. This demand for freedom in human society chiefly regards the quest for the values proper to the human spirit. It regards, in the first place, the free exercise of religion in society. This Vatican Council takes careful note of these desires in the minds of men. It proposes to declare them to be greatly in accord with truth and justice. To this end, it searches into the sacred tradition and doctrine of the Church—the treasury out of which the Church continually brings forth new things that are in harmony with the things that are old.

First, the council professes its belief that God Himself has made known to mankind the way in which men are to serve Him, and thus be saved in Christ and come to blessedness. We believe that this one true religion subsists in the Catholic and Apostolic Church, to which the Lord Jesus committed the duty of spreading it abroad among all men. Thus He spoke to the Apostles: "Go, therefore, and make disciples of all nations, baptizing them in the name of the Father and of the Son and of the Holy Spirit, teaching them to observe all things whatsoever I have enjoined upon you" (Matt. 28: 19-20). On their part, all men are

From *The Sixteen Documents of Vatican II and the Instruction on the Liturgy.* Printed by the Daughters of St. Paul, Boston, Mass. Translation reprinted with permission of the National Catholic News Service, Washington D.C.

bound to seek the truth, especially in what concerns God and His Church, and to embrace the truth they come to know, and to hold fast to it.

This Vatican Council likewise professes its belief that it is upon the human conscience that these obligations fall and exert their binding force. The truth cannot impose itself except by virtue of its own truth, as it makes its entrance into the mind at once quietly and with power.

Religious freedom, in turn, which men demand as necessary to fulfill their duty to worship God, has to do with immunity from coercion in civil society. Therefore it leaves untouched traditional Catholic doctrine on the moral duty of men and societies toward the true religion and toward the one Church of Christ.

Over and above all this, the council intends to develop the doctrine of recent popes on the inviolable rights of the human person and the constitutional order of society.

2. This Vatican Council declares that the human person has a right to religious freedom. This freedom means that all men are to be immune from coercion on the part of individuals or of social groups and of any human power, in such wise that no one is to be forced to act in a manner contrary to his own beliefs, whether privately or publicly, whether alone or in association with others, within due limits.

The council further declares that the right to religious freedom has its foundation in the very dignity of the human person as this dignity is known through the revealed word of God and by reason itself. This right of the human person to religious freedom is to be recognized in the constitutional law whereby society is governed and thus it is to become a civil right.

It is in accordance with their dignity as persons— that is, beings endowed with reason and free will and therefore privileged to bear personal responsibility—that all men should be at once impelled by nature and also bound by a moral obligation to seek the truth, especially religious truth. They are also bound to adhere to the truth, once it is known, and to order their whole lives in accord with the demands of truth. However, men cannot discharge these obligations in a manner in keeping with their own nature unless they enjoy immunity from external coercion as well as psychological freedom. Therefore the right to religious freedom has its foundation not in the subjective disposition of the person, but in his very nature. In consequence, the right to this immunity continues to exist even in those who do not live up to their obligation of seeking the truth and adhering to it and the exercise of this right is not to be impeded, provided that just public order be observed.

3. Further light is shed on the subject if one considers that the highest norm of human life is the divine law—eternal, objective and universal— whereby God orders, directs and governs the entire universe and all the ways of the human community by a plan conceived in wisdom and love. Man has been made by God to participate in this law, with the result that, under the gentle disposition of divine Providence, he can come to perceive ever more fully the truth that is unchanging. Wherefore every man has the duty, and therefore the right, to seek the truth in matters religious in order that he may with prudence form for himself right and true judgments of conscience, under use of all suitable means.

Truth, however, is to be sought after in a manner proper to the dignity of the human person and his social nature. The inquiry is to be free, carried on with the aid of teaching or instruction, communication and dialogue, in the course of which men explain to one another the truth they have discovered, or think they have discovered, in order thus to assist one another in the quest for truth.

Moreover, as the truth is discovered, it is by a personal assent that men are to adhere to it.

On his part, man perceives and acknowledges the imperatives of the divine law through the mediation of conscience. In all his activity a man is bound to follow his conscience in order that he may come to God, the end and purpose of life. It follows that he is not to be forced to act in a manner contrary to his conscience. Nor, on the other hand, is he to be restrained from acting in accordance with his conscience, especially in matters religious. The reason is that the exercise of religion, of its very nature, consists before all else in those internal, voluntary and free acts whereby man sets the course of his life directly toward God. No merely human power can either command or prohibit acts of this kind. The social nature of man, however, itself requires that he should give external expression to his internal acts of religion: that he should share with others in matters religious; that he should profess his religion in community. Injury therefore is done to the human person and to the very order established by God for human life, if the free exercise of religion is denied in society, provided just public order is observed.

There is a further consideration. The religious acts whereby men, in private and in public and out of a sense of personal conviction, direct their lives to God transcend by their very nature the order of terrestrial and temporal affairs. Government therefore ought indeed to take account of the religious life of the citizenry and show it favor, since the function of government is to make provision for the common welfare. However, it would clearly transgress the limits set to its power, were it to presume to command or inhibit acts that are religious.

4. The freedom or immunity from coercion in matters religious which is the endowment of persons as individuals is also to be recognized as their right when they act in community. Religious communities are a requirement of the social nature both of man and of religion itself.

Provided the just demands of public order are observed, religious communities rightfully claim freedom in order that they may govern themselves according to their own norms, honor the Supreme Being in public worship, assist their members in the practice of the religious life, strengthen them by instruction, and promote institutions in which they may join together for the purpose of ordering their own lives in accordance with their religious principles.

Religious communities also have the right not to be hindered, either by legal measures or by administrative action on the part of government, in the selection, training, appointment, and transferral of their own ministers, in communicating with religious authorities and communities abroad, in erecting buildings for religious purposes, and in the acquisition and use of suitable funds or properties.

Religious communities also have the right not to be hindered in their public teaching and witness to their faith, whether by the spoken or by the written word. However, in spreading religious faith and in introducing religious practices everyone ought at all times to refrain from any manner of action which might seem to carry a hint of coercion or of a kind of persuasion that would be dishonorable or unworthy, especially when dealing with poor or uneducated people. Such a manner of action would have to be considered an abuse of one's right and a violation of the right of others.

In addition, it comes within the meaning of religious freedom that religious communities should not be prohibited from freely undertaking to show the special value of their doctrine in what concerns the organization of society and the inspiration of the whole of human activity. Finally, the social nature of man and the very nature of religion afford the foundation of the right of men freely to hold meetings and to establish education-al, cultural, charitable and social organizations, under the impulse of their own religious sense.

5. The family, since it is a society in its own original right, has the right freely to live its own domestic religious life under the guidance of parents. Parents, moreover, have the right to determine, in accordance with their own religious beliefs, the kind of religious education that their children are to receive. Government, in consequence, must acknowledge the right of parents to make a genuinely free choice of schools and of other means of education, and the use of this freedom of choice is not to be made a reason for imposing unjust burdens on parents, whether directly or indirectly. Besides, the right of parents are violated, if their children are forced to attend lessons or instructions which are not in agreement with their religious beliefs, or if a single system of education, from which all religious formation is excluded, is imposed upon all.

6. Since the common welfare of society consists in the entirety of those conditions of social life under which men enjoy the possibility of achieving their own perfection in a certain fulness of measure and also with some relative ease, it chiefly consists in the protection of the rights, and in the performance of the duties, of the human person. Therefore the care of the right to religious freedom devolves upon the whole citizenry, upon social groups, upon government, and upon the Church and other religious communities, in virtue of the duty of all toward the common welfare, and in the manner proper to each.

The protection and promotion of the inviolable rights of man ranks among the essential duties of government. Therefore government is to assume the safeguard of the religious freedom of all its citizens, in an effective manner, by just laws and by other appropriate means.

Government is also to help create conditions favorable to the fostering of religious life, in order that the people may be truly enabled to exercise their religious rights and to fulfill their religious duties, and also in order that society itself may profit by the moral qualities of justice and peace which have their origin in men's faithfulness to God and to His holy will.

If, in view of peculair circumstances obtaining among peoples, special civil recognition is given to one religious community in the constitutional order of society, it is at the same time imperative that the right of all citizens and religious communities to religious freedom should be recognized and made effective in practice.

Finally, government is to see to it that equality of citizens before the law, which is itself an element of the common good, is never violated, whether openly or covertly, for religious reasons. Nor is there to be discrimination among citizens.

It follows that a wrong is done when government imposes upon its people, by force or fear or other means, the profession or repudiation of any religion, or when it hinders men from joining or leaving a religious community. All the more is it a violation of the will of God and of the sacred rights of the person and the family of nations when force is brought to bear in any way in order to destroy or repress religion, either in the whole of mankind or in a particular country or in a definite community.

7. The right to religious freedom is exercised in human society: hence its exercise is subject to certain regulatory norms. In the use of all freedoms the moral principle of personal and social responsibility is to be observed. In the exercise of their rights, individual men and social groups are bound by the moral law to have respect both for the rights of others and for their own duties toward others and for the common welfare of all. Men are to deal with their fellows in justice and civility.

Furthermore, society has the right to defend itself against possible abuses committed on the pretext of freedom of religion. It is the special duty of government to provide this protection. However, government is not to act in an arbitrary fashion or in an unfair spirit of partisanship. Its action is to be controlled by juridical norms which are in conformity with the objective moral order. These norms arise out of the need for the effective safeguard of the rights of all citizens and for the peaceful settlement of conflicts of rights, also out of the need for an adequate care of genuine public peace, which comes about when men live together in good order and true justice, and finally out of the need for a proper guardianship of public morality.

These matters constitute the basic component of the common welfare: they are what is meant by public order. For the rest, the usages of society are to be the usages of freedom in their full range: that is, the freedom of man is to be respected as far as possible and is not to be curtailed except when and insofar as necessary.

8. Many pressures are brought to bear upon the men of our day, to the point where the danger arises lest they lose the possibility of acting on their own judgment. On the other hand, not a few can be found who seem inclined to use the name of freedom as the pretext for refusing to submit to authority and for making light of the duty of obedience. Wherefore this Vatican Council urges everyone, especially those who are charged with the task of educating others, to do their utmost to form men who, on the one hand, will respect the moral order and be obedient to lawful authority, and, on the other hand, will be lovers of true freedom—men, in other words, who will come to decisions on their own judgment and in the light of truth, govern their activities with a sense of responsibility, and strive after what is true and right, willing always to join with others in cooperative effort.

Religious freedom therefore ought to have this further purpose and aim, namely, that men may come to act with greater responsibility in fulfilling their duties in community life.

9. The declaration of this Vatican Council on the right of man to religious freedom has its foundation in the dignity of the person, whose exigencies have come to be more fully known to human reason through centuries of experience. What is more, this doctrine of freedom has roots in divine revelation, and for this reason Christians are bound to respect it all the more conscientiously. Revelation does not indeed affirm in so many words the right of man to immunity from external coercion in matters religious. It does, however, disclose the dignity of the human person in its full dimensions. It gives evidence of the respect which Christ showed toward the freedom with which man is to fulfill his duty of belief in the word of God and it gives us lessons in the spirit which disciples of such a Master ought to adopt and continually follow. Thus further light is cast upon the general principles upon which the doctrine of this declaration on religious freedom is based. In particular, religious freedom in society is entirely consonant with the freedom of the act of Christian faith.

10. It is one of the major tenets of Catholic doctrine that man's response to God in faith must be free: no one therefore is to be forced to embrace the Christian faith against his own will. This doctrine is contained in the word of God and it was constantly proclaimed by the Fathers of the Church. The act of faith is of its very nature a free act. Man, redeemed by Christ the Savior and through Christ Jesus called to be God's adopted son, cannot give his adherence to God revealing Himself unless, under the drawing of the Father, he offers to God the reasonable and free submission of faith. It is therefore completely in accord with the nature of faith that in matters religious every

manner of coercion on the part of men should be excluded. In consequence, the principle of religious freedom makes no small contribution to the creation of an environment in which men can without hindrance be invited to the Christian faith, embrace it of their own free will, and profess it effectively in their whole manner of life. . . .

15. The fact is that men of the present day want to be able freely to profess their religion in private and in public. Indeed, religious freedom has already been declared to be a civil right in most constitutions, and it is solemnly recognized in international documents. The further fact is that forms of government still exist under which, even though freedom of religious worship receives constitutional recognition, the powers of government are engaged in the effort to deter citizens from the profession of religion and to make life very difficult and dangerous for religious communities.

This council greets with joy the first of these two facts as among the signs of the times. With sorrow, however, it denounces the other fact, as only to be deplored. The council exhorts Catholics, and it directs a plea to all men, most carefully to consider how greatly necessary religious freedom is, especially in the present condition of the human family. All nations are coming into even closer unity. Men of different cultures and religions are being brought together in closer relationships. There is a growing consciousness of the personal responsibility that every man has. All this is evident. Consequently, in order that relationships of peace and harmony be established and maintained within the whole of mankind, it is necessary that religious freedom be everywhere provided with an effective constitutional guarantee and that respect be shown for the high duty and right of man freely to lead his religious life in society.

May the God and Father of all grant that the human family, through careful observance of the principle of religious freedom in society, may be brought by the grace of Christ and the power of the Holy Spirit to the sublime and unending and "glorious freedom of the sons of God" (Rom. 8:21).